W9-AOB-694

# SUSAN B. ANTHONY

SUSAN B. ANTHONY
In Her 86th Year

# SUSAN B. ANTHONY

## THE WOMAN WHO CHANGED
## THE MIND OF A NATION

BY

### RHETA CHILDE DORR

ILLUSTRATED FROM PHOTOGRAPHS

WITH AN INDEX

AMS PRESS
NEW YORK

The Library of Congress catalogued this title as follows:

**Dorr, Rheta Louise (Childe)** 1872-1948.
    Susan B. Anthony, the woman who changed the mind of a
nation.   New York, AMS Press [1970]
    xiii, 367 p.   illus., ports.   23 cm.
    Reprint of the 1928 ed.

    1. Anthony, Susan Brownell, 1820-1906.   2. Woman—Suffrage—United
States.

  JK1899.A6D6   1970           324'.3'0924            74-100519
  ISBN 0-404-00626-4           [B]                    MARC

       Library of Congress          70[70]

HOUSTON PUBLIC LIBRARY

. R01029 49726

SSCCA

Reprinted from the edition of 1928
First AMS edition published in 1970

Manufactured in the United States of America

AMS PRESS, INC.
NEW YORK, N.Y.

To

MY GRANDDAUGHTER

# LORA RHETA DORR

THAT SHE MAY KNOW SOMETHING OF HER HERITAGE

# FOREWORD

For a biography of Susan B. Anthony there can never be much new material. The monumental "History of Woman Suffrage," compiled by Susan herself, Elizabeth Cady Stanton, Matilda Joslyn Gage and Ida Husted Harper, contains most of the facts of her work during fifty-three years for woman's right, as she expressed it, to own and possess herself. Mrs. Harper's minute and painstaking biography, published in two large volumes in 1898, and a third volume written immediately after her death in 1906, is a source book of priceless value to every student of the facts of her remarkable career. Mrs. Harper's book suffered the one disadvantage of being written mainly in Susan's lifetime, and characteristically she refused to permit herself to be represented the towering figure she actually was.

To give Susan the historic background against which she lived and moved I have read many contemporary books and magazines, and I have gone through old files of Garrison's *Liberator,* and the short-lived paper she so dearly cherished, *The Revolution.* Especially have I read her many scrapbooks, and those of Elizabeth Cady Stanton, preserved in the Library of Congress, Washington, filled with old letters, speeches and newspaper clippings dating back to 1848, the margins of the books freely scribbled with Susan's comments and corrections. I have searched the yellowing columns of daily newspapers where the activities of Susan and her crusaders were reported, first with astonishment and alarm, next with ridicule and abuse, finally with respect and homage. In those newspaper columns one sees how perceptibly in half a century the whole current of men's convictions about women and their place in society was changed, and how insistently the name of Susan B. Anthony dominates the story.

To Harriot Stanton Blatch and Ida Husted Harper I am indebted for suggestions and personal reminiscences. I have also my own memories, going back to when, as a girl of twelve, I eluded the vigilance of cautious parents to attend my first "woman's rights" meeting, there to be made by Susan B. Anthony and Elizabeth Cady Stanton a life convert to woman suffrage. In later years it was my privilege as a newspaper reporter to attend many conventions of the National American Woman Suffrage Association, and I was present at that historic one when Susan appeared for once without her famous red silk shawl. The press table sent her a note: "No red shawl, no report," and Susan, laughing like a girl, wrote back: "I have sent to the hotel for it." I heard her in Baltimore make her last speech to the association. Few at the reporters' table, even the men, could see very well what they wrote for their tears.

It is to men as well as women that I have wanted to present Susan B. Anthony as a warm and living, faulty, but human and dynamic personality, for men also owe her a great and lasting debt. In the weak and helpless, dependent women of her youth Susan saw something worse than mere chattels of men; she saw a burden that had to be lifted from the shoulders of men. She loved liberty for itself, and she gave her life as much to free the slave owner as the slave. For this Susan B. Anthony deserves to be remembered, not merely as a great name, but as a woman possessing that feminine and emotional sense of humanity which transcends class and sex and embraces with love the whole human race.

# CONTENTS

## PART I

## PART III

# ILLUSTRATIONS

# PART I

*"In ancient Greece she would have been a Stoic; in the era of the Reformation, a Calvinist; in King Charles' time a Puritan; but in the Nineteenth Century, by the very laws of her being, she is a reformer."*

ELIZABETH CADY STANTON.

# CHAPTER I

## A STUDY IN FAILURE

WHEN Susan B. Anthony died, at the great age of eighty-six, the press, liberal and conservative, united in a tribute of respectful homage which nevertheless amounted to a requiem. She was spoken of as one of the great figures of the old Nineteenth Century, now departed to join the honored shade of her equally great colleague, Elizabeth Cady Stanton, and those other reformers of abolition fame, Wendell Phillips, William Lloyd Garrison, Harriet Beecher Stowe, Julia Ward Howe, Charles Sumner. Yet not quite with these last could she be said to have ranked, for what they strove for they accomplished fully, whereas Susan B. Anthony's work remained half finished. It was granted that during her lifetime the progress of women had been remarkable, and that some of it, no doubt, was due to her long crusade for sex freedom. Practically all avenues of industry, the trades and professions, were now open to women. Higher education was theirs for the asking in every State in the Union. Most of the ancient taboos limiting the personal freedom of women were now forgotten. But the final goal toward which Susan B. Anthony had urged American women was still unachieved. Political enfranchisement, for all her fifty years of propaganda, had hardly passed beyond its controversial stage. Honor was due the woman who for more than half a century had endured

3

without flinching ridicule, abuse, calumny, opposition from press and pulpit, opposition from women themselves.  She had set forth early in life to convert the country to the doctrine of political as well as social and economic equality of women and men, but the majority were far from being converted.  In some distant future events might so shape themselves that another might succeed where she had not, but as for Susan B. Anthony she was, like Napoleon at Waterloo, a splendid failure.

In 1906, the year of Susan's death, there was much to warrant this verdict.  The woman suffrage movement was at a standstill.  All the arguments having been advanced, all the facts presented, the question had ceased to be news, hence it was accorded in a year less newspaper space than the editors allowed in a day to baseball, racing and the prize ring.  To the average reader of magazines and books woman suffrage was so uninteresting a topic that no first-class periodical would accept an article on the subject.  Politically woman suffrage was nowhere an issue.  Once in a great while a Senate or House Committee would grant a hearing to its proponents, but their speeches simply went into the waste-basket.  In four Western States of the Union women had indeed been given the full franchise, but no other State seemed ambitious to follow their example.  As for the rest of the world, except in Finland, then an obscure autonomous Grand Duchy of Russia, equal suffrage was unthinkable.

Susan B. Anthony knew this, knew that in dying she left the whole question indefinite and chaotic.  She knew that she left behind her no new leaders, no new plan of campaign, for the devoted women to whom she bequeathed her life-work were all past middle age and very weary, and not one was as able, as aggressive, as radical or as resourceful as the women who, in her youth, had flung into the world that challenge to man's dominance of human interests and activities. She was the last of the old guard, and it is possible that in her hour of death the expiring sigh of Keats, "writ in water," may have found echo. For selfless as she was it is not human to be entirely selfless. To the end Susan B. Anthony believed in the ultimate triumph of her ideals, but her estimate of herself may have been that of the majority of men, a splendid failure.

Yet within eight years of her death new leaders had developed, woman suffrage had suddenly emerged from propaganda to politics, and women all over this country were out in a militant campaign for what was everywhere known as the Susan B. Anthony Amendment to the Constitution of the United States. With amazing rapidity the measure was carried through both Houses of Congress, ratified by more than the requisite three-fourths of the State Legislatures, and in November, 1920, the centennial year of Susan's birth, the women of America went to the polls and voted in a national election. In Great Britain women over thirty were already voters, and within a few years practically every civilized nation in the world had made their women full citizens. This was the only completely democratic achievement of a war waged for democracy, and in Europe as well as in the United States and Canada the debt of women to Susan B. Anthony was reverently acknowledged. She stood then, and she still stands, as the everlasting symbol of women's emancipation.

A quarter of a century after her death is not too late
to begin to write of this woman who, while she neither
began nor ended the upward struggle of half the human race towards equality with the other half, has
left upon the whole movement the stamp of an imper-
ishable personality. Perhaps it is even a little early.
For not until the free woman ceases to be a novelty in
the eyes of men can it clearly be seen that what Susan
B. Anthony did, the yet uncomprehended social revolution she worked for, and in great measure accomplished, belongs not to the history of special
propaganda, but to the history of our civilization. The
threads of the woman movement have woven themselves so subtly into the warp and woof of our emerging
democracy that now they blend harmoniously, almost
indistinguishably, with the whole fabric. The loom
took up each thread without a jar. The proof of this
is that when women made each gradual advance they
were sometimes halted for a space, but they were never
turned back. When the last advance into citizenship
was made it was as though the weaver almost casually
completed his pattern. Woman suffrage was no peace
without victory, as Negro suffrage has proved. It was
no victory without peace, as the prohibition amendment has turned out to be. It is an approved and
undisputed part of the American Constitution.

What then will future students of the history of the
United States think of the men who wrote our text-
books without reference to forces which, under their
very eyes, were steadily at work to create a new social
order in this country and throughout the world? Few
historians have even mentioned the name of Susan B.

Anthony. Only in a recent work, "The Rise of American Civilization," by Charles and Mary Beard, has the woman movement been admitted into the dignity of history. This is at least a guarantee of better interpretation of events which have raised this country into its present predominance among nations.

The newer interpreters, however generously they may concede that women, too, were among the builders, will have difficulty in placing Susan B. Anthony where she belongs in our annals. They may be puzzled to understand exactly what she did that so definitely altered opinions and events in her time. She left behind her no written record, for Susan was not a writer. Compared with Elizabeth Cady Stanton and other colleagues she was not a great orator. Neither was she a statesman nor even a very astute politician. What she possessed was a quality of leadership that amounted to genius. In the earlier stages of the woman's rights movement she served as a quiet but competent secretary. A little later she began to lay out brilliant and audacious plans of campaign and to compel their success. Finally it was discovered that she was commander-in-chief of all the forces. Commander she remained, even after her death, for the women who carried out her policies, some of them children when she died, never thought of themselves except as her under-officers. The Susan B. Anthony Amendment was indeed hers, because as far back as Civil War days she had declared that the charter of women's liberties must be written into the Constitution itself. No action of the separate States, no emancipation proclamation, would ever have satisfied her. Complete victory, not armistice, was her objective. It was the goal of all those liberators who taught Americans that their country could not forever remain half slave, half free.

Susan B. Anthony's life story must therefore be written against the whole background of her United States. Born in the year of the Missouri Compromise, she grew up in that middle period which accepted compromise after compromise, until fire and sword came to destroy all compromises between caste and democracy, between free and slave labor. All but one. That final compromise had to be destroyed by women, and Susan B. Anthony, more than any other, armed women to do it. The time is past when she can be classed with propagandists and special pleaders. She belongs with the history makers of this Republic, and who fails to place her there simply admits that he knows the history of his country not at all.

# CHAPTER II

## AN EARLY AMERICAN IDYL

SUSAN, the second child of Daniel and Lucy Read Anthony, was born February 15, 1820, in Adams, Massachusetts, a little white Berkshire Hills village largely populated by well-to-do and orthodox Quakers. Considering the career to which she was destined this fact assured her, as a female child, a fairly good start in life. The Society of Friends was the first religious sect to put into practice the Christ principle that there is no sex in souls, the first to reject the Pauline precept, "Let your women keep silence in the churches." Quaker women not only spoke in meeting, the ablest of them actually sharing the high seat with elders and preachers, but they had a voice and vote in secular matters affecting the congregations. It followed that in their domestic relations they had considerably more freedom than other women. In the simple and austere home life of Friends father and mother exercised almost equal authority over the children, and girls were not unduly subordinated to their brothers. Friends were narrowly religious, but their theology was a little less dark and gloomy than that of the Puritans, and their rule of life, while severe, was not harsh. Nevertheless it is simple delusion to ascribe to Quakers much ascendancy over Puritans in liberality of mind or tolerance of the individual conscience. Every opinion and every act of a Quaker's life was subject to rule. He had to think, speak and behave in conformity with his fellow religionists. His garments might not vary in color, line or pattern. He could not make an independent move, could not marry, engage in business, make a speech or publish a book without the censorship and consent of the congregation. In dress, speech, manners and conventions generally a Quaker community was as standardized as an ant hill, and it was by consent only that a certain joyousness abounded within it, a love of good things to eat and drink, a social spirit which expressed itself by visiting around, entertaining strangers, interest in and harmless discussion of social and even political events.

Daniel Anthony, Susan's father, had a mind which occasionally transcended the limits of the ant hill. In his youth he had defied a sacred tenet of his order by marrying a girl whose family were Baptists and whose father had been won over to the Universalists, in those days hardly considered a Christian sect because the Universalists rejected a personal devil and a literal hell. Lucy Read, although she leaned towards her mother's faith, was almost the last girl in the village whom a staid young Quaker would be expected to woo. Lucy, in her charming adolescence was a pretty and coquettish young creature, fond of dress, dancing, beaux, and all the pleasures of life which a small community afforded. She was possessed of a phenomenal voice, pure and strong, and her habit of singing at her spinning wheel was one of the principal objections urged against her by the elders. Had she not owned to a longing to go into some open field and, if for only once in her life, let out that voice to the full splendor of its power? What a wife for a godly young Friend! What a wife for any respectable man of that unworldly generation. However, Daniel stubbornly insisted on marrying the girl he loved to infatuation, and it was only because his family was so influential, and he himself a man of importance in the community, that the meeting reluctantly decided not to turn him out.

Lucy Anthony, to the relief of the congregation, developed into a model wife according to their own standards. Two or three days before she married Daniel she went to a party and danced until four o'clock in the morning, but that was the last bit of wildness she ever displayed in her life. The day after her wedding she put away all her pretty gowns, assumed the Quaker drab, and except for low cradle tunes was never again heard to lift her beautiful voice in song. She never joined the meeting or adopted the Biblical thee and thou, but in all other external ways she became one with her husband's people. A modern psychologist might find Lucy Anthony a curious study in frustration. Her real nature she buried like a child in the grave, but all during her young wifehood and motherhood there was evidence that her old self still lived, a pale spirit hovering near to twist and torment her body. No good woman of her time was supposed to be conscious of sex or sex inhibitions, but what would a psychologist make of Lucy's abnormal shrinking from such primal facts as birth and generation? Mrs. Harper, Susan B. Anthony's first biographer, naïvely records that before the birth of each of her eight children Mrs. Anthony suffered such unbearable agonies of humiliation and embarrassment that she literally went into seclusion and would never allow her pregnancy to be alluded to even by her own mother. Grandmother Read used to make baby clothes, take them to the Anthony home and slip them into a bureau drawer, expecting no acknowledgement and getting none from her excessively modest daughter.

The Anthony children were brought up orthodox Quakers, but once in a while their mother's alien mind asserted itself in a bit of trimming on the girls' sober dresses, subtle encouragement of their love of juvenile parties, and once a timid plea to Daniel to allow them to attend the village singing school. She knew that he would have to deny her, but she made the plea nevertheless. Twenty years later, after Daniel had broken with the Society of Friends, or they had broken with him, Lucy Anthony had the sad pleasure of hearing the piano played in her home. But it was too late. The harmonies of her music-starved soul had vanished in a dream.

Susan B. Anthony was thus a child of two unusual parents, a father of courage and independent mind, and a mother who might have been an artist. Susan was always supposed to resemble her father, physically and mentally, but it is certain that she also inherited something of her mother's finer temperament. In her childhood she was distinguished only by being very precocious and self-willed. She learned to read and write before she was five, and a little later startled the village schoolmaster by a demand to be taught long division. Not every teacher of the 1820's was capable of imparting so much of higher mathematics, nor did any of them expect to teach it to girls. A woman might properly use addition, and even a little of the multiplication table to help her count out and weigh the surplus eggs, butter and yarn she sent to market, but as men managed all the important accounts, all business public and private, they alone needed arithmetic. But Susan wanted to learn long division, and somehow or other she managed to learn it. With equal obstinacy she persisted in mastering other branches of learning supposed to be sacred to males. She had a restless energy, a rude health, an abounding vitality which made her the equal of her father and brothers in all outdoor work, although nothing was neglected to train and perfect her in traditional household arts. Daniel Anthony, while not wealthy, was a fairly prosperous man. He was the owner of a small cotton mill, the rapid little stream which flowed through the Read-Anthony acres furnishing power to operate twenty-six looms. Still it never occurred to him to hire a servant to help his wife in the care of a large house and a family of small children. As each child reached seven or eight years a little of the work was delegated to his tiny hands, and with only such assistance Lucy Anthony cooked and baked, washed and ironed, spun, wove and sewed innumerable garments to clothe the family. At times she had to take unmarried factory hands to board, and one summer, with a nursing baby in her arms, she boarded eleven. Such was the life of "protected" women in the good old days.

When Susan was six years old her father's fortunes were materially advanced by a move to Battenville, New York, where he formed a partnership with Judge John McLean, a capitalist interested in the growing importance of cotton manufacturing. Judge McLean had erected in Battenville a large and modernly equipped cotton mill, and he took Daniel Anthony, a practical manufacturer and executive, as a managing partner. In addition to the cotton factory the partners built a large brick store and a number of tenant houses for the accommodation of their operatives, all Americans of original stock, for immigration from Continental Europe, or even from the British Isles, had reached little proportion in the United States. Among other workers attracted to Battenville were not a few unmarried daughters of New York and New England farmers, girls of the type described by Lucy Larcom in her stories of early American mill life. These young girls had to be provided with good homes, for they were proud and would not accept an inferior social status.

Daniel Anthony's attitude towards his people was that of a patriarch, say that of a kindly and beneficent autocrat. Of their morals he was particularly mindful. For example, in his Adams, Massachusetts, business he had handled liquor, for it was the universal custom that all deals were accompanied by a treat from the proprietor. But when the big store in Battenville came to be stocked Daniel refused to buy any rum. Neither would he consent to furnish drinks to the men and boys who came to the "raising" of the tenant houses. The scandalized Judge McLean objected that no one would ever patronize a store where no liquor was sold, or assist in house raisings where time-honored libations were omitted. Daniel Anthony insisted that they would, provided the goods offered at the store were of the best quality and moderately priced, and provided the refreshments attendant on the raising were appetizing. His judgment proved correct in both cases. The store flourished from its first opening, and on the

day of the raising the men found such a generous feast
of cakes, pies, doughnuts, great pitchers of lemonade,
good tea and coffee, all prepared by Mrs. Anthony's
tireless hands, that although they laughed a little ruefully they did the work, afterward no doubt, slaking
their thirst at home or in the village grog shop.

The radical Daniel proceeded farther with his temperance crusade.  He organized among the mill hands
a temperance society, to the indignation of the local
tavern keeper, although the pledge required only abstinence from hard liquor.  Nobody in those days
thought of abolishing wine or good hard cider, and
Daniel himself unwillingly retained a small keg of rum
or gin in his home against the visits of Quaker preachers or old-fashioned customers.  Another of Daniel's
patriarchal enterprises was an evening school in which
he was the principal teacher.  Many of the younger
workers had come from remote farms and had never
before had an opportunity to learn much reading and
writing, so the school was a popular feature.  On Sunday afternoons, for Quakers were not strict Sabba-
tarians, the Anthony home was always open, and many
of the operatives, especially the older men, gathered
there for religious and ethical discussions, the morning
sermon and obscure Biblical passages furnishing endless material for conversation.  It is probable that
current events were also discussed, although village
communities were far removed from the main streams
of thought or of world movements.  The slavery question was beginning to be agitated in a quiet way, and
while the Society of Friends was divided on its rights
and wrongs, Daniel Anthony was a convinced abolitionist.  So strongly did he feel on the subject that he even

tried to buy for the mills cotton that was not grown by slave labor. Daniel, in a word, was an idealist. It was his ambition to build up around his mills an industrial community which should be a model for all manufacturers. He insisted on paying good wages, as wages went then, and though he governed almost every detail of his employees' lives he did it in democratic fashion, assuming for himself and his family no social privileges. Once when there was a shortage of girl workers Daniel allowed his favorite child Susan to go into the mills and work for a few weeks as a spooler, paying her the current wage of three dollars a week. Susan enjoyed the experience, most of all the three dollars a week, the first money she had ever handled in her life. She was permitted to spend it as she pleased, and she pleased to give part of it to her elder sister Guelma and to lavish the rest on a present to her mother.

Daniel Anthony was no Socialist, but his Battenville mill community was benevolent enough to have satisfied a Fourier or a Robert Owen. The workers' houses were mere cottages, but each one had its garden, its chicken yard, cow barn and pig pen to furnish food in plain abundance. In the large kitchens the women cooked over open hearths and baked their bread, pies and Indian puddings in deep Dutch ovens. In the sunniest windows stood spinning wheels and quilting frames to occupy what was felicitously termed their spare time. In this spare time also the housewives canned vegetables and fruit, dried corn, beans and herbs, cured meat, dipped candles, and manufactured clothing for the entire family, including men's garments. Hours of work in the mills and in the home were immoderately long, but Americans of the old stock expected to toil grimly hard and to have few pleasures. As long as what they called their freedom and their liberties were not interfered with they served their employers faithfully and believed themselves to be the happiest and most favored of the children of God,

# CHAPTER III

FROM a romantic point of view it seems a pity that such an almost perfect state of things could not have continued indefinitely. Rural, self-contained communities enjoying so many of the essentials of happiness, small but secure incomes, homes of primitive comfort, innocent recreations, unquestioning religious faith, humane employers, bucolically contented workers, willingly subjected women, every one far removed from the raging storms of politics. But this is not a world where the simple essentials of happiness can long be conserved. Especially was this apparent in the third decade of the Nineteenth Century. The Age of Innocence was passing in the American commonwealth, and the country was entering an era of growth and power that staggers the mind to look back upon. An era of expansion in every possible direction. Land expansion, which between 1803 and 1848 turned a little group of loosely federated States into a mighty empire. Expansion along lines of creative invention such as the world had never known before. Steam applied not only to manufacturing but to transportation on land and sea and inland waters; exploitation on an unheard-of scale of national resources, coal and iron, silver and gold. Above all, a heady development of ideas and national ambitions. Into factories, mines, railroads and power-driven ships poured enormous capital. Into

the vast spaces of the uncharted West streamed the
Pioneers, men of such new and different racial types
that they make us forget that in the beginning all
Americans were pioneers. Changed conditions.
Changed modes of thought. Overnight, it seemed, a
changed conception of government in Washington.

Inevitably the country began to suffer such violent
growing pains that even isolated and unambitious communities such as Battenville, New York, suffered without understanding why. There were newspapers but
no telegraphs, and people generally knew even less
than they do now of the drift of national affairs or the
economic forces underlying them. There were voters
enough in the conservative East, small manufacturers,
shopkeepers, workmen, dreamy socialists, to thrill to
the Jacksonian slogan of rights for the common people,
and when the last of the old Jeffersonian Federalists
were swept out of office they acclaimed the rise to
power of the radical West. There was so much good
statesmanship mixed up with the blatant demagoguery
of the new democracy that its supporters, East and
West, were blinded to its weak economic policies. How
were men like Judge McLean and Daniel Anthony,
for example, to know that Andrew Jackson's ruthless
destruction of the sound money Federal Bank, four
years before its charter had expired; the consequent
triumph of irresponsible wildcat State and private
banks; the Administration's encouragement of land
speculation in the Middle West, and its return to shifting and uncertain tariffs, would so affect their honest
lives as to ruin their business and to plunge themselves
and their employees into sudden poverty? Yet so it
was in 1838, the year of the worst panic the country

had ever faced. Trade and business simply died. Daniel Anthony, paying a hurried visit to New York, possibly to seek credits for his distressed mills, wrote back that all he saw was empty wharfs, shuttered warehouses and streets almost empty of goods traffic.

Out of the general wreck of his affairs Judge Mc-Lean, by rare good luck, managed to save something, but Daniel Anthony saved nothing. The cotton mills, the big store, the tenant houses, the Anthony home and everything in it were seized and sold. Nothing in the house was exempt, the creditor's inventory including furniture, domestic tools and utensils, clothing, food in the larder, the children's school books, even the spectacles of Mr. and Mrs. Anthony. Fortunately, Mrs. Anthony's brother, Joshua Read, was able to fly to the rescue with a little ready cash, enough at least to bid in the actual necessities that enabled the family to begin life over again. In the spring of 1839 the Anthonys removed from Battenville to the little town of Hardscrabble, a place which must have seemed to them almost too appropriately named. Daniel owned there a small satinet factory, a grist mill and a piece of timbered land, all heavily mortgaged, and there for five unhappy years he toiled to make a living and pay his ever-increasing debts. But manufacturing for the time was dead, the consuming power of the people paralyzed. Nobody had any money to buy satinet or even the timber from Daniel's woods. After journeying as far west as Wisconsin in vain search for another business opening Daniel gave up the fight and retired to a farm on the outskirts of Rochester, the same brother-in-law, Joshua, advancing money for the first payments. This money was really Lucy Anthony's share in her father's estate, but of course she had no legal right to possess it. Joshua Read, as trustee under his father's will, could not even give it to her outright, because a married woman could own nothing. The farm and homestead purchased with Lucy's inheritance, became the property of her husband, she and the children having the privilege of working ceaselessly with him to wrest a living out of the thirty-two acres of fields and orchards. It was a losing struggle from the first, and in the end Daniel went into Rochester and obtained a position with the New York Life Insurance Company. Keeping the farm as a family homestead he remained for the rest of his life a more or less contented salaried man.

It was fortunate that before the panic of 1838 destroyed his fortunes Daniel Anthony was able to give his older children, Guelma and Susan, some kind of an education. None of the children had attended the village school in Battenville, mainly because their parents disapproved of the too-freely wielded birch rod. They had a young governess at home for a while, and in 1837, when Guelma was nineteen and Susan seventeen, the two girls were sent to a finishing school in Hamilton, a small town near Philadelphia. Better schools nearer home were available, and if Daniel had only chosen Mrs. Willard's famous academy at Troy Susan would have been given an almost modern education. Certainly she could have gratified her taste for mathematics, for the daring Mrs. Willard had but recently held a public examination in which, to the disquietude of the conservative, a young lady had passed brilliantly in geometry. Perhaps Mrs. Willard's terms were higher than the even then harassed Mr. Anthony

could afford, and in any case a school where dancing
and music lessons were added to advanced science must
have seemed too worldly for staid Quaker maidens. As
things were the school Daniel fixed upon was Deborah
Moulson's Select Seminary for Females, in Pennsylvania, where the terms were $125 a year for board and
tuition, and where vulgar branches of learning were
artfully combined with "The Principles of Morality,
Humility and the Love of Virtue." In fact, the austere
Deborah devoted so much time and attention to Morality, Humility and the Love of Virtue that her pupils
were given scant opportunity to learn anything else.
Deborah Moulson, poor creature, was ill of a con-
sumption and her mind brooded constantly on death and
the probable dread punishment coming to all through
man's first disobedience. The wrath of God was held
before those innocent young girls as something they
courted every day of their lives. Discipline was ex-
alted far above the mere acquisition of learning. One
of Deborah's favorite punishments was to deprive her
pupils of all privileges of study or even reading for
failure of perfection in lessons or conduct. In the
yellow pages of Susan's old school diary may be read
such passages as this:

"Our class has not recited in Philosophy, Chemistry or Physiol-
ogy, nor have we read, since the twentieth of this month, for the
reason of there being such a departure among the scholars from the
paths of rectitude."

A birch flogging could not have been worse torture
to Susan in her ardent school years. Her mind craved
knowledge as the lungs crave air, and every little scrap
of it that came her way was embraced with enthusiasm.
A Saturday afternoon excursion to the Philadelphia

Academy of Arts and Sciences, a lecture on natural philosophy by a visiting professor, a view through a microscope of the dust from a butterfly's wings, even a lecture and demonstration by an itinerant phrenologist, were described in letters home as outstanding events. But the candid Susan said of the phrenologist: "He described only the good organs and said nothing of the bad. I should like to know the whole truth."

Too few of these exciting cultural experiences and too much gloomy theology made Susan's life at this period a very heavy burden. She had the deep respect for constituted authority which tradition and environment had impressed on all women, but her brain was too clear and logical to accept Deborah's God of Wrath. To save her life she could not believe that when she and other conscientious young students tripped in their recitations, forgot to address each other with thee and thou, and especially when they gave way to youthful mirth and levity, they deserved to be treated like candidates for a reformatory. Susan, being the brightest girl in school, received the heaviest batteries of Deborah's displeasure. She failed to give a satisfactory definition for "compendiums,"and the rule for dotting an i, and Deborah thought that this accounted for the unusual suffering of mind and body she had subsequently to endure, her increased cough, her fever and night sweats. One morning Susan overslept, and Deborah sternly bade her remember Ananias and Sapphira who had also withheld some of their substance from the Apostle. Susan couldn't help laughing in class one day, and Deborah pointed out to her the fate of Judas Iscariot. It was a rule of the school that all letters had to be written first on slates and inspected and censored before they were goose-quilled, sealed and committed to the mails. Susan ventured to write a very private letter home and tried to send it to the post uncensored. But Deborah intercepted the epistle, summoned the culprit to judgment and treated her to such a scene that it was long before Susan could even recall it without scalding tears. The worst episode of all was in connection with a weekly housecleaning. In her zeal to get at a dusty ceiling Susan jumped up on Deborah's desk and broke it! That evening, before the whole school, Deborah read a long chapter from the Scriptures, referring no doubt to regions where "The worm dieth not and the fire is not quenched," and then she delivered a homily, saying that where there was no desire for moral improvement there could be no improvement in a certain pupil's mind.

"Cold and sick at heart," Susan tried conscientiously to work herself into a proper condition of repentance. In the stiff and artificial phrases of the day she inscribed in her diary:

"O, Morality, would that I could say that I possessed thy charms! O, the happiness of an innocent mind, would that I could say that mine were so, but it is too far from it! I think so much of my resolutions to do better that even my dreams are filled with these desires."

In a mood much more honest and self-respecting she wrote:

"If I am such a vile sinner, I would that I might feel it myself. . . . Perhaps the reason is that my heart is hardened."

A heart a trifle hardened was needed to survive the cruelties of such a school life. Susan did survive them, but the canting and hypocritical phraseology of the school clung to her, and as she afterwards declared, ruined her literary style forever. "Whenever I take my pen in hand I seem to be mounted on stilts," she complained, half a century after leaving the morbid atmosphere of Miss Deborah Moulson's Select Seminary for Females. When her father broke the news of his bankruptcy and told his daughters that their school life was over, Susan wept for his misfortunes and for the loss of the beloved home in Battenville, but for herself she shed no tears. It was good to be home again, even in Hardscrabble, even though the new poverty meant long days of manual labor to replace house furnishings lost in the creditors' sale. Susan wove carpets, spun great balls of wool and cotton yarn, stitched quilts, and helped her mother and sisters in butter making, cooking, baking ("Made twenty-one loaves of bread to-day," is a careless entry in her journal), and in the entertainment of casual travelers, for the house Daniel Anthony had taken had formerly been a tavern. Soon Guelma became engaged to Aaron McLean, grandson of Daniel's old partner, but Susan's thoughts were far from marriage for herself. The adventure towards which she yearned was self-help, self-support.

This impulse in a girl of Susan B. Anthony's social status was significant of a great change which was dawning on American civilization. A great and permanent change. The fact is that Andrew Jackson's zeal for destroying one political theory and establishing another had had results not infrequently brought about by statesmen and demagogues, results quite different from those expected. The Jacksonian policies had released forces which were never intended, which could not have been foreseen, and which for many decades could not properly be valued. One of the effects of the destruction of the Federal Bank, and the inevitable panic of 1838, was an immense increase in the number of women wage earners. The straits of their fathers forced thousands of girls to go to work, although opportunities for women in the industrial field were sadly limited. The important thing was the effect on the minds and characters of the new wage earners, for it is an axiom that any individual and any class progressing from unpaid to paid labor immediately steps up. The more intelligent the class the more apparent the advance. The Industrial Revolution of the late Eighteenth Century had sent masses of women, first in England, a little later in America, out of the home into the factory. But those women belonged to the half-enslaved and wholly inarticulate working classes. Beginning with the eighteen forties in the United States an entirely new type of woman stepped up into wage earning, a literate, self-conscious type. How far this release of the feminine half of the race was to affect the whole social structure no man of the first half of the Nineteenth Century could know or dream. In the second half of the Twentieth Century we are but beginning to surmise.

# CHAPTER IV

## THE SMARTEST WOMAN IN CANAJOHARIE

TEACHING being the most respectable profession open to women Susan B. Anthony became a teacher. From several positions offered she accepted that of assistant principal of a girls' boarding school in New Rochelle. The head of the school, Miss Eunice Kenyon, was a teacher of reputation, and under her direction Susan hoped to gain valuable experience. But when she reached New Rochelle, after a long journey down the Hudson River, she found Miss Kenyon so seriously ill that she was obliged to take over not only all the classes but the entire responsibility of the household. She also had to act as sick nurse while the doctors dosed the invalid with huge quantities of calomel, bled her until she fainted, blistered her into consciousness and then gave her more calomel. Under this heroic treatment, or in spite of it, Miss Kenyon recovered, and for the rest of the fifteen-weeks' term Susan taught, and between classes read voraciously, some of the books never being included in libraries of good Quakers. From New York newspapers she learned something of the tumultuous political conditions of the times, but as she was still adolescent in years and undeveloped in judgment it is not surprising that neither liberal books nor metropolitan newspapers immediately widened her point of view. Letters home reveal that Susan at least grew rapidly in courage of convictions.

Her father was in advance of most Quakers in his abolition sentiments, but he still hesitated to take the extreme
position of Phillips and Garrison, who were all for removing every social barrier between whites and blacks.
Susan soon ranged herself with the extremists, as a
letter to her brother-in-law Aaron McLean indicates:

"The people here," she wrote, "are anti-abolitionist and anti everything else that is good. The Friends raised quite a fuss about a
colored man sitting in the meeting house, and some left on account
of it. The man was rich, well dressed, and very polite, but still the
meek followers of Christ could not worship their God and have this
sable companion with them. . . . There are three colored girls here
who have been in the habit of attending Friends meeting where they
have lived, but here they are not even allowed to sit on the back seat.
One long-faced elder dusted off a seat in the gallery and told them to
sit there."

Whatever the family thought of the long-faced elder,
Susan's youthful enthusiasm for reform must have
sounded alarming, for Aaron McLean replied hastily
that he was glad her new associates were so prudent
in their attitude towards controversial questions, and he
entreated her not to jeopardize her own position by
trying to "niggerize" the New Rochelle Friends. To
which Susan flung back defiantly: "Since school to-day
I have had the unspeakable satisfaction of visiting four
colored people and drinking tea with them."

Susan's mind was growing like a plant which thrusts
forth large, coarse leaves which are but protective of
fine flowering to come. But it cannot be denied that
it was still a very small-town mind, and why not, since
with the exception of a few closely chaperoned visits
to Philadelphia she had never seen a town larger than
Battenville? New Rochelle was within easy distance

of New York, and Susan may have visited it half a dozen times, but like most travelers she carried away from Rome what she took there. In her lively correspondence with her brother-in-law she tells of hearing, in the Rose Street meeting house, a remarkable sermon on "Vices of the City" by one Rachel Barker of Dutchess County, a discourse which completely demolished his "absurd notion that women have not intellectual and moral faculties sufficient for anything but domestic concerns." The vitality and exceeding charm of New York in 1839 seems to have escaped her, but again, why not? The United States was largely agricultural, and cities and city dwellers were viewed with general distrust. In school Susan had learned little of the history of her country, so the stately Dutch and Colonial mansions still lingering in the neighborhood of Trinity Church and old St. Paul's; the Battery, where fashion promenaded of evenings, viewing the harbor white with ships from farthest lands, while fortified Castle William guarded their entrance and departure; Fraunce's Tavern where Washington bade his officers farewell, and where a great many important political and social events were still staged, meant little to her. What most impressed her appears to have been the crowds, extravagant living and the extremes of fashion adversely commented upon by more sophisticated visitors than herself.

At twenty Susan still measured most of what she observed by Deborah Moulson's yardstick of Humility, Morality and the Love of Virtue. A glimpse of President Martin Van Buren, passing through New Rochelle on his way to dine with Washington Irving at Tarrytown, provoked a fulmination against that mild

wearer of the Jacksonian lion skin which would have
amazed him to read.

"Let us look at his behavior and scan its effects on society. One
day while in New York was spent in riding through the streets
preceded by an extravagant number of military men and musicians,
who were kept in exercise on that and succeeding days of the week
until they were all completely exhausted. On the next day while he
and his party were reveling in their tents on luxuries and the all-
debasing wine, many poor dear children were crying for food and
water to allay their thirst. On Friday evening he attended the Park
Theater, and on Monday the Bowery Theater. Yes, he who is
called by the majority as most capable of ruling this Republic, may
be seen in the theater encouraging one of the most heinous crimes and
practices with which our country is disgraced. Yes, and afterwards
we find him rioting at the wine table the whole livelong night. Is
it to be wondered at that such vast numbers of our population are
votaries of vice and dissipation?"

But Mr. McLean had also seen President Van Buren,
whom he found no gay dog, but a man quite old and
gray, grave and careworn, and very plainly dressed.
He wrote to Susan:

"If you do not like him because he drinks wine how can you like
Henry Clay who drinks it freely? Mr. Webster drinks wine also.
At a Whig festival got up in Boston in his honor, at which he and
1,200 other Whigs were present, there were drunk 2,300 bottles of
champagne, two bottles to each man. Mr. Clay attended balls at the
Springs. He had a slave to wait on him and hand him water to clear
his throat while he was speaking; and this when he was preaching
liberty and declaring what a fine thing this freedom is."

The evil practices of the great and the inconsistencies
of her favorite statesmen ceased to occupy Susan's attention when her personal affairs demanded her to think
soberly of her own future. Her first adventure in wage
earning had not carried her very far in the direction

of independence. For fifteen weeks' teaching in New Rochelle she received thirty dollars, and after spending most of that on necessary clothing she had left barely enough to pay her way home. Several plans for making more money were tried out in her active imagination. Silkworm culture, which she thought might be combined with teaching; the cultivation of a superior variety of cherry she had bought in a New York market; several projects for selling home crafts. All vain. Yet some women had escaped the treadmill she knew, for her reading at New Rochelle had included some of the works of Harriet Martineau, a novel or two of George Sand, a harmlessly feministic "History of Women," by Lydia Maria Child, and a few of Margaret Fuller's scintillant essays in the Boston *Dial*. For Susan there was no immediate escape, so she took charge of a country school near Hardscrabble, the name now changed to Center Falls. The salary was two dollars and a half a week with board, and half of her wages Susan had to send to her father, struggling to support the family on the dwindling returns of his satinet factory and grist mill. The new school, lately given up by a man teacher receiving ten dollars a week, was a hard proposition. Among the pupils were several half-grown farm louts who came not to study but to indulge in the pleasant sport of teacher baiting. They did not bait Susan very long. As soon as she decided which one of the rowdies was the real leader she cut a thick stick and after a desperate battle she beat him into such complete submission that there was never any more trouble from the others.

In vacation Susan visited relatives in Vermont where a young man cousin taught her algebra. After that an-

other school where nobody wanted to study algebra
and where the salary was again one-fourth of what men
teachers were paid for the same work. The trusty
journal occasionally indicates that Susan was at times
tempted to give up trying to escape a dependent life.
The trouble was that she was unable to fall in love with
any of the young men who were then paying her attentions. One suitor offended her taste by sending her a
newspaper with some foolish jokes and love poems
marked. Another suitor she described as a "real soft-
headed old bachelor." One gallant whom she liked a
little better than the others took another girl on a buggy
riding excursion to Saratoga Springs, and to make matters worse, the youth who substituted for him took advantage of the occasion to propose. Why must women
always put up with the second best things of life? In
Center Falls a rich widower with a fine farm, a big
house and a sixty-cow dairy, tried to persuade Susan
to marry him, partly because she looked so strong and
well, and partly because she reminded him of his dead
wife. But Susan shuddered at the prospect of being
the second woman to wear her life out in a dairy of
sixty cows. Although reason ever prevailed over emotion Susan was not a cold or sexless young woman. In
sleep she sometimes dreamed of being married, but
always of repenting it. These dreams are recorded in
her journal, because they puzzled her so much!

In 1843 she became a governess in a certain family
of Taylors, well-bred and cultured people, in Fort Edward, New York. This must have been a pretty dull
experience, as the diary was for some time abandoned.
The Taylors subscribed for the *New York Herald,* and
perhaps also for *Harper's Weekly,* for Susan in her

letters showed an interest in national politics, growing more and more stormy as the conflict over slavery extention in new States and Territories approached a climax. In the two years spent in Fort Edward Susan studied more mathematics, read some good literature, formed a friendship with Abigail Mott, an abolitionist of prominence in Albany, resisted attempts of two friends who tried to convert her to Methodism and Unitarianism, and attended a Whig Convention, her first political meeting, which interested her deeply. When the Anthonys moved to the Rochester farm she went along, and for the better part of a year helped plant and cultivate apple and peach orchards. The following spring she prepared to teach another country school, but at this point something better offered.

Uncle Joshua Read, the same one who had helped the Anthonys when the panic of 1838 closed the cotton mill in Battenville, was at this time a rich and influential citizen of Canajoharie. He was director of a bank, part owner of a turnpike, a toll bridge and a stage line, a hotel proprietor and a trustee of the Canajoharie Academy, one of the few co-educational schools then in the State. Rather tardily it would seem, it occurred to Uncle Joshua to offer Susan a position in the academy. Early in 1843 she was appointed principal of the girls' department, at a salary higher than any she had yet received, but of course lower than a man's salary. She accepted joyfully, and for two years lived and taught in Canajoharie, a paying guest in the home of her cousin Margaret, Uncle Joshua's married daughter. The Reads, it will be remembered, were not Quakers, nor was Quaker influence strong in the town. Removed from the strait-laced traditions and conventionalities of her youth Susan's nature underwent an amazing metamorphosis. From a moralist and a reformer she suddenly bloomed into a gay young lady, eager after the joys of life. She dropped the Quaker garments, the Quaker plain speech, began to go to parties, the theater and the circus, even accepting the escort of gentlemen who, like President Van Buren, hesitated not to taste the all-debasing wine cup. Susan's father was now in a salaried position and there was no need to send any of her salary home. She could spend it all on herself, and she did. She became, in fact, quite desperately dressy, lavishing on her first winter wardrobe $22.50 for a broché shawl; $5.50 for a white silk-ribbed bonnet; $8 for a gray fox muff; adding to all these a plum-colored merino dress at $2 a yard. To make a gown after a new model in *Godey's Lady Book,* a very long skirt draped over a hoop and trimmed with two or three deep ruffles, or if you preferred them, puffs, a tight basque with a fichu or cape edged with fringes, required at least eighteen yards of stuff, so the plum-colored merino represented quite an outlay, and very modish Susan thought she appeared in it. The gown and the white silk bonnet, she wrote her mother, "made the villagers stare," and this pleased Uncle Joshua, for he had impressed on Susan from the first that in order to make a real success it was necessary to make the world notice you. "Make people think you know it all," he advised her.

Canajoharie noticed Susan, admired everything she wore and almost everything she did, but it is doubtful if she was considered very handsome. Beauty standards of the Forties demanded a small woman with a heart-shaped face, large, limpid eyes without too much expression, and an air about her of sweet submission. Susan was tall, five feet six inches, with shoulders broad in proportion. She had a beautifully shaped head crowned with thick and glossy brown hair, brilliant eyes, a little near-sighted, a face square rather than oval, and a mouth large, perhaps, but mobile and healthily red. Nowadays we should ask as soon as she entered a room: "Who is she?" Then they said: "A fine figure of a woman." Nobody questioned that the new school mistress was "the smartest woman who ever came to Canajoharie." That was the verdict, first voiced after a public examination of the girls of her department at the close of her first term. This age knows not public examinations of school children, but in former days they were great events, looked forward to almost like college commencements. Pupils wore their best clothes, palpitant parents and critical trustees, as well as the general public, came to listen, applaud or criticize, the teacher's reputation being at stake on each occasion. The night before her first public examination Susan was too nervous to sleep, but on the crucial day, becomingly arrayed in a new white muslin gown, plaided in purple, blue and brown, blue prunella gaiters with patent leather heels, and a gold watch, chain and pencil generously loaned by Cousin Margaret, she was at her best, and the examination went off with colors flying. Gushing compliments from the trustees, renewed admiration from the townspeople, but no raise of salary rewarded Susan's efforts. Two fresh proposals of marriage from men who thought so much ability wasted in school-teaching were added to the others which she had rejected. Paid labor, however ill-paid, attracted her more than the wedded state, as it then existed.  Susan, who to the end of her life loved good clothes, wrote to her married sisters, Guelma and Hannah, teasingly contrasting their lot with that of an "old maid" who was free to earn and spend her money on fine raiment.  However, as far as social gaiety and the attentions of men were concerned she was already beginning to waver.  She revolted against the custom, common in those days among men in the best society, to indulge too freely in strong drink.  A decent man did not get drunk, but practically all imbibed pretty regularly, and it was usual for young gentlemen to fortify themselves with a few glasses of whisky before attending social functions.  Their bibulous love making was accepted by most women as something inevitable, even flattering, but it simply disgusted the clear-headed Susan.  The morning after a military (militia?) ball she made this single comment in her diary:

"My fancy for attending dances is fully satiated.  I certainly shall not attend another unless I can have a total abstinence man to accompany me, and not one whose highest delight is to make a fool of himself."

A real tragedy was needed to turn Susan definitely away from marriage.  The dearly loved cousin Margaret, in whose home she had lived so happily, gave birth to a fourth child, and after several weeks of suffering she meekly died.  Lingering over her sick bed Susan witnessed an incident which shocked her to her heart's core.  Margaret's husband, supposed to be a very good example indeed, complained to his dying wife that he had a bad headache.  "I have had one for days," ventured Margaret.  "Oh, yes," retorted Joseph, "but I mean that I have a real headache, very painful. Yours is just a natural consequence."

In her grief after Margaret's death Susan began to take serious thought of herself and to what end she was living. She was twenty-eight years old, and after nine years of proved ability she had reached about the highest point a woman teacher could hope to attain. She knew now that she had never been really satisfied with her career in Canajoharie. What she had believed to be happiness was mere excitement and delight in popular success. A common delusion. For a woman of her ability there was but one career to be envied, service to society. Yet what possible chance had she to take part in politics or social movements? Susan was too intellectually honest to over-estimate her own talents. She had a superior mind and knew it as well as anybody. But special gifts she seemed to lack. Margaret Fuller had expended the wealth of her intellect in writing, but Susan had no talent for writing. Several women, Abby Fuller and the spectacular Grimké sisters, especially Angelina Grimké, had smashed all precedents by appearing as anti-slavery lecturers in ultra-liberal churches. Susan had made one speech, at a supper of the local Daughters of Temperance, but while it was applauded she knew that it was good merely because nobody in Canajoharie could have made a better. Measured against the theatrical eloquence of Angelina Grimké it was only a passable performance. In deep depression Susan wrote to her father that, rather than this continued inaction, she would like to join the men who were rushing to the California gold fields. She would like to do anything rather than rotate dully between her classrooms and the home made desolate by Margaret's death. At the end of her resources, her hopes and ambitions, she was like one wandering in a maze, vainly seeking a way out. Meanwhile, a short distance from the scene of her despair, a group of women unknown to her personally, had, more or less by chance, discovered the only way that ever led out of a human impasse—organization.

# CHAPTER V

## THE WOMEN'S DECLARATION OF INDEPENDENCE

THE first attempt to organize women as a social group to obtain equal rights with men was the Seneca Falls Convention of July, 1848. Although not yet fully realized, this convention had an importance difficult to exaggerate. For, as has been well said, the Middle Ages lasted longer for women than for men, and this event marked their passing, first for American women, later for women of all civilized countries. The story of the convention has been told many times, but it needs a retelling, or at least a revaluation. There is an impression that the Seneca Falls Convention was the beginning of the agitation for woman suffrage, and in a sense this is true, since in a republic a demand for political equality is inseparable from a demand for any equality at all. But the women who met in Seneca Falls demanded much more than votes. They declared war on the whole status of women under the English Common Law, on which all American laws are based.* A brief exposition of the old law is necessary, because otherwise it would be impossible to understand the ignoble position of women no farther back than the middle years of the Nineteenth Century.

The theory of the English Common Law made women perpetual minors. An unmarried woman

* In Louisiana the laws are based on the Code Napoléon, the position of women being even more degraded than under English Common Law.

rested under the tutelage and control of her father or male guardian until she was twenty-one; in reality as long as she lived, since a spinster could not live alone, and if she owned any property she had to have male trustees. A married woman lived under the tutelage and control of her husband until death dissolved the union. A married woman had no separate existence from her husband, but was in every legal sense a *feme covert*. She could own no property, real or personal, every vestige of her possessions, acquired or inherited, passing to the ownership of her husband with the marriage ceremony. She could not receive a gift of property, even from her husband. It is true that a pre-nuptial contract could secure, under male trusteeship, a bride's dowry to her use, but as dowries were practically unknown in the United States this did not affect the general situation. A *feme covert* naturally could not make separate contracts, witness a legal document, sue or be sued, claim wages earned, or collect damages for injuries to her person or her character. The children of a marriage belonged to the father alone. He could give or will away from the mother her living and even her unborn children. If a wife divorced her husband for any cause the custody of the children was usually given to him. If he was notoriously an unfit guardian for minors it was customary to award them to his family. Property could be willed to a wife, but if a man died intestate she received only dower, that is, the use for life of one third of his real estate. If he left no real estate she became a dependent, a pauper.

One curious right a married woman possessed, the right to saddle her husband with responsibility for her minor infractions of the law, her torts. He was punishable for any except grave crimes, committed by her in his presence or with his knowledge, the theory being, in the language of the law, that "a woman would not dare to disobey her baron." The law also protected a woman from being beaten, except in moderation, and with a stick no bigger than a man's thumb, the size and weight of the man not being specified. "Such a favorite," declares Blackstone, "is woman under the laws of England." Unmarried women were also favorites to the extent of being excluded from earning a living except in a few ill-paid trades. The law having declared women inferior to men, no institution of higher learning, no professional training was open to them. Skilled trades and business enterprises also excluded women. Against the whole theory of the English Common Law, and social theories growing out of the law, the Seneca Falls Convention of women declared not revolt but revolution. They went a great deal farther than that. They declared revolution against the even more sacred Canon Law! Well they knew that mere legal disabilities of women could not be removed as long as the majority of men believed that the Hebrew Bible, which upholds slavery in many forms, was inspired in every line and paragraph.

English Common Law subjected women on the ground that they were inferior mentally, and physically defenseless. Canon Law subjected them on the ground that they were a sub-species of God's creation, man, and unclean to boot, because they had caused the fall of man. The Church, ignoring the plain teachings of Jesus Christ, adhered to an Oriental conception of woman formed in a desert civilization thousands of years before the present era; on the pronouncements of an Asiatic Jew, Paul of Tarsus; and on the pathological morbidities of monks of the first centuries A.D. A few sentences picked out, it would seem, at random, from the Old and the New Testaments, served to establish woman's status for all time, in all forms of civilization, as far as the Church was concerned. By woman came sin into the world, therefore "the man shall rule over thee." "Wives, submit yourselves unto your husbands as unto the Lord." " . . . As the church is subject unto Christ, so let wives be to their own husbands." "Neither was the man created for the woman, but the woman for the man." Against the accumulated wisdom of legal and divine authority that handful of women in 1848 declared war, successful war as time has proved. Since this is the first recorded instance of a subjected class wresting freedom from its owners and masters it is not exactly to the credit of men that they have overlooked it in their learned works of history and sociology.

The first rift in the English Common Law, in its application to women, was a Married Woman's Property Act passed by the New York State Legislature in April, 1848. Women had petitioned in behalf of the law, but it was really sponsored and passed by a number of rich men, anxious that their wealth, descending to grandsons in the female line, should not be dissipated beforehand by profligate sons-in-law. As far as it went it was a progressive measure, but it affected a comparatively small class of women. The property rights, and what is more important, the human rights of the great majority were left unprotected. But while Church and State still united in keeping women in subjection, mighty forces were moving unseen to make easier the revolt of women against them. The abolition movement, since agitation against involuntary servitude based on color was at least a good talking point against involuntary servitude based on sex; the rise of the working classes, since women now belonged to the working classes, and a dominant class which pays money to any submerged class has already lost a measure of its dominance over it; last of all, the increase of wealth in the United States, with its consequence of increased leisure, and the growth of a national culture in which women shared, and to which not a few contributed.

The two women responsible for the Seneca Falls Convention were Elizabeth Cady Stanton and Lucretia Mott. Both belonged to a social class superior to that into which Susan B. Anthony was born. Mrs. Stanton was the daughter of Judge Daniel Cady, and the wife of Henry B. Stanton, a lawyer eminent in his profession, a member of the New York State Senate, an early abolitionist and a man of very liberal principles. Mrs. Stanton had attended the Emma Willard Academy at Troy, New York, and this almost-collegiate education was supplemented by private instruction in Greek and Latin. Lucretia Mott also belonged to the upper stratum of society. She was a Philadelphian, by adoption if not by birth, a member of that branch of Quakers called the Progressive Friends, and a woman of education and culture. Her husband, James Mott, had made a fortune in the woolen business, and Lucretia's drawing-room was by way of being a salon, not only for intellectual Philadelphians, but for foreign celebrities visiting the United States. Writers, artists, scholars, philanthropists and politicians from abroad naturally gravitated to the Mott mansion, among these being Harriet Martineau, Fanny Kemble, Fredericka Bremer, Lord Morpeth, Lord Amberly and other members of Parliament, all curious to meet the "American reformers," strikingly personified in Lucretia Mott.

Privileged in their lives as they were, both Mrs. Stanton and Mrs. Mott had been made to feel the humiliation attendant on sex subjection, and both smarted keenly under it. In 1840 a World's Anti-Slavery Convention was held in London, and several American societies had named among other delegates four women, probably because the women could pay their own expenses. Lucretia Mott was one of the delegates, as indeed she had every right to be, because her abolitionist activities actually pre-dated those of Wendell Phillips and William Lloyd Garrison. As far back as 1833 she had helped organize in Philadelphia a Women's Anti-Slavery Society, and for years she had been tireless in memorializing Congress to abolish slavery in the District of Columbia and the territories. Two years before the World Convention in London she had played a brave part in a meeting in Philadelphia, when mobs howled around Pennsylvania Hall, smashed windows, and finally burned the building over the delegates' heads. In London she met Elizabeth Cady Stanton, on her wedding journey with Henry B. Stanton, a delegate to the convention and afterward its secretary. Fenced off from public gaze by a grating, like women in a Jewish synagogue, Mrs. Mott and Mrs. Stanton, in company with such distinguished English women as Elizabeth Fry, Mary Howitt, Amelia Opie, Anna Jameson and Lady Byron, witnessed a fight against the admission of the women delegates which, as Mrs. Stanton declared, could not have been surpassed if the news had come that the French were about to invade England. The convention was largely controlled by ministers of the Gospel, and these men, abandoning all dignity, rushed up and down, open Testaments in hand, invoking the commands of Jehovah himself against the participation of women in public meetings. After hours of shrieking debate it was voted, almost unanimously, to reject the credentials of the four women delegates.

Mrs. Stanton and Mrs. Mott walked out of the hall together, and as soon as they could speak for indignation, they told each other that the time would come when women themselves would hold a convention to change these things. A few days later a group of American visitors of distinction were especially invited to view the treasures of the great British Museum, but these two did not accompany the others on their personally conducted tour through the buildings. Sitting on a hard bench in an anteroom they spent the time discussing the possibilities of Philadelphia, New York and Boston as meeting places for women of the best minds. Eight years passed and in correspondence they had tried to arrange conventions in all these cities, but no encouragement offering they had let the idea slumber. In early July, 1848, Mrs. Mott went to western New York to attend a yearly meeting of the Hicksite, or Progressive, Friends, afterward visiting her sister, Mrs. Martha C. Wright, in Auburn, near Seneca Falls, now the home of the Stantons. Talking over the events of London in 1840, Mrs. Stanton, without much difficulty, persuaded Mrs. Mott that their convention to

revise the whole status of women might just as well be
held then and there.  A revision of the whole status of
women in a town of 1,500 inhabitants in rural New
York, seems audacious.  But since under their then
status few women had either money or freedom to
journey to more populous centers, one place was really
as good as another as a starting point, and the little
semi-weekly *Seneca County Courier* was equal to the
*New York Herald* or the *Philadelphia Ledger* as a
publicity carrier.  In its issue of July 14, 1848, the
*Courier* published this modest announcement:

### "SENECA FALLS CONVENTION

WOMAN'S RIGHTS CONVENTION—A Convention to discuss the
social, civil, and religious rights of woman, will be held in the Wesleyan Chapel, Seneca Falls, New York, on Wednesday and Thurs-
day, the 19th and 20th of July, current; commencing at ten o'clock
A. M.  During the first day the meeting will be held exclusively for
women, who are earnestly invited to attend.  The public generally
are invited to be present on the second day, when Lucretia Mott,
of Philadelphia, and other ladies and gentlemen will address the
meeting."

Not many women who read this announcement were
of the mental caliber of Susan B. Anthony who, only
as far away as Canajoharie, could not read it at all.
The women it reached were, for the most part, wives
and daughters of villagers or of farmers living within
a radius of fifty miles of Seneca Falls.  The free woman
of to-day, free to choose her work, her career and her
way of life, may well wonder how that first Declaration of the Rights of Woman impressed the simple, average woman of 1848, and how far her mind was prepared to receive it.  Fortunately we may know.  As
recently as 1920 the last survivor of the Seneca Falls

MRS. STANTON AND HER CHILDREN
About 1848, the Time of the Seneca Falls Convention

Convention was living in Philadelphia, and from her lips this writer heard it described, not as it appeared to one of the leaders, but to a girl of nineteen who sat in a back seat, a silent but delighted spectator. Mrs. Charlotte Pierce, then Charlotte Woodward, was one of a large class of girls, the alarming younger generation, their elders called them, who having been forced into wage earning were not at all satisfied with either wages or conditions of their toil. Outside of mill and factory towns most woman labor was performed in the home, the workers in no degree being freed from their traditional household tasks. Wage earning only meant longer hours of work, and to most women it meant work without money compensation. Generous husbands and fathers sometimes let the women keep their earnings as a dress allowance, but the majority of men simply entered the money in their ledgers against the women's board and keep. The younger generation had begun to object to this arrangement, and some even complained that the industrial field allotted them was dull and uninteresting. In Charlotte Woodward's neighborhood, for example, about the only thing women could do to earn extra money needed for the family income was to sew gloves sent in packages from factories in Gloversville. Now Charlotte, for one, detested sewing. She thought if she had to work at all she would like to set type in a printing office. Other girls believed they would enjoy selling ribbons, bonnets, dress materials in drygoods shops. Of course they might as well have aspired to banking or bridge building.

Over a gulf of seventy-two years Mrs. Charlotte Pierce remembered her excitement when the July 14

issue of the *Seneca County Courier* fell into her hands.
She ran from one house to another in her neighborhood,
and found other women reading it, some with amusement and incredulity, others with absorbed interest.
Half a dozen of Charlotte's intimate friends were interested enough to agree with her that they must attend the convention, at least on the first day when only
members of their own sex would be present. They
knew all about the celebrated Lucretia Mott and Mrs.
Stanton, for although the announcement did not carry
her name they felt sure that Mrs. Stanton was behind
it. Early in the morning of July 19 those country girls
started on their long drive, in a democrat wagon drawn
by fat farm horses. Over country roads we can picture
them traveling, through leafy woods, past fields and
orchards where men toiled with hand plows and cul-
tivators; through quiet villages where white church
steeples reminded them of the sanctity of things as
they were, and over pagan brooks babbling that the
essence of life was movement, progress, change.
Through a world that was, toward a world that was
to be reshaped in the lifetime of most of them.

They had imagined that they would be practically
alone in their adventure, and that few outside their
own families would know that they had done anything
as sensational as to attend a woman's rights meeting.
But as they drove along they perceived an unusual
number of vehicles, family carriages, chaises, surreys,
democrats and even farm wagons, turning in from lanes
and byways to join the procession on the main high
road. Women formed the majority of the passengers,
but some of the vehicles were driven by men. When
the girls arrived at the Wesleyan Chapel in Seneca

Falls they found about fifty men waiting to be admitted
to a meeting advertised for women only. Mrs. Pierce
remembered that it was the presence of these uncom-
monly liberal men that gave her courage to stay over
for the second day's sessions. The chapel, that first
morning, was locked and bolted, possibly because the
minister had repented his hospitality to such a gathering. A young nephew of Mrs. Stanton, later a professor at Yale, volunteered to climb up, loosen a shutter,
and open the door to the crowd which filled the little
church to capacity. James Mott was made chairman,
because none of the women knew enough of Cushing's
*Manual* to conduct a meeting. Lucretia Mott, Martha
C. Wright, Mary McClintock and perhaps one other
woman read speeches, which they had purposely
couched in language much less radical than they used
in private. Several men also spoke: Ansel Bacon, one
of the men responsible for passing the Married
Woman's Property Act; Samuel Tillman, who gave
a clear exposition of women's position under the Common Law; Thomas McClintock, husband of Mary,
and an influential citizen of the county; also Frederick
Douglass, famous ex-slave and prize exhibit of the
Massachusetts Abolition Society. Finally Elizabeth
Cady Stanton read the Declaration and the Resolutions,
both of which were sufficiently startling and inclusive.

The Declaration of Independence of 1776 being as
familiar to Americans of that day as the Lord's Prayer,
the women in their preamble adopted its form, and
substituting for "The present King of Great Britain"
the general term Man, they submitted to a candid
world the facts of their unjustly subjugated condition
and Man's principal usurpations of woman's inalien-

able rights. He had never permitted her to exercise her right to the elective franchise, and had compelled her to submit to laws in the formation of which she had had no voice; he had made her, if married, in the eye of the law, civilly dead; he had taken from her all right in property, even to the wages she earned; he had made her, morally, an irresponsible being . . . compelled to promise obedience to her husband, he becoming, to all intents and purposes, her master; he had made himself, even if divorced, sole guardian of children; he had taxed single women, if owners of property, to support a government which did not recognize them except for its profit; he had closed against woman all the avenues to wealth and distinction which he considered most honorable to himself, leaving her only unprofitable employments in which she received scanty remuneration; he had denied her facilities for receiving a thorough education, allowed her but a subordinate position in the church, had given the world a different code of morals for men and women, usurped the prerogative of Jehovah himself in assigning woman a sphere of action, and lastly had endeavored in every possible way to destroy her confidence in her own powers, to lessen her self-respect, and to make her willing to lead a dependent and abject life.

The resolutions, eleven in number, declared that all these usurpations and disabilities were contrary to the laws of nature, that women everywhere ought to be enlightened concerning them, and should be taught to resist and overthrow them. The right to free education, equality with men in industry and the professions, to free speech and participation in public affairs, including church affairs, and the right to vote, were de-

manded.  The only resolution which was not unanimously adopted was that one which called for the
elective franchise.  Mrs. Stanton and Frederick Douglass, however, held out so stoutly for the clause that it
was included with the others.  Charlotte Woodward
voted for it wholeheartedly, never dreaming that she
alone of all those women present would live to cast her
ballot, with nation-wide enfranchised women, in a
presidential election.  Sixty-eight women and thirty-
two men signed the resolutions, but many of them withdrew their names as soon as the inevitable storm of
newspaper ridicule and vituperation burst upon their
heads.  They had expected disapproval, but "atheists"
and "hermaphrodites" they were not quite prepared
to be branded.  Undaunted, the leaders prepared at
once for a second convention to be held two weeks later
in the important city of Rochester.

# CHAPTER VI

## THE TEACHER BECOMES TEMPERANCE CRUSADER

THE Seneca Falls Convention got almost as much publicity as is in these days accorded a sensational crime—and much the same kind of publicity. "The Hen Convention," which was about the most polite term applied to it, was denounced as a defiance of Divine revelation, a conspiracy against public morals and the home, the purity of American women (a purer purity than existed elsewhere), in general a conspiracy against all known and approved rules of society. A few thoughtful writers said it was interesting, a few contemptuous ones dismissed it as just another "ism," one of those crank ideas which had broken out like measles in intellectual centers as far west as Cincinnati. Abolition, temperance, vegeterianism, spiritualism, Fourierism, free love. In Canajoharie Susan B. Anthony read with absorbed interest everything published in the village newspaper. Most of the resolutions, better education for women, enlarged industrial opportunities, equal pay for equal work, the right to property and wages; above all, the right of women to free speech on public platforms, she approved, but when she read the eleventh resolution, calling for the right to vote, she laughed. The fact is that Susan, being Quaker born, despised the ballot for anybody. It was a rule of the Society of Friends to abjure all voting, because, as professional pacifists, they thought it positively wrong to support any government that upheld war. Daniel Anthony had never voted in his life, never did vote until 1860, when, convinced that nothing but war could wipe out slavery, he went to the polls and cast his first ballot for Abraham Lincoln.

Great was Susan's surprise, therefore, when, home on a brief holiday, she heard that her whole family had attended the second woman's rights convention, held in Rochester two weeks after the Seneca Falls meeting, and that her father and mother, and even her shy sister, Mary, had signed the resolutions, including the demand for equal suffrage. The family could talk of nothing but the Rochester convention. The women of their intimate circle had sponsored it, and had gone a great deal farther than the Seneca Falls women had dared, for they conducted all the sessions themselves without the help of any men. This bold performance so dismayed the star speakers, Lucretia Mott and Elizabeth Cady Stanton, that when they heard that Mrs. Abigail Bush had been chosen president of the convention, and that several women were to serve as secretaries, they threatened to go home. Ignorance of the sacred Cushing's *Manual,* they protested, would so embarrass the women, would give such advantage to disturbers of the meeting, that the whole thing would break up in confusion. Frederick Douglass, in their opinion, should be made chairman, and Mr. Douglass, no doubt, would have been glad to oblige. But the Rochester women could not be persuaded to alter their program. Women, they said, had found their tongues at last, and whatever cause they had they must now present to the world in person. Nothing disastrous occurred. At first, it is true, Mrs. Bush and the women secretaries, all of them frightened as rabbits, and unaccustomed to raise their voices above a genteel drawing-room pitch, could not make themselves heard beyond the first row of seats. But Sarah Burtis, an Anthony cousin and a teacher in the public schools, came to the rescue with vocal cords grown vigorous in calling recalcitrant youngsters to order, and after that things went swimmingly. Mrs. Burtis read the minutes of the previous meeting and as often as necessary acted as interpreter between the audience and the more inarticulate speakers.

One whole session of the convention had been devoted to the wretched condition of women wage earners in the flourishing city of Rochester, and it was these revelations which really converted Daniel Anthony to woman's rights. In his cotton mills, as we have seen, Daniel had been extremely mindful of the welfare of his women operatives. He had paid them a living wage, as living and wages went in those days, and he had seen to it that they were decently housed and kindly treated. To hear "The Song of the Shirt," not as sung by the English poet Hood, but as lived in anguish in his own community, had plowed up his heart and troubled his dreams. And small wonder. The organizers of the convention had brought to the platform two of the earliest investigators of women's working conditions, and they reported such facts as could only be matched by Lord Shaftsbury's records of factory and mine labor in the previous decades. Rochester seamstresses were paid for a day of twelve to fourteen hours, from thirty-one to thirty-eight cents. Inside workers had deducted from their wages $1.25 to $1.50 a week for board, and the pitiful remainder, if there was a remainder, was often paid, not in cash but in due bills on certain stores where the women were charged exorbitant prices. Married women, of course, had no claim to their own earnings, and these were frequently used by husbands for drink or to support other women. The finest sewing was done at these starvation wages. Men of fashion thought women could not make their clothes, but, it was revealed, when these men patronized expensive tailors, the garments, after being cut and fitted in the shops, were sweated out to women whose needlework was finer than the tailor's own. For making a costly satin vest these accomplished craftswomen received thirty cents; for making a coat, about forty cents; for a pair of trousers, from twelve to thirty cents. They could not refuse to accept such starvation wages, because sewing was practically the only trade open to them. "And yet," said the speaker,

"an experienced cashier of this city remarked to me that women might be as good bookkeepers as men; but men have monopolized every lucrative situation, from drygoods merchant down to whitewashing. Who does not feel, as she sees a stout, athletic man standing behind a counter measuring lace, ribbons and tape, that he is monopolizing a woman's place, while thousands of rich acres in the western world await his coming? . . . Let men become producers, as nature has designed them, and women be educated to fill all those stations which require less physical strength, and we should soon modify many of our social evils."

Following these revolutionary proposals Mrs. Stanton read the Seneca Falls Declaration of Independence and the resolutions for women's emancipation, social, industrial and political, and she challenged any clergyman present to voice his objections then and there, instead of in the pulpit where nobody could answer him.

The fire she hoped to draw came promptly. Several clergymen, their eyes moist over the miseries of women wage slaves, asked how even such deplorable conditions could be removed without substituting a greater evil, destruction of the God-ordained authority of men. What if bookkeeping and other well paid avenues of work were opened to women, and their husbands and fathers objected, as well they might, to the women leaving the home? What if women insisted on leaving nevertheless? Who was to decide such questions? The United States had no Lord Chancellor. In the case of married women the case was clear, because if Christians, they were obliged to obey their husbands. As for unmarried women, any rebellion against man's dominant position would be dangerous because it would tend to break up the home. Such subjects could hardly even be discussed by women without violating the command of St. Paul, "Let your women keep silence in the churches." To which the mild spoken but sardonic Mrs. Mott replied, St. Paul nevertheless gave specific directions how women were to appear when they *did* speak, and he seemed glad enough to have Phœbe, Priscilla, Tryphena Tryphosa, and the four daughters of Philip carry on his provincial parishes. Moreover, Paul had strongly recommended celibacy to men, but most of the clergymen who opposed free speech for women had disregarded his advice. A shocking remark for a lady to make in mixed company, but Mrs. Mott and Mrs. Stanton were saving their really shocking remarks for future meetings.

Susan laughed, and said she wished she might meet those women, especially Mrs. Stanton, to whom with prophetic intuition she felt strongly attracted. But

the woman's rights movement, for all her father's enthusiasm, left her rather cold. Other reforms must
come first. With such a monster as intemperance de-
vouring the land, and the still greater evil, slavery,
oppressing millions, the women's demand for their own
rights seemed premature. Susan had come to the
end, or almost to the end of her own self-life. She was
through with the minor glory of the social conquest of
a small town like Canajoharie, the possession of a purse
ample enough to buy herself fashionable gowns, shawls
and bonnets. Her success as a school-teacher no longer
satisfied her, and she was growing more and more
restive in a profession where the brightest woman com-
peted on unequal terms with the dullest man. Her
whole instinct was toward public life, social service,
but she was acutely conscious of the fact that any
woman who occupied a place in public life had first
to create the place. How to do it and at the same time
earn a living was a question which found no solution in
her brain. She must continue to support herself,
and since her father's business position was not yet very
definitely established, she might be called upon to help
in the education of younger members of the family.
Were she situated like her friend Lydia Mott in Albany, who supported herself by her exquisite needlework, she might have found a place in anti-slavery
propaganda. By now the slavery agitation was passing
from its purely propaganda stage and was becoming
abolitionism, a larger thing and different. In 1844
Susan's old hero, Henry Clay, had been defeated for
the Presidency by the innocuous James Polk, the Abolitionists contributing to this end by diverting enough
Whig votes to the Liberty Party candidate, James G.

Birney. Abolitionism was now a real political factor, and by the time the 1848 campaign came on there were enough Northern Democrats under its influence to return the Whigs to power, and to send Zachary Taylor to the White House. In four years more the Abolitionists might elect their own candidate. If it were only possible to devote herself to this great cause— But the Abolition leaders had no money to pay speakers and organizers. It was a mystery then as it is now how William Lloyd Garrison found money enough to support his own family.

Next to the abolition cause Susan was interested passionately in temperance, and in that field, even with her limited resources, she believed she might be useful, for there surely the social influence of women, if exercised vigorously, would be decisive. "All that is needed to produce a complete temperance and social reform," she had told the Canajoharie Daughters of Temperance, "is for our sex to cast their united influences into the balance." Susan had never read the Greek classics and she was unaware of the fact that the same theory, and its discouraging conclusion, had been laughed at on the Athenian stage more than a thousand years before. Neither the ladies' anti-war society of Athens nor the Daughters of Temperance of Canajoharie were economically in a position to redeem men from their pet vices by boycotting marriage, or as Susan put it, "to speed the day when no young man . . . who pollutes his lips with the drunkard's cup shall presume to seek the favors of our precious daughters."

To tell the truth there were no other kinds of young men. Or very few. Practically all Americans were immoderate drinkers, and had been from the earliest

SUSAN B. ANTHONY
At the Age of Thirty-two. From a Daguerreotype.

times. Those who accuse women of foisting prohibition on this country would do well to examine the soil in which Anti-Saloon League fanaticism was nurtured. Almost from the landing of the Pilgrims the dragon's teeth of the present situation were sown, and it is easy to understand why. Puritanism ruthlessly crushed out all the joy of life, as necessary to the soul's sustenance as bread and meat to the body. Every outlet of the natural man was forbidden by the gloomy religion of the Puritans, singing, dancing, card games, outdoor sports, Christmas revels, the theater, even the boisterous play of growing children. For nearly two hundred and fifty years after the founding of the colonies the poison of Puritanism was virulent in the veins of Americans, nor is it wholly eliminated yet. Not the blessings of life, but the fear of death and damnation was dinned into the minds of our people. Joy was forbidden. But man must have his saturnalia, and inevitably he gets it somewhere. In this country he got it in alcohol. It might not have been so bad if his escape could have been found in ordinary wine drinking, but the first Americans did not make wine. They were forever on the move, forever pioneering westward. They never paused long enough to plant and cultivate the genial grape. Besides, the New England climate was unfavorable, and western forests and prairies offered too much resistance. It was labor enough to clear ground for ordinary grain and root crops. The grains might have included hops for mildly stimulating beer, if in the ceaseless movement of the pioneers it had been possible to transport beer. A keg of whisky or rum from the Barbados, fire water indeed, took up less room in the wagon, besides offering more immediate effect after the day's grinding hardships.

In the course of time city dwellers who could afford it did drink imported wines, especially at banquets and public dinners. But the amount of wine necessary to satisfy their alcohol-tanned gullets would have staggered the traditional three-bottle English aristocrat. Two bottles of champagne per guest at the little Whig affair of Daniel Webster's were probably mere chasers to the real liquid refreshments served on that occasion. Long before the champagne corks began to fly the gentlemen, if we can trust old menu cards of the period, had taken aboard a full cargo of brandy and whisky cocktails, claret, Rhine wines, sherry, madeira and port. A hardy race, our revered ancestors! An important point is that most of this excessive drinking was done by men only. In every country, except those in which wine is cheap and abundant this is the case. Only in city slums where cold and starvation reduce the population to despair are gin-soaked women to be found, and it is a fact that follows our relatively high standard of living that few of our native American women ever drank immoderately. The American housewife, unlike the French and Italian, knew not wine as a part of diet, nor did women, until a very recent date, know it as an aid to festivity, for in men's festivities women were not included. Sometimes after the feast was finished and the bottles emptied, the ladies were permitted to occupy secluded boxes or upper galleries, and as a rare treat, listen to the speeches of the men.

Thus to women of the mid-Nineteenth Century the drinking habits of men were incomprehensible, and where they were not a bitter curse they were an intolerable nuisance. In hardly any State was drunkenness a cause for divorce, nor was any man seriously handicapped, socially or professionally by a known predeliction for liquor. Fuddled lawyers pleaded before fuddled judges in the highest courts; fuddled physicians came to the childbeds of women; merchants and bankers served liquor to their patrons; whisky, rum and gin could be bought, even by children, not only in grog shops and saloons, but in grocery and drug stores. Indeed the drug stores were almost as completely stocked with liquors as with calomel, quinine, morphia and patent medicines. Even ministers of the Gospel drank, in moderation, they claimed. At all events it was not uncommon for them to accept part of their salaries in kegs of liquor.

This was the situation when Susan B. Anthony began her work as a temperance reformer. Against intemperance, especially in the younger generation, and of course, in the working classes, serious men had instituted a movement before Susan's time. But from it women, the worst sufferers from the evil, were excluded. This was partly because they were excluded from all men's organizations, and partly because, in the early days of the reform, one had to be a converted drunkard to qualify as a total abstinence orator. The Washingtonians, the first important temperance society, were made up entirely of reformed "old soaks," and their confessions, told in every lurid detail, were more thrilling to listen to than the most earnest arguments in favor of a godly, righteous and sober life. In a day when the theater was generally agreed to be the nearest gateway to hell, the Washingtonians, it must be admitted, put up a pretty good show. Nearly all of them had gone through delirium tremens, or claimed the experience anyhow, and their battles with snakes and demons, their hideous agonies of body and mind were graphically described. If in their cups they had nearly or quite murdered a loved one, preferably a favorite child, so much the better. All patterned themselves as nearly as possible after John B. Gough whose dramatic gifts were equaled only by his talent for violent backsliding. Most of the orators backslid occasionally, as a sad fact, but then, all the more effective was their return to the platform, for who does not love a redeemed sinner—provided his sex is right?

Even the lesser lights among the temperance lecturers had a good sense of the theater. One prime favorite carried along his little boy whom he carefully planted in an obscure corner of the church or hall. At the moment of his speech when the audience was exactly at the proper pitch of emotion, the speaker demanded: "As for the rum seller, the rum seller, my friends, what name black enough shall we find to call him?" He paused and gesticulated wildly, searching for a sufficiently scurrilous word, which was the little boy's cue to shrill out at the top of his lungs, "Devil! Devil!" Hysterical screams from the women, and loud "Amens" from the men. Another successful platform light was accompanied by a pathetic little girl who sobbed an obligato during her father's speech and afterward, in blue-ribboned ringlets and frilled pantelets, stood beside his chair and sang temperance songs. The classic "Father, dear father, come home with me now," or the even more tear-compelling "Father's a drunkard and mother is dead."

> "Mother, Oh! Why did you leave me alone?
> With no one to love me, no friends and no home.
> Dark is the night and the storm rages wild.
> God pity Bessie, the Drunkard's lone child!"

# CHAPTER VII

## SUSAN MEETS ELIZABETH CADY STANTON

THE Washingtonians were succeeded by the Sons of Temperance, locally organized, and the women, following the men's example, formed the Daughters of Temperance, their lodges however receiving no official recognition from the men. Susan, who had infused a great deal of vitality into the Canajoharie branch of the Daughters, became convinced that the next thing to do, in order to make the movement effective, was to unite the two societies. Her first work must be to organize as many new lodges as possible, and she began to employ all her leisure time, all her holidays, visiting nearby towns and villages and forming branches of the women's society. In Rochester she gave a series of suppers and entertainments to raise money for the cause and to impress on the Sons the value of Women's influence in the great reform. The public came to the entertainments ("One dollar will admit a gentleman and lady"), ate the suppers and praised both, especially the suppers. But the Sons still held off from coöperation. Still, some things, for example, a toast offered by a Rochester gentleman at one of Susan's functions and preserved for posterity by Ida Husted Harper, appeared to the women to be a promise of surrender on the part of the men.

"The Daughters—Our characters they elevate,
Our manners they refine.
Without them we degenerate
To the level of the swine."

Sure enough, when a local organization of the New York Sons of Temperance, early in 1852, called in Albany a convention of all the lodges of the State they extended an invitation to the women to send delegates. The Rochester branch sent Susan, and her credentials, with those of other women, were accepted, and seats in the hall were assigned them. But when Susan rose to speak to a motion the chairman silenced her, saying harshly that the sisters were asked there not to speak but to listen and to learn. Blazing with indignation Susan rose and walked out of the hall, a few women having the courage to follow her. With Lydia Mott she went to the office of the powerful *Albany Evening Journal,* the editor of which was Thurlow Weed, and discussed with this astute politician the feasibility of holding a separate meeting for women. Mr. Weed was sympathetic, and in his paper that evening he published the story of the men's treatment of the women delegates and advised the public to attend their meeting at the Hudson Street Presbyterian Church. A bad snow storm, a chimney that filled the room with smoke and a stove pipe that fell down in the middle of the program failed to discourage the women who filled the hall, and the result of the meeting was a resolution proposed by Susan to summon at an early date a Woman's State Temperance Convention. In getting this convention together Susan displayed a genius for organization, a publicity sense, an ability to work and to make other people work, which won the warm admiration of Elizabeth Cady Stanton, who gladly accepted Susan's invitation to be present and to speak. Almost unaided Susan wrote hundreds of necessary letters, raised money, held meetings in many towns, hired a hall, arranged for ushers, advertising, speakers, and succeeded in attracting to the April convention in Rochester some of the most prominent men and women in the State. Horace Greeley's interest was aroused and he wrote Susan a letter full of encouragement and good advice. He begged her to see that all nominations for officers, all resolutions and all speeches were prepared in advance and put in proper shape for the press, that only the best speakers be presented and that their remarks should be clear and to the point. If Susan would hold her committee to these suggestions Horace promised to publish in the *Tribune* telegraphic reports of the convention and to give as much space as possible to the women's speeches.

As far as attendance, enthusiasm, publicity and the achievement of its immediate object were concerned the convention was a huge success. A Woman's State Temperance Society, the first of its kind ever dreamed of, was formed, with Elizabeth Cady Stanton as President, Mrs. Gerrit Smith, the Rev. Antoinette Brown and several others as Vice-presidents, and Susan B. Anthony and Amelia Bloomer as Secretaries. To Susan, naturally, the heaviest work of the society was assigned. She was appointed State Agent, "with full power to organize auxiliary societies, collect money, issue certificates of membership, and do all things which she may judge necessary to promote the purposes for which our society has been organized." Authority to collect money meant that Susan was expected somehow to raise it, and somehow she did. She had resigned her position in Canajoharie by this time, and now she began traveling, paying her own expenses, obtaining halls and churches for meetings, doing all the speaking, when she could get no one else to speak, organizing new lodges, and generally waking up enthusiasm for the society. Within a short time she had increased the membership over a thousand, all this without a dollar except what she collected at her meetings or coaxed from women who in turn had to coax it from reluctant husbands. The rapid growth of the women's temperance movement at once attracted the attention and even the approval of the men's societies, and when the State Sons of Temperance, the name now changed to the Men's State Temperance Society, held their next convention in Syracuse, the local branch again tendered Susan's organization an invitation to send delegates. This the women did, happy in the belief that at last the men were ready to work with them to a common end. Alas! When Susan and Mrs. Bloomer reached Syracuse they were waited on by the famous clergyman, the Rev. Samuel J. May, who told them that he had been asked to advise them quietly to withdraw. The Syracuse committee had been sincere in their invitation, but a majority of the visiting delegates were clergymen, and one and all they objected to the presence of the women. Would the ladies then retire? Susan, and after her Mrs. Bloomer, flatly refused, and Mr. May assured them that he was delighted with their refusal. He would do all he could to have them recognized, although he feared he could do nothing. The convention opened stormily, the clerical delegates, with one or two exceptions, declaring that no business should

be transacted until those females—or rather those creatures—"a hybrid species, half man and half woman,
belonging to neither sex" were put out into the streets.
Susan got the floor long enough to remind the delegates
that over one hundred thousand signers of the petitions
for the Maine prohibition law the previous winter
had been women, but she was howled down, and in a
babel of abuse and insults the two women were ejected.

Defending their action on the floor of the convention the reverend gentlemen charged that the females,
while they might be temperance advocates, might even
have societies of their own, were really not worthy to
be admitted to the temperance movement. Apart from
their temerity in crashing men's meetings, an indecent thing in itself, they but waited an opportunity to
confuse the temperance question with dreadful doctrines of woman's rights, divorce, atheism, and for all
the men knew free love. Could they afford to have
their work for temperance mixed up with such propaganda? A thousand times no.

As before Susan protested by organizing a woman's
meeting in Mr. May's church, and for one evening at
least she drew away all but a handful of the audience
expected at the men's meeting. She got some pretty
good newspaper notices into the bargain, reporters saying generously that the women's speeches were far more
lucid and entertaining than any made by visiting clergymen. That was very well, but just the same Susan went
home pretty sick at heart. Could it be that Mrs. Mott
and Mrs. Stanton were right in their conviction that
all of women's freedom must be demanded before any
of it was attained? Susan was not quite sure even after
she attended the following September, her first woman's

rights convention, this also in Syracuse. This convention, by far the most important the women had yet organized, was attended by delegates from eight States and from Canada, for despite ridicule from the press and thunders from the pulpit the "detestable doctrine" had spread like a prairie fire, and woman's rights societies were now flourishing in communities as far west as Ohio, Indiana and Wisconsin. Garrison, Greeley, William Henry Channing, George W. Johnson, chairman of the New York State Committee of the Liberty Party, Angelina Grimké Weld and other notables, sent letters of endorsement. Greeley published glowing notices in the *Tribune* and Mr. Johnson even sent a contribution of ten dollars. Lucretia Mott presided, and Mrs. Stanton pressed Susan into service as one of the secretaries. In fact, Susan must at this time have become a member, because she figured in the nominating committee, objecting very strongly to a nominee for President, Elizabeth Oakes Smith, of Boston's exclusive literary circle. This lady had come to the convention in a short-sleeved, low-necked frock, and although she wore over it a light jacket, her bare arms and neck were much in evidence, and Susan argued that in such array no woman could represent the hard working wage earners for whom she desired woman's rights. Mrs. Smith was not elected.

Susan spoke at one session, very briefly, and her plea was less for woman's rights than for her temperance society and in favor of a projected People's College, which afterward became Cornell University. But she listened to many speeches, all of them calling for the ballot as the very structure of women's emancipation. She heard for the first time Lucy Stone, a delightful young creature with a voice of gold; Paulina Wright Davis, a most accomplished woman of Providence, Rhode Island; the benign Mrs. Mott and her husband, James Mott; Gerrit Smith, the rich reformer and philanthropist of Peterboro, N. Y.; and Ernestine Rose, at that time called "The Queen of the Platform." Ernestine Rose was a remarkable woman whether or not her powers of eloquence have been exaggerated. She was a Polish Jewess, daughter of a rabbi, and in her childhood had been a pattern of piety. But Ernestine was one of those accidents which happen in the best regulated families, a girl child with a better mentality than that of any male member, even her father, the rabbi. By the time she reached early womanhood her mind and her sensibilities had revolted against the daily prayer of the men: "I thank thee Lord that thou hast not created me a woman," and she utterly refused to offer the orthodox prayer of the women: "I thank thee Lord that thou hast created me according to thy will." From this revolt it was but a step to renouncing not only the Judaism of her fathers but all theological dogma. Obliged to leave Poland she fled to England where she married a British abolitionist, and with him she went to America, at once and fervently embracing woman's rights. It is said that Ernestine was beautiful, but her pictures do not bear this out very convincingly. An effective speaker and a magnetic personality she must have been, for she drew crowds wherever she appeared. Ernestine was audacious beyond most Americans of the period in publicly admitting that she was an agnostic, an infidel, if any one preferred the name. She horrified the Rev. Antoinette Brown, the first ordained woman minister,

**ERNESTINE ROSE**
"Queen of the Platform" in the Early 'Fifties

and she furnished endless copy to antagonistic news-papers. Susan found her a fascinating type.

Of this convention the *Syracuse Standard* said that it was attended by over 2,000 persons, and that no one could deny that it showed a greater amount of talent "than has characterized any public gathering in this city during the last ten years, if ever before." The *Standard* said of Susan B. Anthony that she had a capital voice and deserved to be made clerk of the Assembly. The *Syracuse Star* received quite another impression.

" . . . The poor creatures who take part in the silly rant of 'brawling women' and Aunt Nancy men," said the *Star,* "are most of them 'ismizers' of the rankest stamp, Abolitionists of the most frantic and contemptible kind, and Christian (?) sympathizers with such heretics as William Lloyd Garrison, Parker Pillsbury, C. C. Burleigh and S. S. Foster. These men are all woman's righters and preachers of such damnable doctrines and accursed heresies as would make demons of the pit shudder to hear."

We do not know as much about demons of the pit or what caused them to shudder as men did in the Fifties, but if William Lloyd Garrison caused them concern, the elder Bennett, arch foe of all social reforms, must have given them delight with his account of the Syracuse Convention. Bennett was one of those Rabelaisian men, common in his day, who could think of women only as sex animals, breeders if in captivity, prostitutes otherwise. The following is an extract from a long editorial which Mr. Bennett published in the *New York Herald,* September 12, 1852:

" . . . How did woman first become subject to man, as she now is all over the world? By her nature, her sex, just as the negro is and always will be to the end of time, inferior to the white race and, therefore, doomed to subjection; but she is happier than she would be in any other condition, just because it is the law of her nature. . . .

What do the leaders of the woman's rights convention want? They want to be members of Congress, and in the heat of debate subject themselves to coarse jests and indecent language like that of the Rev. Mr. Hatch.* They want to fill all other posts which men are ambitious to occupy, to be lawyers, doctors, captains of vessels and generals in the field. How funny it would sound in the newspapers that Lucy Stone, pleading a cause, took suddenly ill in the pains of parturition and perhaps gave birth to a fine bouncing boy in court! Or that the Rev. Antoinette Brown was arrested in the pulpit in the middle of her sermon from the same cause, and presented a 'pledge' to her husband and the congregation; or that Dr. Harriot K. Hunt, while attending a gentleman patient for a fit of the gout or fistula in ano found it necessary to send for a doctor, there and then, to be delivered of a man or woman child—perhaps twins. A similar event might happen on the floor of Congress, in a storm at sea or in the raging tempest of battle, and then what is to become of the woman legislator?" †

After Syracuse, Susan's temperance speeches included arguments for woman's rights, although she subordinated the latter to what she still believed to be the more immediate social necessity. But she was wavering. Perhaps after all in her temperance crusade she was dealing with effects rather than causes. She wavered still more after, in January, 1853, she held at Albany a mass meeting of her State Temperance Society to petition the Legislature for a Maine prohibition law for New York. The men's society also called a meeting, but the women had the greater popular success and much more newspaper publicity. As an

---

* Mr. Hatch was a minister of the Gospel whose speech from the floor at Syracuse was so obscene that he was forced, even by those opposing the women, to leave the hall.

† None of the women mentioned were at this time married.

unheard-of concession the Assembly Chamber was given up to a women's evening meeting, and one morning the rules were suspended in order that they might present personally their petition to the legislators. Twenty-eight thousand names were attached to the petition, most of them having been gathered by Susan, but, as one Assemblyman put it afterwards: "Who are these asking for a Maine Law? Nobody but women and children." A man of wealth who happened to be in Albany at the time was otherwise influenced. Mr. S. P. Thompson was building up a great fortune in the soft drink business, but that *might* not have had any bearing on the case. At all events he invited Susan, Mrs. Bloomer and the Rev. Antoinette Brown to New York, at his expense, and got them up a large temperance meeting in Metropolitan Hall, where Jenny Lind had sung, and other meetings in Broadway Tabernacle and the Brooklyn Academy of Music. Crowds paid admission to get a thrill out of women speaking in public, and Mr. Thompson, after paying the expenses of the halls, gave the rest of the money to the women. They used it to tour the principal cities and towns of New York lecturing on temperance and woman's rights. As usual Susan came in for her share of editorial rebuke:

"Miss Anthony may be a very respectable lady, but such conversation is certainly not calculated to enhance public regard for her. . . . She announced quite confidently that wives don't de facto love their husbands if they are dissipated. Everyday observation proves the utter falsity of this statement, and if there is one characteristic of the sex which more than another elevates and enobles it, it is the *persistency* and intensity of woman's love for man."

Thus the *Utica Evening Telegraph,* before easy divorce reared its hideous head to dissolve unlovely unions.

Susan continued her temperance activities through that year. There was a disreputable incident in connection with a World's Temperance Convention in the old Brick Church, Franklin Square, New York, which all friends of temperance, even women, were invited to attend. The women delegates' credentials were accepted, but when a business committee from each State was appointed, and Susan's name was proposed for the New York committee, Mayor Barstow, in a speech which even the *New York Herald* declared was too indecent to publish, threatened to resign if any female was admitted to office. Other delegates, including clergymen and Doctors of Divinity, moved that the women's credentials be withdrawn, and the motion was carried. Although the coarsest speeches of the men were omitted the newspapers generally approved their action. The *New York Commercial Advertiser* said:

"The delegates at the Brick Church who took the responsibility of knocking off these parasites deserve the thanks of the Temperance friends. . . . Such an association would mar any cause. Left to themselves such women must fall into contempt."

One more failure before Susan was through. When her cherished Woman's State Temperance Society was formed, a clause in the constitution admitted men to membership, allowed them to speak at all meetings, but made women only eligible to office. Most of the men and a great many of the more timid women objected to any disabilities for the men members, and at the first anniversary meeting, in the Spring of 1853, Mrs.

Stanton, yielding, though against her judgment, to these importunities, said that since any limitations seemed to some a violation of men's rights, and as the women had now learned to stand alone, it might perhaps be safe to admit men to all the privileges of the society, but she hoped that they would modestly permit women to continue the work they had so successfully begun.   How unsafe the new ruling was became at once apparent. The men dominated the convention, monopolized the floor, moved to have the name of the society changed to The People's League, and by bullying a sufficient number of subservient women members, they ousted Mrs. Stanton from the presidency.   Susan, to be sure, they reëlected secretary, but she indignantly declined to serve, and with Mrs. Stanton resigned from the society they had organized.   Within two years the Woman's State Temperance Society went to pieces, and not until twenty years later, when the Women's Christian Temperance Union was founded, did women again figure prominently in temperance reform.   They were encouraged to organize praying bands and, of course, to contribute money to the men's organizations.   But the majority of the men, forever torn between their temperance zeal and their business interests, worked so half-heartedly that the saloon and saloon influences more and more gained ascendancy in politics.   It mattered not that true temperance, thanks largely to educational propaganda of the Women's Christian Temperance Union, made tremendous progress, and the disgraceful conditions of earlier days disappeared among decent men.   The saloon finally became such an intolerable evil that the American soul was maddened by its very existence, and a hasty, drastic and unenforceable prohibition amendment was added to the Constitution of the United States. A logical result of long exclusion of such women as Susan B. Anthony from all social reforms, and forcing them to demand political power.

After the collapse of her State Temperance Society Mrs. Stanton said to Susan: "Do you see, at last?" And Susan said: "At last, I see." Thus woman's rights made its essential convert.

# CHAPTER VIII

## AND JOINS THE BLOOMER BRIGADE

THE year 1853 marks Susan's hegira from temperance and all other minor reforms to the ever-widening field of woman's rights. In the five years which had passed since the Seneca Falls Convention she had changed a great deal. Not only was her mind fully matured, but she had progressed beyond most of the narrow conventionalities of her Quaker girlhood. In part this was due to the fact that her family also had progressed beyond them, for the independent Mr. Anthony had at last been read out of the Society of Friends. He got into trouble in his Battenville days by purchasing, on one of his business trips to New York, a camlet cloak with a cape and, as a further protection against the extreme cold, a colored silk muffler. These were declared "out of plainness," but Daniel kept on wearing them just the same. In his house in Hardscrabble, formerly an inn, there was one room which had been used for public dances. Daniel had no intention of continuing the dances, but when a committee of young people called on him to protest that the only other available hall was in a rather disreputable tavern with a barroom attached, he could see no way out of letting them have the room. Lucy Anthony begged him to do so, and he consented, with the clear understanding that his children should never learn to dance. That settled it with the elders. "We are sorry to disown

Friend Anthony," they said, "but we cannot condone such an offense as allowing a dancing school in his house." Daniel keenly resented their verdict. "For the two best acts of my life," he commented bitterly, "my marriage and the protection of these young people, I am turned out of the best religious society in the world."

The Anthonys continued for some time to attend Friends' meeting, but Daniel's opinions on life and religion grew steadily more tolerant. When he removed to Rochester he found a society more congenial than any he had previously known, wider in its outlook, in the advance guard of social and political questions of the troubled times. In Rochester lived a number of Quakers who had separated from the society because they could not endure its vacillating policy toward slavery. This group, perhaps a dozen well-to-do and cultured families, formed, with certain Unitarians, a center of liberal thought not only in their city but in that whole section of the State. Their names are forgotten now, dimmed by the years like old daguerreotypes, but in their youth they represented all that was modern and idealistic, prophetic of the new United States, struggling in painful birth-pangs. Isaac and Amy Post, James and Abigail Bush, the Kedzies, the Fishes, the Burtises, the Hallowells, stood for those brave ideas sponsored in Boston by Sumner, Garrison and Phillips, and in the west by a yet obscure young lawyer, Abraham Lincoln. Their Unitarian Church had for its minister William Henry Channing, a man of the same large vision as his friend the Rev. Samuel J. May of Syracuse. The Anthonys joined

Channing's congregation and very soon were drawn into the intimacy of the radical group.

The Anthony farm, on the outskirts of Rochester, became a favorite Sunday afternoon rendezvous, and Susan, on holiday visits from Canajoharie, found herself in a wholly new atmosphere, a whirlpool of advanced ideas. Instead of the plain speech, the mild discourses of other Sunday afternoons at home, she took part in exciting political discussions, denunciations of the opportunist Missouri Compromise, and the danger of slavery extension in California and the territories of the southwest. She heard accounts of the workings of the revived fugitive slave law, of free negroes fleeing in terror to the Canadian border, of escaped slaves hiding in stations of the underground railroad, some of these in the homes of the Anthonys' new friends. She met Frederick Douglass, whose paper, the *North Star,* was edited in Rochester; and once in a while she had a glimpse of the great leaders, Garrison, Phillips, Parker Pillsbury, Theodore Parker, Francis Jackson, who on lecture trips often found time to join the Sunday afternoon "conventions" at the farm. These dauntless spirits, their scorn of the watchful waiting policy of the "best minds" as represented by leaders in Congress, by the Boston followers of Emerson and William Ellery Channing, and by the evangelical respectables typified by the Beecher family, thrilled Susan to her heart's core, woke in her boiling wrath against ancient prejudices which forbade women to take part in this struggle of the ages, brought her to the conviction that her life work must be the destruction of those prejudices. It was through the Abolitionists, who had the hardihood to declare that not even the sacred Constitution was above the enlightened conscience of mankind, that Susan B. Anthony came into her destiny. Her resolve once made was forever unbreakable. For her there was to be no turning back, no compromise, no more moderation of speech or action. "Shall I tell a man whose house is on fire to give a moderate alarm; tell him moderately to rescue his wife from the hands of a ravisher; tell the mother gradually to extricate her babe from the fire into which it has fallen. . . . I am in earnest—I will not equivocate—I will not excuse—I will not retreat a single inch—and I will be heard!" Many a Sunday afternoon Susan had heard that credo of the Garrisonians recited, renewed, and sworn to as a rule of life, until it became a burning agony in her blood. And from the course on which she set out she never did retreat a single inch—and she was heard.

Elizabeth Cady Stanton's home in Seneca Falls now became Susan's second home, for between these two women there sprang up one of the most remarkable feminine friendships in history, a friendship which lasted without an hour's break for fifty years, until the death, in 1902, of Mrs. Stanton. Their mutual understanding began at Susan's Rochester Convention to organize the Woman's Temperance Society. On that occasion Mrs. Stanton had shocked almost every one present except Susan by one of her bombshell speeches advocating divorce for drunkenness. Divorce was then a tabooed subject, but Mrs. Stanton managed to sandwich it into most of the speeches she made around that time. She believed in divorce, with custody of the children to the mother, and worse still, she believed in birth control for drunkards' wives. She called upon women to refuse to bear children to men whose souls and bodies were degenerate through drink, and she even suggested laws fining women fifty dollars for each potential drunkard they brought into the world. Birth control was by no means unknown in the highly moral Nineteenth Century. Not a few respectable newspapers carried advertisements of quack remedies for surplus population—that is, for unwanted or unfathered children, and some, not quite so respectable, published thinly camouflaged advertisements of abortionists. But nobody *talked* about such things, and Mrs. Stanton's utterances were deemed excessively indelicate, if not positively law defying.

To the downright Susan they seemed simple common sense, and she greatly admired a woman who not only had the courage of her convictions, but who could with such eloquence as well as with such purity of language, give voice to them. It was this fearlessness, this almost juvenile recklessness of consequences when she believed herself right, that won Susan's allegiance to Elizabeth Cady Stanton. She was fearless herself, but although she had as many ideas as Mrs. Stanton, and was even more capable of marshaling them in logical order, she had not her friend's amazing fluency of speech. The fact that each had something which the other lacked was the secret of their long association, their half century of faithful collaboration. Physically and mentally the women differed, yet complemented each other. Mrs. Stanton was short and plump, ease-loving, humorous, equable of temper, quick at repartee, and thoroughly aware of her own intellectual abilities. Susan was tall, spare as an athlete and as active, serious and sarcastic rather than humorous, introspective, analytic, and toward herself singularly detached. She had a marvelous memory for facts and statistics, the instinct of an artist in perceiving under cold statistics pulsing life, a dynamic energy, a total disregard for hardships and discomforts, and a great impatience with laziness in her fellow workers. Mrs. Stanton for all her unusual capacity for work, was lazy, and she shrank from discomforts. It was Susan's task for many years to spur her on to write, to speak, to attend conventions —Mrs. Stanton disliked conventions, always preferred sending letters and addresses for Susan to read—and above all to keep her mind on one issue instead of half a dozen.

In formative influences and experiences the two women differed. Mrs. Stanton was born an aristocrat. She was related to a dozen great American families, a granddaughter of that Col. James Livingston whose lucky cannon shot sent His British Majesty's warship, the *Vulture,* speeding down the Hudson, leaving the hapless Major André to his fate. Through her ties of kinship and her social connections she had ready access to politicians and legislators, and from them she learned much useful strategy. (Susan was of the people, and she understood a great deal better than Mrs. Stanton the workings of the common mind.) Both women had emerged successfully from the narrow confines of domestic life, but they had arrived by different routes. Judge Cady reluctantly admitted that his daughter had what was called "a masculine mind," but he was of the older generation which distrusted and deplored intellect in women. He opposed her at every step of her career, quarreled with her, and once even went so far as to disinherit her. In 1847 he rescued her from what he thought were dangerous influences in Boston, where her husband, Henry B. Stanton, was doing very well indeed in the law firm of Rufus Choate, and on the plea that Boston east winds were threatening his son-in-law's health, induced them to move to his estate at Seneca Falls.  Through his influence Henry was elected to the New York State Senate, and Elizabeth was told that since she possessed such extraordinary executive ability, she might use it in the development of the estate.  She developed the estate, but she found time also, to her father's deep disgust, to organize the woman's rights movement.  She was an admirable housekeeper, a loyal wife, and the devoted mother of seven children, but that did not prevent her from becoming a writer, a public speaker, a pleader before law-making bodies, and a leader of women.  To the day of his death his rebellious daughter was a thorn in the stern old man's side.

Susan's father, on the other hand, not only recognized his daughter's great gifts, but he encouraged her to develop them.  He taught her, in the first place, that work and endeavor were as much a part of woman's life as man's.  He admonished her when she distrusted her abilities, pushed her forward when she held back, and when at last she allied herself with Mrs. Stanton in the cause of women's advancement, bade her think no more of the necessity of wage earning but to count on him for financial backing when her own resources were exhausted.  Susan had worked for a living, had endured the hardships of "boarding round" in mean and cramped farm homes; she had known and felt in her own person the humiliations of a subjected member of society, whereas Mrs. Stanton, belonging to a protected class, knew them only in theory. Thus each supplied what the other needed. As Mrs. Stanton wrote in after years:

"In thought and sympathy we were one, and in the division of labor we exactly complemented each other. In writing we did better work than either could do alone. While she is slow and analytic in composition I am rapid and synthetic. I am the better writer, she the better critic. She supplied the facts and statistics, I the philosophy and rhetoric. . . . Our speeches may be considered the joint products of our two brains."

And Susan declared: "She is my sentence maker, my pen artist," insisting that without Mrs. Stanton she might never have been able to make any speeches at all. Here Susan was unfair to herself, or else her mind was still in thrall to the fallacy, common in her day and far beyond it, that good speaking must be oratorical, full of flowers of language and cast in rounded periods. Susan's gift, little appreciated then, but prized above rubies now, was having something to say, saying it in a few terse sentences, and sitting down. Who knows, if Demosthenes had adopted that method instead of hypnotizing the Athenians, he might not have galvanized them into rising against Philip of Macedon and saving their country? At all events Susan's philippics had a similar effect on women, and as time progressed on men also. The first one of these she launched, not at a woman's rights meeting, but in an annual convention of the New York State Teachers' Association, of which she was a member. Women formed two-thirds of the membership, but up to the day and year of Susan's first speech they had never done anything in a convention but sit modestly with their veils down while the men talked, voted and managed the affairs of the association.  At this particular session, in 1852, the presiding officer was Charles Davies, LL.D., professor of mathematics at West Point, and author of a series of standard text-books.  The question under discussion was the still unanswered one:  Why is the profession of teacher not as highly respected as that of lawyer, doctor or minister?  For several hours men deplored the fact but offered no solution to the problem.  Susan listened, growing more and more disgusted with the platitudes of the men and the bovine inaction of the women.  Finally she rose abruptly and said: "Mr. President."

In the midst of a shocked silence Dr. Davies inquired: "What will the lady have?"

"The lady," said Susan, "would like to speak to the question."

In the history of the association no woman had demanded such a privilege, but after half an hour's earnest debate it was voted, by a bare majority, that Susan might speak.  During the entire time Susan stood, fearing that if she sat down she might lose the floor.  Straight and slim as a young pine tree, in her fine broché shawl and close fitting bonnet she stood, but her knees trembled, and to hide the shaking of her hands she had to keep them tightly clasped together.  When it came her time to speak her voice did not tremble at all.  In clear, concise tones she said: "It seems to me that you fail to comprehend the cause of the disrespect of which you complain.  Do you not see that so long as society says that woman has not brains enough to be a lawyer, doctor or minister, but has plenty to be a teacher, every one of you who condescends to teach tacitly admits before all Israel and the sun that he has no more brains than a woman?" Then she sat down.

Having had all the wind taken out of their sails the men voted to adjourn for the day, the delegates gathering in groups outside to discuss the scandal. Susan walked out of the hall, women drawing their hoop-skirts aside and whispering audibly that they never were so mortified in their lives, that they wished the floor had opened and swallowed them up. But a few women walked with Susan, thanked her, and confessed themselves ashamed of their own supineness. The next day Dr. Davies made a flowery speech, explaining that it was from pure chivalry and a desire to protect the women teachers that the men had never invited them to speak or take part in the onerous duties of committee work. To his annoyance another woman, Mrs. Northrop of Rochester, arose and said, "Mr. President." Having with difficulty obtained the floor this convert of Susan B. Anthony introduced a resolution over which the two had worked the evening before. The resolution provided that thereafter the New York State Teachers' Association would recognize "the rights of female teachers to share in all the privileges and deliberations of this body." Mrs. Northrop also called attention to the grossly inadequate salaries paid female teachers, and asked the association to take action against the evil. Against every effort of the chairman to ignore the resolution it was read, and by the combined votes of the women and the more liberal men it was actually passed.

Susan, from this time on, was a power to be dreaded by the men and leaned on by the women teachers of New York State. For years after she ceased to teach she retained her membership in the association, and year after year she found time to attend the conventions, working for better educational methods, abolishment of the rod as a means of discipline, coeducation in the higher schools, and above all equal pay and equal opportunities for women. "Miss Anthony," said a leading educator after listening to one of her short and telling speeches, "that was a magnificent address. But I must tell you that I would rather see my wife or my daughter in her coffin than hear her speaking as you did before a public assembly."

Even after such tributes as this Susan could not believe, nor could Mrs. Stanton convince her, that she was a really good speaker. All Susan knew was that she could not produce the literary orations which Mrs. Stanton wrote with such ease and which had such marked effect when read or spoken on the platform. She was absolutely incapable of putting her thoughts on paper, and even when Mrs. Stanton did it for her she could not commit the thing to memory. Finally she adopted one speech, Mrs. Stanton's in form, and by untiring labor managed, more or less, to memorize it. The first part of this masterpiece was devoted to women's legal disabilities, the second to their industrial handicaps, and when Susan had to take the platform alone she delivered one or both parts of the speech. Soon she began to interpolate observations of her own, especially the specific instances with which she was familiar, and after that through life she spoke extemporaneously from a few scattered notes held in her hand.

When these two women began working together Mrs. Stanton was thirty-eight, Susan thirty-three. Mrs.

Stanton being in her late thirties was called a matron, and although her hair had not begun to thin she wore a cap. Susan, of course, was an "old maid." Thus being quite beyond the age of coquetry it was considered safe for them to travel unaccompanied and to engage in public work—as far as it was decent for any woman to do these unconventional things. During the first year or two of their association Mrs. Stanton was the leader, Susan her willing neophyte. Soon their positions became equalized and finally they were completely reversed, but it was a long time before Susan realized this. During the first years she figuratively sat at her friend's feet, drinking in her wisdom, helping, not only in the work dearest their hearts but in the housekeeping and the care of the five—afterward seven—children. Susan assisted in the kitchen and upstairs work, played nursemaid and governess to the children, while Mrs. Stanton read, studied and wrote speeches for them both, much of the material being Susan's. Henry B. and the boys became as accustomed to having Susan around the house as though she were Elizabeth's twin, and all grew familiar of evenings with the sight of mother and Susan sitting opposite each other at a large mahogany table covered with books, pamphlets, manuscripts, pens and ink, always scribbling, consulting, talking about conventions, the laws, women's disabilities, the church, men's hostility to reforms, new strategies against opposition, a victory here, a failure here, and never-ending plans for a next campaign. There was no superficial scratching of the soil for these women. They read newspapers, magazines, every public document they could lay hands on, proceedings of Congress and the legislatures, accounts or conventions, church and reform assemblies the country over. When Mrs. Stanton went off for a lecture trip Susan stayed on and ran the house. When Mrs. Stanton needed rest or leisure to do some especially important piece of writing Susan gathered up the more obstreperous of the boys and carried them off to the Rochester farm. Susan did almost everything Mrs. Stanton wanted her to, and at that particular time Mrs. Stanton wanted everybody to adopt, as a symbolic gesture of emancipation, the horrific bloomer costume. This was characteristic, for Mrs. Stanton had through life a propensity to stray from the main highroad into bypaths of adventure. She wanted all the heads of the hydra at once, but occasionally she made the mistake of whacking at the tail instead. The bloomer episode, into which between 1851 and 1854 she inveigled many of the woman's rights advocates, is a striking, but not an unusual case in point. No one knows what it cost Susan to leave off her becoming clothes, crop her beautiful hair and put on bloomers, but she did it, because Mrs. Stanton thought it almost the most important thing women could do for the cause.

Bloomers, or the short dress, as its votaries preferred to call the costume, have quite incorrectly been handed down to history as the invention of Mrs. Amelia Bloomer, whose husband was postmaster at Seneca Falls, and who herself edited a small reform paper called the *Lily*. Mrs. Bloomer had nothing whatever to do with the reformed dress besides adopting it, and in her little monthly newspaper giving it so much publicity that it became celebrated under her name, and as one historian records, set the world rocking with laughter. The real creator of the bloomers was Elizabeth Smith Miller, daughter of Gerrit Smith, wealthy reformer and philanthropist of Peterboro, New York, and a cousin of Elizabeth Cady Stanton. Mrs. Miller, out of all patience with the fashionable dress of the period, six or seven layers of underwear, starched and quilted petticoats, tight corsets, long and sweeping skirts, had made for herself an elegant costume which she fondly believed to be Turkish, probably getting the idea from steel engraved illustrations of Lord Byron's poems. She wore her new gown on a visit to Seneca Falls, where cousin Elizabeth rapturously acclaimed and adopted it, in spite of the fact that it revealed the hitherto suppressed fact that woman was a biped. A lady who wore bloomers displayed under a full skirt reaching half way between the knees and ankles, a pair of trousers either full gathered or straight, but in either case covering the instep. She wore no corsets, but a blouse and loose coat, and usually in the street a concealing cape. In such a smother of clothes a woman to-day would be ready for a cross country airplane flight, but in the early Fifties she was practically nude. Hoopskirts were not worn as much as is popularly supposed, conservative women dreading accidents from sitting down carelessly in the treacherous things. But crinolined and quilted skirts and many starched petticoats gave the proper silhouette, something between an old-fashioned dinner bell and a feather duster, and no woman was modestly accoutered unless her dress touched the ground. To show an ankle, much less a leg—a limb—even when getting into a carriage, was something no well bred female ever dreamed of doing. As for wearing trousers, that was a direct defiance of Scripture, as many preachers thundered, taking their

MRS. STANTON AND MRS. BLOOMER
In the Reform Dress of the Early 1850's

text from Deuteronomy xxii: 5, which plainly says: "The woman shall not wear that which pertaineth unto man; neither shall a man put on a woman's garment, for all that do so are an abomination unto the Lord thy God."

Besides Mrs. Stanton, Mrs. Bloomer and Susan, about a hundred "strong minded" women, in the face of the prophet's admonition, wore the bloomers for periods varying from one to four years. Lucy Stone, the Grimké sisters, Celia Burleigh the writer, Charlotte Wilbour, among others, were enthusiastic supporters of a dress which, however unesthetic, did allow a freedom of movement utterly unknown to slavish followers of *Godey's Lady Book*. Elizabeth Smith Miller wrote it in Washington during her father's term in Congress, and because she was one of those women who can be charming in any clothes, she was less ridiculed than most of the others. Gerrit Smith was such an ardent admirer of the bloomer that when the women finally discarded it he wrote a letter to Mrs. Stanton formally withdrawing his support from the whole woman's rights movement. The dress, he insisted, was the essential feature of the reform and its abandonment was complete proof that women were not fit to vote. Gerrit Smith was exactly that kind of a man. The bloomer costume was finally abandoned not only because it was crucifixion for the women who wore it, but because it proved a real hindrance to their work. Whenever a bloomer came in sight men stopped, not to think of the cause for which it was worn but to grin and jeer. Women pulled their skirts aside in scorn, and ribald urchins sprang up in numbers from nowhere at all to dance behind singing doggerel verses:

"Hi-yo!
In sleet and snow,
Mrs. Bloomer's all the go.
Twenty tailors take the stitches,
Plenty o' wimmen wear the britches. . . ."

Mrs. Stanton gave up her bloomers at the end of two years, perhaps to Henry B.'s tears, for Henry B. and the other husbands must have shed a good many private tears, and Susan soon followed her example.  In anguish of soul she wrote Lucy Stone:

"Mrs. Stanton's parting words were 'Let the hem out of your dress to-day, before to-morrow night's meeting.'  I have not obeyed her, but have been in the streets and the printing offices all day long, had rude and vulgar men stare me out of countenance and heard them say as I opened a door, 'There comes my bloomer!'  Oh, hated name!  Oh, I cannot, cannot bear it any longer!"

To which Lucy, secure in her Boston home from the jeers of rude and vulgar men, replied severely, asking Susan how she could think that a great cause hung on such trivialities as dress.  "I don't think I can abandon it," she declared.  Adding with her habitual caution, "but I will have two skirts."  It was not in Susan's nature to have two skirts either to her dress or to her mind.  She had put on the reformed dress because her reason told her that it was rational, sanitary, convenient and comfortable, and she clung to it until she was convinced that audiences could not listen with undivided attention to arguments for woman's rights as long as the speakers appeared in bizarre and unusual apparel.  It was absurd that it should be so, but there it was, and nothing could alter the fact.  The average mind, Susan learned, is incapable of assimilating more than one idea at a time.  "To be successful," she wrote Mrs. Stanton, "a person must attempt only one reform, and I shall always fight to keep woman's rights free from every other issue." To this resolution she adhered through life, although she had to fight a multitude of cranks, and sometimes even her dearest friend, Elizabeth Cady Stanton.

There is one thing however that can be said for the bloomer crusade. Like Mrs. Pankhurst's window smashings in Piccadilly, it gave the cause a million dollars worth of free advertising, and that is something no man's publicity department would be likely to turn down in a hurry.

# CHAPTER IX

## NAPOLEON TAKES THE FIELD

UP to the day and year when Susan B. Anthony
assumed its direction the woman's rights movement
had been limited to propaganda, widely diffused
through lectures, pamphlets, newspaper discussions,
pulpit fulminations, and especially through conventions, state and national. The idea of woman's rights
was of course no new thing. Mary Wollstonecraft's
epoch-making book, "A Vindication of the Rights of
Women," was published in 1792, and although many
men agreed with Horace Walpole that the author was
a hyena in petticoats, the book made a profound impression, not only in England but in His Majesty's
lately rebellious colonies where, some years before,
certain ladies had brought the subject up. At least,
Abigail Adams was annoying John, her husband, and
Mercy Otis Warren was importuning Thomas Jefferson, her friend, to have "the blessings of liberty to
ourselves and our posterity" guaranteed for women as
well as men in the Constitution of the United States.
In 1844 Margaret Fuller's "Women in the Nineteenth
Century," and her virile pamphlet, "The Great Law-
suit," circulated all over the United States and reminded thousands of women that they had never been
satisfied with a condition of legal subjection. The discontent however was an individual affair until 1848,
when something new did come into the world, a sense

of sex solidarity, a consciousness among women that they had ideals and interests in common, quite apart from what, under one name or another, had always been considered woman's sole existence. This sex solidarity, sex trust and confidence, a thing which men had always known, was to women so novel, so startling, and so enchanting, that the majority might have been content for years merely to meet and talk about it. To hear, in convention assembled, leaders like Elizabeth Cady Stanton, Lucretia Mott, Antoinette Brown, Lucy Stone, and the exotic Ernestine Rose, men like Phillips, Pillsbury, May, Channing and Douglass, restate, define and defend their great charter of liberty, women from all parts of the Union flocked like harts athirst for the water brooks. From the speakers and from their unusual contact with each other they gathered inspiration to go home and convert more and more women to the new religion. Considering that few of these women had any money of their own, and that long distance traveling was both expensive and hazardous, the wonder grows that so many contrived to leave their homes, their complicated housekeeping and their enormous families of children on such an errand. We can only conclude that the American Husband, that white blackbird among created males, was already a developing institution, in the United States. To the everlasting credit of the American Husband let it be remembered that he, first among men, at a time when complete self-suppression was the ideal for wives, granted to his the elemental right to go away from home and talk about themselves.

A place in the public forum, or even the right of free speech therein, was not enough for Susan B.

Anthony. To a mind like hers ideas and action are always inseparable, and to her the newly developed sex solidarity of women was of no value unless it could be put to work to remold the whole of society. Like another pioneer, ax in hand facing the unbroken wilderness, Susan paused only long enough to consider in which direction to blaze the first trail. She was not long in doubt. Returning in September, 1853, from the fourth annual Woman's Rights Convention in Cleveland, where as usual she had been placed on the business and financial committee, she set out on an organization tour through the southern tier of counties in New York. Just a year before she had been over the same territory in the interests of her State Temperance Society, and now she found that practically every lodge she had founded had languished and disappeared. Always for the same reason; the women had no money, no way of getting money, to continue the work. Women, on whom the perpetuation and the nurture of the race depended, were as propertyless as slaves. In a civilization which could not exist without their creative labor they were a pauper class. A sweeping survey of this situation was enough to show Susan where her first trail must lead. In her journal she wrote, with an indignation she hardly knew how to put into words:

"Thus as I passed from town to town I was made to feel the great evil of woman's utter dependence on man for the necessary means to aid reform movements. I never before took in so fully the grand idea of pecuniary independence. Woman must have a purse of her own, and how can this be, so long as the law denies to the wife all right to both the individual and the joint earnings? There is no true freedom for woman without the possession of equal property rights, and these can be obtained only through legislation. If this be so the sooner the demand is made the sooner it will be granted. It must be done by petition, this too at the very next session of the legislature."

Back to Rochester she turned, and by the time the slow and erratic train service got her there she had a complete program, first for a preliminary convention in her home town to draft the petitions and arrange for their circulation, and next for a State Convention at Albany and a descent on the Legislature. Mrs. Stanton must write an address—two addresses—for Susan determined to face the legislators herself, and this Mrs. Stanton agreed to do, although her many domestic cares, she feared, would probably make it impossible for her to attend the Rochester meeting. Susan must furnish the material for the speeches. Susan usually did.

"Can you not get an acute lawyer—," wrote Mrs. Stanton, "perhaps Judge Hay is the man—sufficiently interested in our movement to look up just eight laws concerning us—the very worst in all the code? I can generalize and philosophize easily enough by myself but the details of the laws I have not time to look up. . . . While I am about the house, surrounded by my children, washing dishes, sewing, baking, etc., I can think up many points, but I cannot search books. . . . Men who can, when they wish to write a document, shut themselves up for days with their thoughts and their books, know little of what difficulties a woman must surmount to get off a tolerable production."

Judge William Hay, of Saratoga, to whom Susan wrote post haste, consented to look up the eight worst laws, but apparently when he got into the code he could not make up his mind which of all the bad ones were the worst, so he sent Susan thirteen. In passing, some of these still adorn the statute books of the great State of New York. The radical Quakers and the Rev. Mr. Channing gladly agreed to help Susan with her Rochester convention, but it was her hand that penned most of the letters, scores of letters, to influential people throughout the State, asking for their signatures; to editors begging for publicity; to men and women inviting them to come to Rochester and help circulate the petitions. Susan hired a hall, arranged for ushers, speakers, advertising, lights, all the troublesome minutiæ. The convention unanimously elected her chairman of the committee on petitions, and immediately after the meeting she selected sixty women as captains, and dividing the State into districts she assigned each woman her place. Susan and her captains then went out into the cold and storm of a New York winter in a house to house canvass for names. Like itinerant tin pedlars or book agents they tramped the streets and country roads, knocking at every door, presenting their petitions, arguing with women who half the time slammed the door in their faces with the smug remark that *they* had husbands, thank God, to look after their interests, and they needed no new laws to protect their rights. After each rebuff the women simply trudged on to the next street, the next row of houses, the next grudgingly opened front doors. In ten weeks' time they secured 6,000 signatures to the petition asking for laws granting married women the right to collect and control their own earnings, and the right of equal guardianship of their children. Surprisingly they secured on the petition for equal suffrage 4,000 names.

The State Convention met in Albany, February 14, 1854, with Mrs. Stanton presiding, and Susan very

busy in the background, seeing that Mrs. Stanton's
splendid address was printed in time to have a copy on
each legislator's desk on the opening day of the convention, and 50,000 copies printed and mailed to every
corner of the State. The two bills were introduced and
were referred to a joint committee of the Senate and
Assembly, and these gentlemen Susan was, as a great
favor, permitted to address. She came before them in
bloomers, the last she ever wore, but even her despised
"shorts" did not detract materially from the seriousness
of the occasion. With her clear contralto voice, her
perfect enunciation, her fine economy of words, she
could not fail to impress on the men the earnestness of
her errand. Yet they must have been sorely puzzled,
those politicians, to hear solemnly recited a long cata-
logue of laws which they had always taken for granted
as right and proper, and to be told that she, Susan B.
Anthony, and all her colleagues proposed to come before the Legislature every year, as long as they lived,
until these laws were erased from the books. Married
women must have all the rights of single women, exactly as though the husbands did not exist. They must
own and control their property, their wages; they must
be allowed to will and devise their property like men;
they must be allowed freely to contract, to sue and be
sued; they must be equal guardians of their minor children, and while joint property laws should be enacted,
women should be subject to proportional liability for
the support of children; homesteads must be made in-
violable and inalienable for widows and children;
habitual drunkenness must be made cause for divorce;
and finally, in order that they might aid in the securing
of equal laws, women married and unmarried, must be

given the right to vote. They must be eligible to all offices, occupations, professions, be entitled to serve on juries, and to be employed in public offices. The whole code must be revised, extending the masculine designation to women. One committeeman went on record as saying that it gave him gooseflesh to hear an unmarried female advocate such destructive changes in the protected status of loved and cherished wives.

More of the assembled legislators must have experienced cold chills when they listened to the longer and more passionate speech of Elizabeth Cady Stanton, for although the chairman of the joint committee, James L. Angle of Monroe County, recommended a bill allowing married women to collect and control their own earnings, whenever their husbands were proven dissolute or neglectful, and providing that children of tender years might not be apprenticed to trades without the written consent of their mothers, House and Senate alike, by a very large majority, voted adversely. The speeches of the opposition were in essence identical.

"Are we, sir," demanded Mr. Burnett of Essex, addressing the speaker of the Assembly against the bill granting married women their right to wages and the guardianship of children, "to give the least countenance to claims so preposterous, disgraceful and criminal as are embodied in this address? Are we to put the stamp of truth upon the libel here set forth that men and women in the matrimonial relation are to be equal? We *know* that God created man as the representative of the race; that after his creation the Creator took from his side the material for woman's creation; and that by the institution of matrimony, woman was restored to the side of man, and that they became one flesh and one being, he being the head. . . ." If such a felicitous arrangement were ever interfered with by law makers, said the speaker, there would be no way of preserving men's honor except by locking wives behind bolts and bars, "as in Italy."

From the galleries the women delegates listened with sick hearts, but the iron-nerved Susan heard it all without even a sign of impatience. She knew that neither Mr. Burnett of Essex nor any of his colleagues really believed such nonsense. They were simply uttering inherited opinions, very conveniently brought forth and aired for their own defense. If some did believe it, very well, they must be made to change their minds. Before a larger and more insistent public opinion they would have to change. Therefore, to work again, collecting more petitions, more and more names, until the Legislature was swamped with them. "Napoleon," as Mr. Channing now christened her, decided on the preliminary of testing out national as well as local sentiment, and in March she gathered up Ernestine Rose and went to Washington. But Washington proved entirely apathetic. Not a newspaper, except the *Star,* would even publish advertisements of meetings, nor would any large church consent to open its doors for a meeting. Susan therefore audaciously applied for the use of the Representative Chamber for an evening meeting, but Chaplain Milburn sternly refused, on the ground that Mrs. Rose was notoriously hostile to the church. The hall of Smithsonian Institute was also refused her for, as Professor Henry explained, it was necessary to keep out of those dignified precincts all discussions of exciting questions, and besides, "it would dis-

turb the harmony of feeling" for women to speak there.
Gerrit Smith, then in Congress, arranged one or two
drawing-room meetings, and then Susan and Ernestine
moved on to Baltimore, Alexandria, Virginia, and
finally to Philadelphia where James and Lucretia
Mott took them in and made much of them among
their rich friends, and in one large meeting actually
collected enough money almost to pay the expenses
of their journey.

In Washington and Baltimore and in Virginia Susan
came in contact for the first time with slavery, and she
notes with a certain horror how quickly even an abolitionist might become hardened to the South's peculiar
institution.

"This noon I ate my dinner without once asking myself, 'Are
these human beings who minister to my wants *slaves* who can be
bought and sold?' Yes, even I am growing accustomed to slavery;
so much so that I cease to think of its accursed influence and calmly
eat from the hands of the bondman without being mindful that he
is such. O, Slavery! Hateful thing that thou art, thus to blunt the
keen edge of conscience!"

The appalling laziness and dirt, the general in-
efficiency everywhere attendant on slavery repelled
Susan very much as it had shocked Aunt Ophelia from
Vermont in Mrs. Stowe's immortal "Uncle Tom."
Like Aunt Ophelia Susan perceived that it was the
whole system of slavery that was wrong, not its brutal
floggings, its adulteries, its negation of family life and
its callous separation of mothers and babies. The system itself was rotten to the core, and its effect on slave
owners even more deadly than on the slaves. Remembering those awful speeches in Albany she reflected
that in like manner the effect of the subjection of

women was worse on men than on women. This became the text of Susan's speeches as she tramped up and down the State, often with no money in her purse save what every little meeting yielded in the collection basket. Her father, however, made good his promise of financial backing, and as he could spare the money, he paid back instalments on the few hundred dollars Susan had loaned him in the days of his adversity. Aside from Daniel's practical support Susan got little, except letters of warm commendation from the women who stayed home.

"God bless you, Susan dear," wrote Lucy Stone, "for the brave heart that will work on even in the midst of discouragement and the lack of helpers. Everywhere I am telling people what your State is doing, and it is a great deal to the cause. The example of positive action is what we need."

Susan went on being an example, sometimes not in the mildest of tempers. The Saratoga incident that summer was typical. Susan heard that a large temperance convention was to be held in Saratoga, and simultaneously an Anti-Nebraska meeting, and to that renowned summer resort she immediately repaired to hold a woman's rights meeting the same week. She dispatched hasty letters to Mrs. Stanton, Mrs. Mott, Lucy Stone, and Rev. Antoinette and the ardent Ernestine, every good speaker she knew, urging the great advantage of holding meetings, and of circulating petitions in such audiences as they should certainly draw from the two other conventions. Confident that some of the women at least would respond, Susan went on with her arrangements, with great difficulty renting a hall and advertising her meeting. But when the morning of the day arrived not a single one of the faithful was on hand. Each woman was preoccupied with her domestic or professional duties, each relied on the others to go, and of course nobody turned up. So here was Susan, in debt for a hall, for handbills and newspaper notices, without a speaker or even a presiding officer. To add to her troubles she had had her pocket book lifted by some adroit thief, and the money, fifteen dollars, happened to be every penny she possessed. However, she said nothing about that to her friend Judge Hay, to whom in despair she now turned. The Judge was no speaker, but he encouraged Susan to get out and polish up that speech Mrs. Stanton had written for her a year ago, and together they scoured the town for a possible chairman. To their joy they found at one of the huge hotels two woman's rights adherents, Matilda Joslyn Gage and Sarah Pellet, a recent graduate of Oberlin, the first coeducational college. Both consented to speak, and Susan, in addition to presiding, gave her speech, by this time enriched with pungent interpolations of her own. Twenty-five cents admission was charged, but even so the hall was not large enough to hold the curious crowd. Bored and sated Saratoga hailed the woman's rights meeting as an oasis in their dry pursuit of pleasure amid the heat and the crowded conditions of the Summer city. Belles and beaux came together, well chaperoned, of course, the ladies light as soap bubbles in their crinolined Summer silks and muslins, their wasp waists, bare shoulders, and pink and white beflowered bonnets; the gentlemen smart in wide gray or plaided trousers, pinched-in waistcoats, high collared coats and choking black silk cravats intricately wound and knotted around stiff collars above their beautiful shirts. Southern planters accompanied by frail, camelia-complexioned wives and daughters; foreign visitors agape at the spectacle; even the gamblers and race track followers who were inevitable in any Saratoga crowd, came to Susan's meeting. And how the place must have smelled of frangipani, patchouly, bay rum and cigars! No matter. The meeting was a wonderful success, many names went on the petition and so many tracts were sold that, what with admissions and all, Susan had money to pay her expenses, give ten dollars apiece to her speakers, and forgetful of the stolen fifteen dollars go home in comfort. And that took money, in 1854, for the journey from Saratoga to Albany alone involved eight hours in jolting railroad trains, with several changes of cars and much waiting on hard benches between trains. From Albany to Rochester—"but travelers must be content."

Seven months of this sort of thing in one year might have dscouraged some, but to Susan the campaign of 1854 was but an appetizer of what was to come in the two years following. She now conceived the idea, which after a national convention in Philadelphia, in October, became a stern purpose, of canvassing every county in New York State with petitions to be rained down on the next legislature. No woman had ever done such a thing, and at first even Susan hoped she might not have to do it alone. But Elizabeth wrote from Seneca Falls:

"I wish I were as free as you, and I would stump the state in a twinkling. But I am not, and what is more, I passed through a terrible scourging when last at my father's. I cannot tell you how deeply the iron entered my soul. I never felt more keenly the degradation of my sex. To think that all in me of which my father would have felt a proper pride had I been a man, is deeply mortifying to him because I am a woman. The thought has stung me to a fierce decision—to speak as soon as I can do myself credit. But the pressure on me just now is too great. Henry sides with my friends, who oppose me in all that is dearest to my heart. . . . Sometimes, Susan, I struggle in deep waters."

There was no time for sighing, so Susan went ahead with her solitary preparations. With her father as security she went into debt for a few thousand handbills advertising her lectures, and these her younger brother Merritt and his pretty fiancée, Mary Luther, folded and addressed and sent out to sheriffs and postmasters, with letters asking that the handbills be conspicuously displayed at least two weeks in advance of her scheduled meetings. Editors to whom Susan wrote were kind and obliging about publishing her notices, and even the great Horace Greeley promised them a place in the *Tribune*. Susan had offered to pay for the advertisements, but Greeley, not having the bowels to quote her metropolitan rates, offered to publish the notices free of charge. Having spent every dollar of her surplus Susan wrote to Wendell Phillips who had taken a prominent part in the Philadelphia convention, asking him if there had been any money left over. He replied that the funds were quite exhausted, but he enclosed a personal check for fifty dollars, a loan, he said, although he never did allow Susan to pay it back. With this fifty dollars in hand, not a penny besides, Susan left home on Christmas day, 1854, with a head full of plans, a heart full of courage, and a carpet bag full of campaign literature and petitions for the legislature. Her mother and sister wept to see her go, and even

Daniel held his daughter fast in his arms for a moment before he could bring himself to let her board the shabby train out of Rochester. The winter was the coldest and snowiest known in ten years, the wooden cars were furnished with wood stoves which alternated between being red hot and stone cold, and in whatever town tavern or country farm house she would be sleeping for the next months her hardships would be great. But at least her father left her free to go wherever conviction led her, and that far Susan was better off than most women of her generation.

The adventures of that winter deserve much more space than can possibly be given them here. In some towns she had fine meetings, enthusiastic audiences, and no end of "York shillings" in the collection box. In others not a church or schoolhouse could be obtained, and at one town, Olean, the meeting would have had to be abandoned had not the landlord of the hotel offered his dining-room. At Angelica, nine towns represented, as the diary records, crowded houses. A young minister signs his name to the petition, but hastily scratches it off when one of his rich parishioners threatens to leave the church unless the name is withdrawn. At Mayville, Chautauqua County, she has to spend fifty-six cents for four pounds of candles to light the hall. At Elmira she takes tea with Mrs. Holbrook and meets the Rev. Thomas K. Beecher, younger brother, or half-brother, of Henry Ward. "His theology, as set forth that evening, is a dark and hopeless one. He sees no hope for the progress of the race, does not believe that education even will improve the species." A true son of that gloomy Puritan, Lyman Beecher. The clergy on the whole are a pretty hard lot to deal with. At Corning not one would give a notice of the meeting, but fortunately this so incensed the men "that they went to the printing office, struck off hand bills and had boys standing at the doors of the churches as the people passed out." Who was responsible for that Sabbath breaking, Susan asks a candid world.

In February Susan broke off long enough to visit the Legislature with hugely augmented petitions, but she could get no new bills introduced that session, so off again, this time into the icy fastnesses of the Lake George and Schroon Lake districts. Nowhere in the State were all towns connected by railroads, and in this isolated region Susan had to depend almost entirely on stage-coaches. She finds it almost too much to endure at times, she confesses, but once in a while a little relief arrives. A gentleman who had been an interested auditor in Albany turns up mysteriously just as she is about to take the stage for Lake George. He has a thick plank baked delightfully hot, and begs permission to place it under her feet. As often as the stage halts he dashes out and has the plank reheated, and with his own hands brings her cups of steaming tea. A day or two later the same handsome, bearded stranger turns up again, this time with a fine sleigh and a pair of spanking gray horses, and drives her to his sister's home for an over-Sunday rest. From town to town he insists on driving Susan, buried in fur robes and her feet deliciously warm on the hot plank. Several days of her unusual conversation, the proximity of her vital body, and the gentleman's heart suddenly overflows, and he totally ruins the situation by bursting forth and imploring Susan to leave this terrible life and share his heart, his home and his hot plank forever. Susan cannot make him understand that this terrible life is the only one she finds endurable, and so he turns back, swearing by heaven that these modern women are too much for the ordinary man's comprehension. Stage-coaches seem pretty uncomfortable for a while after that. The snowdrifts are over the fences in many places and roads are so badly blocked that vehicles have to take to the ice-covered meadows. Susan's feet, frost bitten no doubt, begin to give her serious trouble. She soaks them in cold water, then wraps them in woolens, but the pain merely transfers itself to her back. All the way to Malone she has to sit doubled over, clinging to the seat in front in order not to groan aloud. She holds her meeting in spite of suffering, gets to Ogdensburg, then to Canton. But when the time arrives to leave this point she has to be carried to the stage. Ten miles from Watertown she changes to the train, barely able to walk, and arriving at the hotel in late afternoon she determines to give the "water cure," sovereign remedy of the age, a final test. She sends for a chambermaid, orders two buckets of ice water, and sitting in a coffin-like tin tub, has both buckets poured over her aching body. Wrapped in hot blankets she sleeps through the night and, believe it or not, wakes up in the morning as good as new.

The first of May Susan reached home, exhausted but triumphant. In four months she had lectured and circulated petitions in fifty-four of the sixty counties of the State, collected $2,367, expended $2,291, and has a balance left over of $76. For herself? What a question! For the first expenses of the campaign of 1856.

# CHAPTER X

BUCHANAN KEEPS US OUT OF WAR

SUSAN promised her father that she would take a good rest that summer, and of course she meant to keep her word, but there were one or two anti-slavery meetings not too far away that she just couldn't keep away from, and a woman's rights meeting at Adams, Mass., her birthplace, to which, as guest of honor, she had to repair. The meeting was held at the Baptist Church, and as Susan rose to speak who should come tottering up the aisle but her venerable grandfather, Humphrey Anthony, born in 1770, and therefore a patriarch indeed. In all his life before the old gentleman had never set foot in a "worldly" church, but on this occasion he came proudly to sit on the platform and at the close of the meeting to pay his granddaughter a compliment as gushing as a good Quaker could with propriety utter: "Well, well, Susan, that is a very smart talk thee has given us this evening." He was but one of Susan's men folk who now began to realize that she was a personage. When she appeared in Canajoharie old friends crowded around the platform, told her how much they missed her at the Academy, and begged her to return. But Uncle Joshua Read silenced them peremptorily. "No!" he said, "some one ought to be going around setting people thinking about the laws, and it is Susan's work to do it."

Alas! Too many of Susan's colleagues also thought

it was Susan's work to do it. Mrs. Stanton, in spite of household cares and the demands of a large family, kept her pen flying, but most of the others felt that they had done their full duty when they spoke at an annual convention. Two of the best speakers that year threw Susan into despair by getting married, the Rev. Antoinette Brown to Samuel Blackwell, and Lucy Stone to Henry B. Blackwell. Lucy's marriage, at which Thomas Wentworth Higginson officiated, was the sensation of the day, for she and Henry published a statement announcing that, as a protest against the subjected status of wives, Lucy would continue to bear her maiden name. Lucy at once became a celebrity, and after the manner of celebrities, she henceforth held a little aloof from the rougher work of reform. Both women wrote Susan the cheeriest and most reassuring letters. They weren't going to let marriage make the slightest difference; in fact they would really bring more power and enthusiasm to the cause, since the men they had married were such paragons of sympathy. But Susan knew better. Like Queen Elizabeth, though from different motives, she always resented the marriages of her favorites. Well she knew the effect on women of honeymooning, housekeeping, domestic bliss and the inevitable advent of babies, babies, and more babies. Why, even her loved sisters, Guelma and Hannah, hardly ever now had time to write to her.

Defection in the ranks and probably the after-effects of cold and frostbites brought on an illness, but still she managed by August to get up a new speech and to carry through a successful convention at gay and opulent Saratoga Springs, where again rank and fashion poured out and the financial returns were most satisfactory.

Home again for a brief season, Susan "rested" by super-intending the printing of new circulars and campaign literature, and addressing with her own hand nearly a thousand envelopes to contain these. In September she went to Boston to the Massachusetts Woman's Rights Convention at which Ralph Waldo Emerson, who three years before had refused to endorse the woman's cause, was now, as an ardent advocate, to speak. He did speak, making one of those flowery addresses that always caused Susan to writhe in her seat. When women voted, declared the incorrigible dreamer, polling places would be no more in barber shops and up back alleys, but in beautiful halls decorated with paintings and noble statuary, and fragrant with fresh flowers!

Despite back and legs that ached incessantly Susan, judging from her letters home, has a lovely time in Boston. She stops with the Francis Jacksons, rich and cultured abolitionists, foregathering there with Garrison, Phillips, Higginson, Samuel J. May, Jr., Caroline H. Dall, Elizabeth Peabody, Dr. Harriot K. Holt, and others long admired from afar. Mr. Jackson takes her to see the sights, and in Mount Auburn tries vainly to locate for her Margaret Fuller's monument. Garrison escorts her to Charlestown and together they climb the interminable stairs of the Bunker Hill monument. There is a tea at the Garrisons, where Susan meets all the literati, for times have changed, and instead of being dragged through the streets with a rope around his neck, Garrison is now a lion in Boston. She calls on Theodore Parker and is fascinated by his book-lined study, 16,000 books, many in old and rare editions. She has talks with Wendell Phillips in his home,

**WILLIAM LLOYD GARRISON**
Abolitionist and Suffragist

and writes a letter to Emerson, securing all three of these men for a liberal lecture course she is arranging in Mr. Channing's church in Rochester. As if she hadn't enough on her hands already.

From Boston Susan dashes over to Worcester to attend a great meeting of the young Republican Party on which the abolitionists are building such bright hopes. The times were growing steadily worse, and old political parties were breaking up and re-forming along strictly sectional lines. The year before, that perfect politician, Stephen A. Douglas, had forced through Congress the iniquitous Kansas-Nebraska bill, automatically repealing the Missouri Compromise of 1850 and allowing the extension of slavery into all the new territories. Southern Democrats were jubilant, but Northern States were passing "personal liberty" laws for the express purpose of nullifying the fugitive slave laws. Into Kansas were streaming thousands of pro-slavery Missourians and Carolinians, and thousands more "Sharpe's rifles," Eastern and Middle-Western anti-slavery men, each side determined to control the terms of the constitution soon to be submitted to Congress. Out there, in the midst of a situation growing daily more dangerous, was Susan's young brother Merritt, and this gave her an added interest in the fortunes of the new Republican Party. She was the only woman present at the Worcester meeting, but the chairman, Senator John P. Hale, welcomed her warmly and invited her to the platform where she listened spellbound to fiery speeches by Charles Sumner, Henry Wilson, Anson Burlingame, and other founders, and with the thrill of it yet in her blood she wrote to her father:

"Had the accident of birth given me place among the aristocracy of sex, I doubt not that I should be an active, zealous advocate of Republicanism; unless perchance, I had received the higher, holier light which would have lifted me to the sublime height where now stand Garrison, Phillips and all that small but noble band whose motto is "No Union with Slave Holders.""

Susan, because she could never be a non-resistant, felt that she was not quite a perfect Garrisonian, and through life she strongly inclined toward the Republican Party, in spite of its mean and many times repeated betrayals of the women's cause.

In the autumn, not yet finding herself in condition for the hard campaign ahead, Susan determined to give the water cure a last test, so she retired for a few weeks to the institute of her cousin, Dr. Seth Rogers, at Worcester. She hated to miss the Cincinnati Woman's Rights Convention, but Sister Mary consented to go in her place and bring back a full report. Susan's account of her régime at the water cure is worth handing down to this softer generation.

"First thing in the morning, dripping sheet; pack at ten o'clock for forty-five minutes, come out of that and take a shower, followed by a sitz bath, with a pail of water at 75 degrees poured over the shoulders, after which a dry sheet and then brisk exercises. After four P. M. the program repeated, and then again at nine P. M. My day so cut up with four baths, four dressings and undressings, four exercisings, one drive and three eatings, that I do not have time to put two thoughts together."

She found time however to get in some pretty solid reading, Sartor Resartus, Gerald Massey, in choice fragments, George Sand's "Consuelo," Mme. de Stael's "Corinne," Currer Bell's "Villette." The water cure, and perhaps even more the daily drives through sunny fall days with Dr. Rogers, a most congenial companion, restored Susan so that by November she felt ready for anything. She had counted on several of her colleagues as speakers, but one by one they failed her. Mrs. Stanton was nursing her second daughter,* and the newly married Antoinette and Lucy could not tear themselves away from home. Lucy was so aghast at the prospect of a winter campaign that she wrote: "Now, Susan, I am going to retire from the field; and if you go out too soon and kill yourself, the two wheel-horses will be gone, and then the chariot will stop."

Commenting a little warmly on Lucy's idea of wheel-horses Susan prevailed upon an almost untried speaker, Frances D. Gage, to start out with her. And just then her perplexities were increased by a letter for Samuel J. May, Jr., secretary of the American Anti-Slavery Society, of which Garrison was President, offering her a job as agent and lecturer for central and western New York. Here, after long years, was the coveted opportunity to hurl her dart against the arch-evil of the times, slavery, but on the other hand here was her bounden duty to descend on the Legislature with longer and stronger petitions demanding the right of women to their earnings and their children. If she took Mr. May's offer she would be relieved of the anxiety of paying her way by uncertain collections, for the Society would pay not only expenses but a small salary. To decide definitely was too much even for Susan's straight thinking brain, so she wrote Mr. May that she would have to go on with her original program through January, then if Mrs. Gage seemed ready to carry on alone with the petitions she would accept his offer. But

* Harriot Stanton Blatch.

wintry storms and snow set in so fiercely that Mrs. Gage was soon discouraged, and reading Susan's casual records of the first weeks of their journey you can't honestly blame the poor woman.

/ "Well, well good folks at home, these surely are times that try women's souls. / After writing you last, the snows fell and the winds blew and the trains failed to go and come at their appointed hours. We could have reached Warsaw if the omnibus had had the energy to come for us. The train . . . got no farther than Warsaw, where it stuck in a drift eleven feet deep and a hundred long, but we might have kept that engagement at least. Friday morning we went to the station; no trains, and no hope of any, but a man said he could get us to Attica in time for an evening meeting, so we agreed to pay him $5. He had a noble pair of grays, and we floundered through the deepest snowbanks I ever saw, but at seven o'clock we were still fourteen miles from Attica."

### From Hall's Corners she writes:

"Just emerged from a long line of snowdrifts and stopped at this little country tavern, supped and am now roasting over a hot stove. No trains running. . . . Once we seemed lost in a drift fully fifteen feet deep. The driver went on ahead to a house and there we sat shivering. When he returned we found that he had gone over a fence into a field, so we had to dismount and plough through the snow after the sleigh; then we reseated ourselves, but oh, the poor horses!"

At these country taverns, and in homes all along the route Susan found plenty of material to work into her pleas for the petitions. At one tavern, where the landlady was not yet twenty and had a baby fifteen months old, the travelers arrived to find the baby crying and the supper dishes waiting to be washed.

"She rocked the little thing to sleep, washed the dishes and got our supper; beautiful white bread, butter, cheese, pickles, apple and mince pie, and excellent peach preserves. . . . She prepared a six o'clock breakfast for us, fried pork, mashed potatoes, mince pie, and for me, at my especial request, a plate of delicious baked apples and a pitcher of rich milk. . . . When we came to pay our bill, the dolt of a husband took our money and put it in his pocket. He had not lifted a hand to lighten that woman's burdens, but had sat and talked with the men in the bar room, not even caring for the baby, yet the law gives him the right to every dollar she earns, and when she needs two cents to buy a darning needle she has to ask him and explain what she wants it for."

Every time Susan encounters a case like this she fairly explodes with wrath. From one snow-bound tavern she writes:

"The baby is very sick with the whooping cough; the wife has dinner to get for all the boarders, and no help; husband standing around with his hands in his pockets. She begs him tc hold the baby for just ten minutes, but before the time is up he hands it back to her, saying, 'Here, take this child. I'm tired.' Yet when we left he was on hand to receive the money and we had to give it to him."

In spite of snow and storms and delayed transportation audiences were generally good, people driving eight and ten miles to get to meetings and to give their signatures. Near the end of January Mrs. Gage gives up. Besides, there is illness in her home. So on goes Susan alone, sending out letter after letter, sometimes getting a speaker for an evening, once in a great while finding some one to help out for a few days. She had to write to Mr. May asking her release from anti-slavery work for the time, and he consented, begging her to inform him the moment she was at liberty. The women had arranged no convention at Albany that year, but Susan was on hand with rolls and rolls of petitions, which were referred to the Senate Judiciary Committee, the chairman of which reported so wittily on the proposal to give women their own wages and the right to protect their young children that, as the Albany *Register* said, the entire Legislature was thrown into roars of laughter. The bachelors on the committee, said the chairman, Samuel J. Foote, perhaps because they were still suitors for the favors of the gentler sex, had left the subject pretty much to the married gentlemen, and they had considered it with the light of experience married life had given them.

"Thus aided they are able to state that the ladies always have the best place and the choicest tidbits at the table. They have the best seat in the cars, carriages and sleighs; the warmest place in Winter and the coolest in Summer. They have the choice on which side of the bed they shall lie, front or back. A lady's dress costs three times as much as that of a gentleman, and at the present time, at the prevailing fashion, one lady occupies three times as much space in the world as a gentleman. . . . On the whole the committee have concluded to recommend no measure, except that they have observed several instances in which husband and wife have both signed the same petition. In such case, they would recommend the parties to apply for a law authorizing them to change dresses, so that the husband may wear petticoats, and the wife breeches, thus indicating to their neighbors and the public the true relations in which they stand to each other."

Susan heard this brilliant utterance with a heart blazing with anger and contempt, yet not without a certain sense of gratification. At least the committee had abandoned the argument of Adam and his rib, and perhaps a few more petitions, signed by husbands as well as wives, would compel them to give a sober consideration to the bills. She went back to work more convinced than ever that the slavery of women as well as the slavery of negroes demanded her best fighting powers. She wrote ahead to those arranging her meetings: "I should like a particular effort made to call out the teachers, seamstresses and wage earning women generally. It is for them rather than for the wives and daughters of the rich that I labor." Even then Susan B. Anthony knew that rich women would be the last converts to justice for their sex.

The summer of 1856 was disheartening as far as conventions were concerned. Susan managed one at Saratoga almost without assistance, but it was not very successful. The approaching presidential campaign and the troubles in Kansas occupied the public mind to the exclusion of every other question. Both nominees, the Republican Frémont and the Democrat Buchanan, were supposed to be favorable to the admission of Kansas as a free State, but as Buchanan's congressional record, to quote the Richmond *Enquirer,* revealed that "he never gave a vote against the interests of slavery, and never uttered a word which could pain the most sensitive Southern heart," New England, the East and most of the Middle Western States gave their support to the romantic Frémont. Henry B. Stanton was speaking all over his State for the Republicans, and Mrs. Stanton was so preoccupied with national politics that Susan feared she was losing interest in the woman movement. She had an address on coeducation to deliver before the State Teachers' Association in August, and although she had furnished the data for the speech to her "pen artist," the finished paper was not forthcoming. She wrote a terrible letter to which Mrs. Stanton replied with her usual good humor, and in June the two women, alternating between nursery and writing table, got it ready. The success of the speech however was forgotten in tragic events on the border, for by now Kansas was actually in a condition of civil war. In early September John Brown's horrible Pottawatomie raid was avenged by the "Border Ruffians" in an equally horrible foray on his district, the news dispatches reporting thirty killed. For the Anthony family this was frightful news, since it was known that John Brown sheltered in Merritt's cabin the night before the battle, and it was long before they could get word if he were alive or dead. At last letters came telling that Merritt had been in the fight, against John Brown's orders, because the boy was weak from a recent illness. After doing his share of fighting on the banks of the Marais des Cygnes he had barely strength left to crawl back to his cabin where for two weeks he lay in delirium with hardly a soul to visit or care for him.

In November Buchanan was elected, Frémont carrying only eleven States. Buchanan, in his inaugural, spoke with a complacency maddening to the free staters of the rapidly declining war scare, and of sectional differences approaching an end; and he prophesied cheerfully that "Bleeding Kansas" would be heard of no more. On the contrary Kansas and the Dred Scott case now were heard of even above the clamor of office seekers shamelessly besieging the White House. In December Susan wrote Samuel J. May, Jr., that she was ready to take the field for the American Anti-Slavery Society. "Heaven knows there is need of earnest, effective radical workers," she said. "The heart sickens over the delusions of the recent campaign and turns achingly to the unconsidered *whole question.*" The committee answered by putting all New York State under Susan's control. "We want your name to all letters and your hand in all arrangements," wrote

Mr. May. "We like your form of posters; by means let 'No Union with Slave Holders' be conspi uous upon them." The success of the whole campaigi in the State, he assured her, depended more on her attendance and direction than upon any other worker.

Susan was now more than a woman's rights agitator. She was an anti-slavery, woman's rights impresario. For the committee she engaged such speakers as Parker Pillsbury, the veterans Stephen and Abby Foster, Aaron Powell, Benjamin and Elizabeth Jones, and an able colored man, Charles Redmond, and his sister Sarah, dividing them into three companies and keeping them constantly at work, speaking, agitating, collecting money, over the routes she had marked out and at meetings which she arranged. She worked like a navvy herself, in the face of the usual disharmony and complaints of her speakers, who were always objecting to going where they were sent, always falling ill at critical moments, and always railing against apparent indifference of the committee, which, to tell the truth, were having a desperate struggle to find funds to pay Susan the ten dollars a week they allowed her above expenses, so say nothing of the salaries and expenses of the speakers. The speakers were expected to be self-supporting through collections, but very early it transpired that a campaign of "No Union With Slave Holders" was not going to be self-supporting. The North was growing more and more Republican, but the November defeat had made its adherents wary of any element that might weaken its influence, and the majority were not yet committed to immediate emancipation of slavery. Thus Susan's radicals had not only to meet the opposition of the remaining pro-slavery Democrats but also that of the timid and vacillating Republicans. To make a bad matter worse, Buchanan's first year in office saw the country plunged into another financial panic, and the people who came to the meetings had little or no money to contribute. On the whole it was the most devastating experience Susan had ever passed through, but it had the result of making her into a finished speaker. She was always at her best in debate, and there were debates every night, sometimes ending in near-fisticuffs between speakers and audience.

The Garrisonians, with Susan as their leader, preached a fiery doctrine, and death to all compromise between freedom and slavery. They had material to their hands, for in Washington the Secretary of War, Jefferson Davis, no less, by his ability and his powers of office, had recently succeeded in causing the removal of Governor Geary of Kansas who, although a Democrat and no abolitionist, was the one man who could be trusted to hold the honest and impartial election on which depended the terms of the constitution. They had other exciting news events to talk about, among them Walker's astounding filibustering expedition to Nicaraugua, where that swaggering Southron made himself president and issued decrees establishing slavery on soil which had been free for over thirty years. These and other crowding pro-slavery demonstrations were cogent arguments to offset the claims of the conservatives that the Great Question could still be solved by letting the South alone. The South could not be let alone, declared Susan's speakers, because slavery, like yellow fever, was a contagious disease. Susan herself argued constantly, like another Harriet Beecher Stowe, against the system of slavery rather than against its cruelest aspects, dwelt upon by such sentimentalists as Harriet's own brother, the pastor of Plymouth Church, Brooklyn. There was no such thing as a good master, said Susan, for the words were in themselves a contradiction. "Defend a Constitution that defends the slave owner, and you become a slave holder yourself," she cried. This was the sort of thing that got audiences out of their seats, some of them to cheer and some to invite the men on the platform to fight it out with their bare hands. The campaign ended in early Spring with Susan completely exhausted, and with a deficit of $1,000 in her budget. Nevertheless the committee retained her for the next year's activities.

Her fame as a speaker had so increased that she was invited to Maine to lecture on woman's rights in a Lyceum course which included among its stars men like Senator Henry Wilson, John B. Gough, Henry Ward Beecher and Theodore Parker. The fee was fifty dollars and expenses, a fortune to Susan who, at the beginning of her winter's tour had had to have her ten-years-old Canajoharie finery dyed and remodeled in order to appear decently on the platform. Her reputation also brought large audiences to the Binghampton convention of the New York Teachers' Association, which she threw into an uproar by a strong resolution condemning discriminations against colored teachers and children in the public schools. Academies, colleges and universities still excluded colored youths, while even in New York colored teachers could not be given their diplomas in public, and colored children were barred from free school concerts. All these proscriptions from educational advantages and honors, Susan called upon the association to remove, for they were "in perfect harmony with the infamous (Dred Scott) decision of Judge Taney, that black men had no rights which white men were bound to respect." Pandemonium followed Susan's resolution, which was hastily referred to a committee. Although several on the committee upheld her, the association adopted a weak minority report and a vague resolution that "colored children should enjoy equal advantages of education with the white." Whereupon Susan proceeded to introduce another resolution in favor of co-education and identical advantages for both sexes in all schools, colleges and universities. This provoked an even worse storm, Professor Davies, Susan's long-suffering adversary, declaring that ever since she made her first appearance at their conventions he had been expecting just such an attempt on her part to introduce "this vast social evil." It was "the first step in the school which seeks to abolish marriage, and behind this picture I see a monster of social deformity." The State Superintendent of Public Instruction, Henry H. Van Dyck, shook his fist at Susan, exclaiming fiercely: "Do you mean to say that you want boys and girls to room side by side in dormitories? To educate them together can have but one result."

The resolution, of course, was lost, but Susan's defense of it won her the admiration of even the opposition press, which was about all the press that was. Said the Binghampton *Daily Republican*:

"Whatever may be thought of her notions or sense of propriety in her bold and conspicuous position, personally, intellectually and socially speaking, there can be but one opinion as to her superior energy, ability and moral courage; and she may well be regarded as an evangel and heroine by her own sex."

Elizabêth wrote jubilantly:

"The *New York Times* was really quite complimentary. Mr. Stanton brought me every item he could find about you. 'Well, my dear,' he would say, 'another notice of Susan. You stir up Susan and she stirs up the world.' . . . Oh, Susan, I will do everything to help you on. You and I have a prospect of a good long life. We shall not be in our prime before fifty, and after that we shall be good for twenty years at least."

There was no possibility of holding the usual woman's rights convention that year, because every one of the leaders except Susan was kept at home by domestic emergencies. It seemed to her that almost every woman she knew was in an interesting condition, or recently emerged from it. Useless to try to tear young mothers away from cradles, so for the first time since 1848 there was no convention in New York. Susan was as cheerful as she could be about it, but she told her unmarried sister Mary that at last she understood why Divine Providence had created some women to be old maids.

# CHAPTER XI

## SUSAN WINS HER FIRST VICTORY

THE 1858 anti-slavery campaign was harder than ever on Susan's band of speakers, although she worked them no more mercilessly than she worked herself. Parker Pillsbury said ruefully that there would soon have to be societies for the protection of men, "in the cause of which we will all be martyrs." The worst of their woes was not the traveling in bitter weather, not the discomforts of rude taverns, not even the too-frequent hostility of audiences. Heaven knows the abolitionists were used to hostile audiences. What caused the men to fall by the wayside was the ghastly food they were obliged to eat in country hotels and even in private homes. Susan's diary shows that she too suffered. "Oh, the crimes that are committed in the kitchens of this land!" Yeast and baking powder were unknown, white flour was too expensive for general use, and bread, in consequence, was often lead-heavy and sour. Fresh vegetables there were none in cold weather, and most of the meat—and the omnipresent "dyspepsy"—came out of the salt pork barrel. This probably explains why, at that period, so many food cranks abounded, people who lived on raw vegetables, fruit and bran. On one occasion, as Ida Husted Harper records, "Miss Anthony, Aaron Powell and Oliver Johnson were entertained by prominent and well-to-do people near New York, who had not a mouthful for any of the three meals except nuts, apples, and coarse bran stirred into water and baked.  At the end of one day the men ignominiously fled and left her to stay over Sunday and hold the Monday meeting. She lived through it, but on Tuesday started for New York and never stopped until she reached Delmonico's where she reveled in a porterhouse steak and a pot of coffee."

By the middle of March all the speakers had broken down with colds, bronchitis, lame backs, and chronic indigestion.  Susan longed desperately for her own comfortable home, and when at last she reached it she stayed in bed two days.  Then up again to begin the drudgery of organizing a woman's rights convention in May, for she simply could not allow a second year to go by without a State meeting.  Mrs. Stanton and Antoinette Blackwell added to their crop of babies just before the convention, but Susan made a success of it just the same.  She held it in Mozart Hall, New York City, immediately after the anniversary celebration of the American Anti-Slavery Society, which also she helped to organize, and secured as speakers some of the most famous people who had come to New York to attend it.  These included Wendell Phillips, Lucretia Mott, Thomas Wentworth Higginson, and for the first time on a woman's rights platform, George William Curtis.  It was a turbulent convention throughout its six sessions, for, incited by the anti-abolition *New York Herald* and other reactionary newspapers, mobs invaded Mozart Hall, and at times their yells, hisses and catcalls made it impossible for the speakers to be heard. But Susan was callous to mobs, and she never budged from the platform until the program was completed and the convention formally adjourned.

Her great reward came in the closing days of the year, when Wendell Phillips wrote her that an anonymous donor had given him $5,000 for the woman's rights cause, Susan, Lucy Stone and Phillips to be a committee to spend the money for the publication and circulation of tracts, for conventions, and lecturers' expenses, and for any other purposes they saw fit. Five thousand dollars! To the women it looked like the United States Treasury, and no wonder that avid hands reached out from all over the country to grab it. Antionette Blackwell wanted a generous slice wherewith to establish a church in which she could preach both woman's rights and the Gospel; Lucy thought that a liberal portion should be allotted for suits to prove the illegality of laws imposing taxes on voteless women; from a dozen States came letters begging for money to pay lecturers and organizers in local communities. But Wendell Phillips made it plain that he meant to stand by Susan in her campaign for extended property rights of women in New York, for if those laws were passed, other States would follow. In this he had the approval of the donor, whom Phillips, if no one else, knew to be Francis Jackson of Boston. Thus the first draft on the fund, a check for $1,500, went to Susan for the great drive on the Legislature which she and Mrs. Stanton were planning for the summer months. One more big campaign, a few thousand names more on their petitions, and they knew they could push through their bills giving women control of their wages and joint guardianship of their children. For when Susan visited Albany in February, 1859, she found that her sworn vow to change the minds of those legislators on these first elementary rights of women was about to be realized. The men no longer flung Genesis at her head; they no longer used the weak defensive of flippancy and cheap jokes. They actually consented to argue the case on its merits, and a number of men privately promised Susan their votes. Now, at last, with money enough in the bank to pay expenses and to hire speakers at twelve dollars a week—quite a salary in 1859—victory seemed certain.

Susan knew exactly where to go in order to get at the really influential people. In July she and Antoinette Brown Blackwell opened the campaign at Niagara Falls, and from there traveled to Avon, Trenton Falls, Saratoga Springs, Ballston Spa, Sharon, Lake George; pleasure cities the like of which exist not in this age, and indeed can hardly be imagined. Old time summer resorts, as different from Atlantic City as Coney Island is from Newport in the Nineties. To them used to repair for weeks, if possible for the entire season, the élite of America, everybody in fact who made the slightest pretense of being "anybody." It was a pretty poor excuse of a man who couldn't afford to send his family, especially his wife and marriageable daughters, to a summer resort every year. Nor was he considered so very good unless he could contrive to spend at least part of the season with them. The summer resort was the nearest substitute for, or contact with, outdoor life and the beauties of nature known to our pre-Civil War ancestors. Except in the South, country life, old style, had gone out with the Revolutionary period, and country life, new style, awaited the invention of the automobile. Men went to summer resorts to drink the medicinal waters, to bet on the races, to play poker, to talk politics, stocks, bonds and investments, with other men, over an endless succession of whisky sours, brandy highballs, juleps, cobblers, flips, fizzes, punches, and other variants of the cup that once through freedom's halls. Women went to dance, flirt, play croquet and otherwise display their charms before the eyes of eligible young gentlemen, and above all to show off their incredible wardrobes. A humorous poem of the time describes the woes of a much abused lady—

> "Whose husband refused, as savage as Charon,
> To let her take more than ten trunks to Sharon."

"Saratoga" trunks, they were called, and when you remember that each approximated in size to a kitchen range you have an idea of just how incredible those wardrobes were.

Not a very good audience for woman's rights propaganda, you might say, but that is where you would be mistaken. Susan knew that those people, for all their drinking and dancing, were bored to death. She knew also that if she got the ears of only a few of the men they would be the right ears. One signature on her petitions of a man, or even a woman, of wealth and prominence was worth twenty unknown names. So to all the summer resorts went Susan and her speakers, the best she could by any means secure. They held crowded meetings in halls, dancing pavilions, hotel parlors, even in picnic grounds and groves, for outdoor oratory was by no means the invention of the later day suffragettes. Everywhere they attracted amused but interested audiences, and everywhere people willingly signed their petitions. No doubt most of the women regarded Susan with disfavor, no doubt also men warned their women folk against emulating her regrettable example, but the only thing Susan cared about was their attention and their signatures.

How unblushingly those "unsexed" woman's rights crusaders transcended all current etiquette is set forth in one of Antoinette Brown Blackwell's stories. Their group went down to breakfast one morning in the old Fort William Henry Hotel, Lake George, the only man in the party being Aaron Powell. The colored waiter handed him the menu card, for no lady was expected to give her own order or to address a waiter directly. Susan glanced carelessly over Mr. Powell's shoulder and said, with her usual impetuosity: "You may bring me a beefsteak, some cornbread and a pot of coffee." The embarrassed colored man again presented the card to Mr. Powell who, somewhat embarrassed himself, hesitated. Again Susan said:

"Bring *me* beefsteak, cornbread and coffee."

It was too much for the dignified waiter, accustomed to the manners of the most genteel society. Turning his broadclothed back squarely on Susan he demanded of Mr. Powell:

"Do I unduhstan' suh, that this am an' orduh fo' yo' whole pahty?"

Said Susan, very distinctly: "I told you I would have—"

But the man had fled, and it was a scandalized head waiter who finally took the orders.

Ladies, as Susan scornfully notes in her diary, never, on a journey left the train for meals at station restaurants. The men went out, ate their fill of hot food, returning with sandwiches, hard boiled eggs, pie and other cold provender for their wives. Depend on it, Susan and her campaigners never subsisted on any station handouts.

When the gay season closed the women and their petitions moved on to the cities, their campaign progressing famously through the Autumn. It was brought to an abrupt close by one of the most tragic events in this country's whole history, the raid on Harper's Ferry by John Brown and his fanatical eighteen followers, October 17, 1859. Even to-day reason and emotion can hardly be divorced in contemplation of that deed of unwarranted violence and single handed vengeance. At the time emotion swept reason and all sanity aside like a simoon in a desert. The country was shaken as by an earthquake shock. To Mrs. Stanton and Susan, as well as the other abolitionists, it was a personal calamity, not only because they knew John Brown and reverenced him as a prophet, but because his act criminally involved so many of their nearest friends. Merritt Anthony had fought with him in Kansas. After that bloody affair John Brown had gone East, and it was perfectly well known that he had conferred in the Peterboro home of Gerrit Smith, Mrs. Stanton's cousin, with a dozen men conspicuous in the abolition movement. They knew his plans and had even contributed a considerable sum—about $4,000—to his mad enterprise. Every one of them now was liable to arrest, imprisonment and possibly execution. It was a time of terror and suspense for their families and friends. But they need have had no fears. The old Puritan went through his trial and to his death on that benign morning, that pitying dawn, steadfastly refusing to name a single one of his accomplices, insisting indeed that he had none. But they were known, and those principally involved, George L. Stearns, merchant prince of Boston, F. L. Sanborn, a young aristocrat just out of Harvard, Dr. Samuel G. Howe, husband of Julia Ward Howe, fled to Canada; the Rev. Theodore Parker was already in Europe, and to Europe also fled Frederick Douglass, although that intelligent mulatto, while cognizant of the plot, had refused to sanction it. Only that parson unafraid, Thomas Wentworth Higginson, refused to leave his home, and as for Gerrit Smith he could not, for the catastrophe so wrought upon his mind that he went temporarily insane and after some days was carried raving to a madhouse.

The John Brown tragedy did not precipitate the Civil War, but without any question it brought nearer the "irrepressible conflict" which one year before William H. Seward had warned the American people was sooner or later to decide whether the United States would become entirely a slave-labor or a free-labor nation. The whole South rose in fury, fury mingled with fear, for their zealots, long before John Brown's act of terrorism, had been guilty of law breaking on a much more extensive scale. Enraged by the increasing strength of the abolitionist, and of the growth and power of the Republican Party, they had gone back to the hideous business of importing slaves from Africa, or at least of permitting foreign "black birders" to land their cargo in obscure inlets of the South Carolina and Louisiana coast. They had financed filibustering expeditions to the Antilles, and had fought in Congress for the annexation of Cuba and other West Indian islands as additional slave States, a plain invitation to war with Europe.

The North was paralyzed with grief and horror, but very few except the boldest dared give expression to their feelings. In Rochester the abolitionists turned instinctively to Susan B. Anthony for leadership, and she, blind to danger, engaged Corinthian Hall for a memorial meeting on the very evening of the execution. A few members of the Liberty Party, soon to be amalgamated with the Republicans, helped her, and of course the Channing congregation stood by. Susan went from door to door selling tickets, priced at fifty cents to keep the rabble away, and although the "best" people were afraid to attend, the meeting passed off without interruption, and the proceeds were sent to John Brown's widow. Susan was but one of the brave who dared consequences by voicing their indignation and sorrow. Louisa Alcott spoke of Brown as Saint John; Longfellow said of his death sentence, "This is sowing the wind to reap the whirlwind which will come soon"; and Emerson, before an immense audience in Tremont Temple, Boston, called him "that new saint, than whom none purer or more brave was ever led by love of man into conflict and death."

Recovering, as best they could, their poise, and remembering immediate duty, Susan and Mrs. Stanton began preparations for the State Woman's Rights Convention to be held February 3 and 4, 1860, in Albany. Everything hung on the success of their appeal to the Legislature. Anson Bingham, chairman of the Judiciary Committee, wrote them that he intended to bring in a report favorable to their bills, but he advised them, previous to the submission of the report, to forward their strongest arguments to the committee. Susan implored Mrs. Stanton to be on hand with the best speech she ever made in her life, and Elizabeth replied: "If Napoleon says cross the Alps, they are crossed. You must come here and start me on the right train of thought, as your practical knowledge of just what is wanted is everything in getting up the right document."

Together they worked to produce what proved to be one of the noblest and most eloquent addresses ever made before a legislative assembly. On March 19, 1860, Elizabeth Cady Stanton, occupying the speaker's desk, and facing a joint session of Senate and Assembly, presented an unanswerable argument, an irresistible plea for the repeal of barbarous laws affecting the women of her State, and at its conclusion the bill then in the hands of the Judiciary Committee was actually objected to as being too illiberal. Susan B. Anthony had ready the text of a very radical bill just introduced into the Massachusetts State Legislature, and this she pressed into the hands of Andrew J. Colvin, one of their staunchest supporters. The substitute was accepted by the committee, and within a short time was passed by both houses and signed by Governor Edwin D. Morgan. After twelve years of unceasing agitation, ten years of work in Albany, a corporal's guard of women had succeeded in smashing the thousand years old English Common Law, to the extent of writing this statute into the laws of New York:

"Any property, real or personal, which any married woman now owns, or which may come to her by descent, etc., shall be her sole and separate property, not subject to control or interference by her husband.

"Any married woman may bargain, sell, etc., carry on any trade or perform any services on her own account, and her earnings shall be her sole and separate property and may be used or invested by her in her own name.

"A married woman may buy, sell, make contracts, etc., and if the husband has wilfully abandoned her, or is an habitual drunkard, or insane, or a convict, his consent shall not be necessary.

"A married woman may sue and be sued, bringing action in her own name for damages, and the money recovered shall be her sole property.

"Every married woman shall be joint guardian of her children with her husband, with equal powers, etc., regarding them.

"At the decease of the husband the wife shall have the same property rights as the husband would have at her death."

The passage of this act, and of similar acts speedily passed in other States where the women were organized, was a legal and social revolution which profoundly affected the history of the United States, but for any mention of it do not turn to standard historical works before the Beards' "Rise of American Civilization." Older authorities evidently attributed the change to an immaculate conception occurring in the minds of legislators.

The rest of that winter Susan divided between antislavery and woman suffrage speeches, for the vote was the next objective of the women's crusade. She spent some time in New York City where began her friendship with many of the greatest men and women of the day, some of them destined to figure not too pleasantly in future episodes of her career. In this year of 1860 Henry Ward Beecher, undoubtedly the most popular preacher and the most influential leader of middle class and evangelical thought in America, decided to espouse the women's cause, despite the fact that Mrs.

Beecher was then and ever afterward bitterly anti-suffrage in her views. Paxton Hibben, in his notable biography of Henry Ward Beecher, says that Theodore Tilton, editor of the *Independent*, forced the great preacher to come out openly for equal suffrage, and he is probably right, although it is questionable whether that shrewd opportunist would have done it before the women's property acts were passed in Albany. At all events, as Hibben says, "Between Lucy Stone and Robert Dale Owen, the Communist, on the stage of Cooper Institute, Henry Ward Beecher burned his domestic bridges behind him," in a magnificent speech which for many years circulated as one of the best suffrage leaflets in the association's whole stock. Although she admitted that he was incomparable as a pulpit orator, Susan did not care terribly for Henry Ward, but the Tiltons, both Theodore and Elizabeth, she loved dearly, and they, fated creatures, divinely happy at this time, loved her equally well. Their house was hers as often as she could be induced to visit it, and the pages of the *Independent* were as open as their home to whatever she might wish to be made public.

Susan had need, about that time, for people to love her, for a thing she did, near the end of the year, lost her many friends, and even threatened to disrupt the Woman's Rights Association of the State. One evening in Albany a veiled woman came to Lydia Mott's house, where Susan was staying, and gaining admission threw herself at Susan's feet sobbing out a shocking story. She was the wife of a State Senator in Massachusetts and a sister of a United States Senator from New York. Discovering that her husband had become involved in a disreputable affair with a woman, she had made a scene, threatening to expose him to his constituents. His first reply was to knock her down, his second to have her railroaded to an insane asylum, something easily accomplished in those days. After a year and a half she was released on a writ of habeas corpus and taken to the home of her brother. Through his insistence her children, first her son and after him her thirteen-year-old daughter, were permitted to make her brief visits. But when the time came to let the girl go the mother could not possibly bear it, although her brother told her that, by Massachusetts law, the child was her father's sole property and that he could not abet her in resisting. In wild despair the woman rushed to Susan B. Anthony, whom she had never seen, but of whom she had heard much.

What could Susan do? Well, this is what she did do. She abducted that woman and her child. Muffling them in the best disguise she and Lydia could contrive, the child in old and dilapidated clothes, the mother in a washerwoman's bonnet and green goggles, she fled with them that night to New York. But getting them to the concealing city was but the beginning of their troubles, for no respectable hotel would take in women unaccompanied by a man. From one place to another, through a drizzling rain they tramped for hours, looking for a night's lodging. At the last hotel although as in the others refused admittance, Susan halted. She told the clerk that in his place she and her charges proposed to remain until morning even if they had to sit up in the lobby. The clerk threatened to call the police, and Susan told him go ahead. At least they would have rest and shelter until the police arrived. He gave in then and allotted them a poor room without a fire before which to dry their drenched clothing. The next day Susan found a safe retreat for the forlorn pair in the home of Mrs. Elizabeth F. Ellet, a feminist writer, who kept them both, found the mother a seamstress's job, and for over a year prevented the recapture of the child by her father, although in the end she was kidnaped from Sunday school.

Susan's part in the affair could not be concealed, and she became the object of continuous persecution from the Massachusetts Senator and his wife's brothers. She never denied that she knew where the woman was, but she told them, "There is no reason or justice in a woman's submitting to such outrages, and I propose to defy the law and you also." She was then engaged in a series of anti-slavery lectures which were assailed by rowdies in almost every town she visited, for the mob spirit, born of the people's dread of fast approaching war, was unchecked by the authorities, and Susan's meetings were more than once broken up by hooligans who threatened the very lives of her speakers. Her arrest for abduction was constantly threatened, but nothing under heaven would induce her to betray the fugitive wife and child. The worst of it was that practically all the abolitionist men took the part of the father, or at any rate upheld his legal claim. Phillips telegraphed Susan: "Let us urge you at once to advise and insist upon this woman's returning to her relatives." Garrison not only wrote a six page letter, but at an anti-slavery convention in Albany publicly pleaded with Susan not to injure both the abolition and the woman's rights causes by further obstinacy in law breaking.

"Don't you know," cried Garrison, "that the law of Massachusetts gives the father the entire guardianship and control of the children?"

"Yes, I do know it," flamed Susan, "and does not the law of the United States give the slave holder the ownership of the slave? And don't you break the law every time you help a slave to Canada? Well, the law which gives the father the sole ownership of the children is just as wicked, and I'll break it just as quickly. You would die before you would deliver a slave to his master, and I will die before I will give up that child to its father."

All the quarrels and dissensions, the differences among the woman's rights adherents themselves over Mrs. Stanton's insistence on divorce as a part of their program, Susan almost alone upholding her, were swept away and buried under the surge of events which followed the election of Abraham Lincoln and his inauguration in March, 1861, under the protection of Federal troops. Fort Sumter was attacked, and the United States flag lowered before the gunfire of its own sons; the Southern Confederacy was declared, with a former United States Senator and Cabinet member as President; the compromises and evasions and political panaceas of two generations of statesmen were discarded; bloody and fratricidal war had come to decide the fate of this nation. From the North and West, and from the South, each side as brave, as idealistic, as determined as the other—for all were Americans—came men to fight and die for what they conceived to be liberty. Every town and city, every country road resounded to the roll of drums, the scream of fifes, the tramp of marching feet, the roar of war songs.    And oh, thou, who so lately died in Virginia the death of an outlaw and a felon, the Union Army sang—

> *"John Brown's body lies a-mouldering in the grave,*
> *But his soul goes marching on."*

# PART II

*"Still another form of slavery remains to be disposed of; the old idea yet prevails that woman is owned and possessed by man, to be clothed and fed and cared for by his generosity. All the wrongs, arrogances, and antagonisms of modern society grow out of this false condition of the relations between man and woman. The present agitation rises from the demand of the soul of woman for the right to own and possess herself."*

SUSAN B. ANTHONY, *at the close of the Civil War.*

# CHAPTER XII

## WAR AND EMANCIPATION

NOT until Abraham Lincoln breathed his last in a dingy lodging house in Washington did Edwin M. Stanton utter the unforgettable requiem: "Now he belongs to the ages." Before that the eminent Secretary of War had habitually alluded to Lincoln as "the original gorilla." Not until a murderer's hand had struck him down did the people begin to erect those monuments to his greatness which have continued to rise, and will for centuries. In 1860 a majority of the States had given him the electoral vote, but the people gave him no popular majority. In 1864 they tried desperately to prevent his renomination and election. Only after the grave closed over him did the people discover that the one man indispensable in peace and reconstruction, as he had been indispensable in war and revolution, was gone forever and could not be replaced.

The generations who read only the requiems and the eulogies; who behold only the towering bronzes and marbles; who are taught from childhood to think of Abraham Lincoln as one of the world's mightiest prophets and seers; before they can begin to understand the mind and the psychology of Civil War days, have need to be reminded that those things above are true. In any life of Susan B. Anthony it is essential that they be reminded, since Susan and her associates, men and women, through Lincoln's first term opposed him bitterly. They had reason on their side. All free labor advocates, including many men who, like Daniel Anthony, had never voted before, cast their votes for Lincoln in 1860, because he alone of the several candidates, Bell, Breckinridge, Douglas, was an anti-slavery man. But Lincoln did not go to the country on an anti-slavery platform, and by his own utterances was disposed to let the South keep its peculiar institution intact provided it dropped all talk of secession from the Union. Immediately after the November elections, in which the Republicans were victorious by a bare margin, the country was thrown into a condition of complete demoralization. The South prepared for secession. The North was divided. War seemed inevitable, but war for what? To many Northerners it seemed enough if only the most troublesome Southerners in Congress could be got rid of, and the South's control of the Senate through extension of slavery into free territory, permanently checked. Lincoln to this class of people was acceptable mainly because he was "safe." They cared little about the preservation of the Union, less still what became of the slave States. Henry Ward Beecher, when asked if he thought the Southern States would secede, said lightly: "I don't think they will, and I don't care if they do." And Beecher, at that time, represented not only the conscience but the mind of almost the entire middle class of Northern and Western America.

The Abolitionists, on the other hand, saw in the election of Lincoln only their fondest hope lost in another fatal compromise. Driven to desperation lest all they had fought and suffered for during twenty-five years was about to disappear like a puff of smoke, they launched a great campaign from New England to the farthest West under the slogan: "No Compromise with Slaveholders! Immediate and Unconditional Emancipation!" Susan B. Anthony was placed in command of the forces in New York State, her party consisting of Elizabeth Cady Stanton, Rev. Samuel J. May, Aaron Powell, Stephen S. Foster, and the Rev. Beriah Green. A series of mass meetings in all the principal cities and towns of the State was arranged, but soon it transpired that their demand for immediate emancipation was hardly more appealing than it would have been in South Carolina or Georgia. In the anguished uncertainty of the hour the majority of good citizens agreed on at least one thing: it was a bad time to talk about slavery.

"A bad time to talk about slavery!" cried Elizabeth Cady Stanton "Rhett, Yancey, Iverson, Keitt, Chestnut and Davis; Seward, Hale, Wade, Wilson, Sumner and Fessenden, are all talking about it. James Buchanan, the immortal platform, is fasting and praying and crying over it. The merchants and bankers and brokers are trembling over it. The priests, like faithless nurses, are on all sides giving their people anodynes, that they may sleep over it. The rowdies in all our northern cities and towns stand ready to bluster and swear for it. And the South declares that they will die for it. . . . Why, in the name of common sense, should we be forbidden to open our lips?

"If we descendants of the Puritans had any self-respect, any true love of liberty, any just appreciation of the blood-bought rights left by our forefathers, we should ourselves have scceded long ago from these heathen idolaters, who set all law, human and divine, at defiance; these cannibals who sell babies by the pound, and feed on their own flesh! These polygamists who have many wives and sell their own children! These hunters whose game is men!"

Such speeches, if heard, might well have stirred the consciences of the people, and for precisely that reason the Democrats and the more cautious Republicans saw to it that they were not heard. Led by hoodlums and paid rioters, but sometimes by responsible men such as the son of Governor Horatio Seymour, and a son of ex-President Fillmore, by constables and justices of the peace, furious mobs invaded the halls, dispersed audiences by extinguishing lights or throwing cayenne pepper on the stove; yelled, sang, howled curses and threats, until the voices of the speakers were completely drowned out, and one after another they retreated from the platform. In some towns the Abolitionists found the doors of halls they had rented locked against them. At Syracuse, a city which hitherto had boasted that there the right of free speech had never been denied, the meeting was a disgraceful rout. As Ida Husted Harper tells it, from Susan's own description:

"The hall was filled with a howling, drunken, infuriated crowd, headed by Ezra Downer, a liquor dealer, and Luke McKenna a pro-slavery Democrat. Even Mr. May, who was venerated by all Syracuse, was not allowed to speak. Rotten eggs were thrown, benches broken, and knives and pistols gleamed in every direction. The few ladies present were hurried out of the hall, and Miss Anthony faced that raging audience, the only woman there. The Republican chief of police refused to make any effort towards keeping order. The mob crowded on the platform and took possession of the meeting, and Miss Anthony and her little band were forced out of the hall. . . . That evening the rioters dragged through the streets hideous effigies of Susan B. Anthony and the Rev. Samuel J. May and burned them in the public square."

In Albany the mayor was a man. Although a Democrat and probably a foe of all Abolitionists, he gave notice to his townsmen that he intended to keep his

*affec<sup>y</sup> thine*
*Lucretia Mott*

**LUCRETIA MOTT**
One of the Three Great Pioneers of Woman's Freedom

oath of office and prevent disorder. Mayor Thacher called in person at the Delavan House and escorted Susan, Mrs. Stanton, Lucretia Mott and Martha C. Wright to Association Hall, and during the meeting, at which Gerrit Smith and Frederick Douglass also appeared, he sat on the platform with a loaded revolver in his hand. A number of plain clothes policemen had been distributed through the hall, and every manifestation of violence was met with prompt arrest. Toward the close of the evening, however, Mr. Thacher told Susan that he doubted whether he could control the passions of the people through another session, and he asked her, as a favor, not to try to hold a second meeting. Of course she yielded, and so ended, as far as New York was concerned, the Garrisonian campaign for immediate emancipation.

A woman's rights convention was held in Albany that week, William Lloyd Garrison, Lucretia Mott, Ernestine Rose, Mrs. Wright and Mrs. Stanton speaking, and Susan, as usual, in the foreground. It was a sadly memorable convention, for it was the last one to be held until the Civil War was fought and over, and it was the last of all in which the old leaders would ever foregather in their fine spirit of harmony and fraternity. Characteristically Susan would not admit that the war need hinder the progress of the movement, and she went ahead with plans for a national convention in New York the following May. But before May came war was a grim fact and no one could think of anything else. While the country waited with drawn breath for the development of President Lincoln's policies, no speakers, no audiences, could be attracted to conventions. Even the Anti-Slavery Anniversary meeting was abandoned, and when that happened Susan gave up and went home to the farm. In answer to a letter from the Rev. Beriah Green, she wrote:

"I have tried to persuade myself that I alone remained mad, while all the rest had become sane, because I have insisted that it is our bounden duty to bear not only our usual testimony but one even louder and more earnest than ever before. . . . Our position seems to me most humiliating. . . . Expediency, not principle."

In Washington President Lincoln suffers between expediency and principle. He watches in agony the rout of the Union troops after the first Bull Run. . . . He appoints McClellan to command the Army of the Potomac, McClellan, who builds a magnificent army but will not let it advance. . . . Lincoln replaces in the War Department the inadequate Cameron with the vigorous but sneering Stanton. . . . He removes Generals Frémont and Hunter who have nearly cost him the border States by their illegal emancipation orders. . . . He faces war with England over the *Trent* affair. . . . He argues with Chase, Sumner, Carl Schurtz, his favorite plan of buying the slaves and colonizing them in Hayti and Liberia, a scheme exploded by Garrison years before. . . . He witnesses defeat after defeat until at last the Peninsula campaign ends in disaster at Harrison's Landing, and it is necessary to call out 300,000 more men to be fed into what people are calling "McClellan's death-trap." . . . Wracked to the edge of human endurance the two-fold nature of the man, rigid Constitutionalist, but war President and Commander in Chief of the Army and Navy, seeks blindly for justification of what he knows he must do, free the slaves in the Confederate States and arm them against their masters.

Susan B. Anthony cannot possibly understand why such struggle, such hesitation is for an hour necessary. It is no doubt desirable to keep the border States, Kentucky, Missouri, Arkansas, loyal to the Union, but how much more desirable to wreck the economic power of the South by stopping her exports of cotton. How can a President have it in his power to end slavery and yet hold back? While Lincoln is placating the border States with his no emancipation policy, a doomed race are cementing their shackles anew by supplying the Confederate Army with rations, the rebel Government with money to buy munitions and allies in Europe. While they are singing under the burning sun, "Let my people go," the President questions his constitutional right to smite a cruel Pharaoh. What price a Constitution which defends and protects the thrice damned doctrine of ownership of human beings? What excuse for shedding an ocean of blood in order to restore a *status quo ante* proved unbearable and unenduring? Thus Susan B. Anthony and her like, forerunners of thousands who, during the World War cried out against President Wilson's academic "peace without victory."

On the farm near Rochester Susan finds a certain grim pleasure in working her physical body to exhaustion every day. Daniel Anthony goes to Kansas leaving the management of the farm in her hands. She helps plant and harvest crops, sells them herself in Rochester. She does most of the housework besides, cooks, washes and irons, scrubs, puts up fruit, weaves yards of rag carpet, quilts, sews, paints and varnishes old furniture, goes to meetings wherever held in the neighborhood, speaks when there is no one else to do it—and finds comfort in none of these futile occupations. Her journal is written in scraps:

"Tried to interest myself in a sewing society; but little intelligence among them. . . . Attended Progressive Friends' meeting; too much namby-pambyism. . . . Went to colored church to hear Douglass. He seems without solid basis. Speaks only popular truths. . . . The teachers' convention was small and dull. The women's committee failed to report. I am mortified to death for them. . . . Washed every window in the house to-day. Put a quilted petticoat in the frame. Commenced Mrs. Browning's Portuguese Sonnets. Have just finished Casa Guidi Windows, a grand poem and so fitted to our terrible struggle. . . . I wish the Government would move quickly, proclaim freedom to every slave and call on every ablebodied negro to enlist in the Union Army. How not to do it seems the whole study in Washington."

Elizabeth Cady Stanton is equally wretched over her seclusion and inaction in an hour that calls for action on the part of every strong will and intelligence. She and Susan write mainly about novels of George Eliot which both are reading. Susan cannot understand why Hetty's illegitimate child should have wrought such havoc in her life and in the lives of Adam Bede and Arthur. Why aren't some irregular unions as sacred as legal marriages? Here Susan shows her innate contempt for Puritanism and all laws bearing hard on women. She throws a curious light on her own nature when she asks Mrs. Stanton: "What is the irresistible power so terrifically pictured in both Hetty and Arthur, which led them on to the very ill they most would shun?" Susan, who would passionately have embraced flames in order to free the negro or to enfranchise women, could not even imagine a sex love carried to any point beyond common sense! Elizabeth replies that such books explain why the marriage question is so inevitably a part of the whole woman's rights question, something she has never succeeded in impressing on the other women. She writes despairingly: "O, Susan, are you never coming to visit me again? It would be like a new life to spend a day with you. How I shudder when I think of our awful experience with those mobs last winter, and yet even now I long for action."

Henry B. Stanton was in Washington as a correspondent for the *New York Tribune,* and Elizabeth was preparing to move the family to New York. Susan helped with the packing, went on ahead with the four boys and stayed with her friend until the house in 46th Street was in order. It was some joy to visit the Tiltons again in the little house in Brooklyn; to meet and talk with Horace Greeley, and be assured by him that emancipation was on the way; to attend a belated Anti-Slavery Anniversary meeting; to go on to Boston and see the Garrisons and Wendell Phillips . . . to be with others of her kind. For 1862 had been a grievous year even without the war horror. In April the New York Legislature, taking advantage of the preoccupied public mind, had amended the law of 1860, repealing that section which gave mothers equal guardianship of their children and widows control over the property of minor children. Susan heard first of this dastardly betrayal from Lydia Mott, to whom she wrote:

"I knew some weeks ago the abominable thing was on the calendar, with some six or eight hundred bills before it, and hence felt sure that it would not come up this winter, and that in the meantime we should sound the alarm. . . . We deserve to suffer for our confidence in 'man's sense of justice'; but nothing short of this could rouse our women again to action. I am sick at heart, but I cannot carry the world against the wish and will of our best friends. What can we do now, when even the motion to retain the mother's joint guardianship is voted down? Twenty thousand petitions rolled up for that—a hard year's work—the law secured—the echoes of our gratitude in the hard Capital scarcely died away, and now all is lost."

More clearly than ever did Susan and Mrs. Stanton see that the thing they must henceforth work for was not beneficent legislation but the full and complete citizenship of women. And when in late summer it began to be whispered among the initiate that Lincoln had actually drafted his emancipation proclamation they took heart anew. This even after the President's discouraging letter in the Washington *National Intelligencer*—"What I do about slavery and the colored race, I do because I believe it would help save the Union, and what I forbear, I forbear because I do not believe it would help save the Union. . . ." Even after that letter, published August 23, Greeley wrote Susan: "I am still at work with the President in various ways and believe you will yet hear him proclaim universal freedom. Keep this letter and judge me by the event." On September 18 the preliminary draft of the emancipation proclamation was published.

Universal freedom! It had more meaning to these two women than to the public at large. The same thought was in the minds of both. After the emancipation of the negro must come his enfranchisement. After the war a new interpretation of the Constitution. Real government of the people . . . by the people. Women as well as men. Less was unthinkable. They would organize women all over the country to demand votes for negroes and women, and no white man would dare advocate the one without consenting to the other. They believed it. Who wouldn't?

While they waited in hopeful patience for Lincoln's final proclamation, one more terrible blow fell on Susan B. Anthony, the death of her father, her best and dearest friend on earth. She was filling a few lecture engagements but had gone home for a week-end visit. In the warm sunshine of an Indian Summer Sunday morning she and her father sat talking of the events which had filled the newspaper columns that week, when Daniel Anthony, without a moment's warning, fell forward in his chair, death-struck. Neuralgia of the stomach, the doctors called it. Acute appendicitis, perhaps. In great suffering he lingered briefly, and on November 25, 1862, he died. For weeks Susan moved in a world without sun or moon or any light. It had rarely occurred to her that she might some day have to get along without that companionship, that perfect communion and understanding. Daniel Anthony was sixty-eight years old, but he was youthful and vigorous, for he had hardly known a day of illness in his life. The relation between Susan and Daniel had been more like that of a father and son than father and daughter. From the first he not only acknowledged her right to an independent career, but had encouraged her, helped her with money as well as counsel. There never would be anyone to take his place in her life. On Susan now rested the responsibility of the family. Lucy Anthony was an invalid. Her sons were far away, her daughters, except Susan and Mary, were married. None of them could remain long after the funeral, and on Susan, more bereft even than poor Lucy, rested the burden of reorganizing their shattered lives.

It was well for her that she was quickly recalled to public work. On January 1, 1863, Lincoln's emancipation proclamation was published to the whole world, and the doom of slavery in the United States was pronounced. But the proclamation, although school textbooks do not always say so, did not abolish slavery. It merely suspended it in the States of the Confederacy, and did not affect slave owners in the border States fighting against the Union. Lincoln himself said that the proclamation would become void as soon as the war ended unless Congress confirmed it. If the Confederacy won the war it would be entirely vain. In January, 1863, things looked very dark for the Union side. Desertions from the army had reached appalling proportions, and after the proclamation they increased, in the Army of the Potomac alone, as General Hooker reported, to a rate of two hundred a day. Copperhead agitation was rife in all the armies, and thousands of soldiers who disagreed with total abolition of slavery were induced to abandon their arms and desert. Lincoln's known aversion to capital punishment in the army made this the easier.

On January 16 Henry B. Stanton wrote Susan from Washington:

"The country is rapidly going to destruction. The army is almost in a state of mutiny for want of its pay and for lack of a leader. Nothing can carry the North through but the Southern negroes, and nobody can marshal them into the struggle except the Abolitionists. . . . Such men as Lovejoy, Hale and the like have pretty much given up the struggle in despair.—We must not lay the flattering unction to our souls that the proclamation will be of any use to us if we are beaten and have a dissolution of the Union. Here then is work for you. Susan, put on your armor and go forth."

In Washington Senator Charles Sumner and other Republican leaders were working on a Constitutional Amendment forever abolishing slavery throughout the United States, but there was serious doubt if both Houses of Congress would give the necessary two-thirds majority. Susan B. Anthony, Elizabeth Cady Stanton, Ernestine Rose, Lucy Stone decided together on a course of action. A call for A Meeting of the Loyal Women of the Nation, to meet in the Church of the Puritans, New York, on May 14, 1863, was widely published. Women of every State were urged to send representatives.

" . . . When every hour is big with destiny and each delay but complicates our difficulties, it is high time for the daughters of the Revolution in solemn council to unseal the last will and testament of the fathers, lay hold of their birthright of freedom and keep it a sacred trust for all coming generations."

The call was signed: "on behalf of the Women's Central Committee. Elizabeth Cady Stanton, Susan B. Anthony."

# CHAPTER XIII

## THE WOMEN'S LOYAL LEAGUE

AN enormous crowd filled the famous Church of the Puritans in Union Square, on May 14, when Susan B. Anthony called to order a meeting of women who were to figure importantly in ending slavery by Federal Amendment. Lucy Stone was elected President of the convention, and Mrs. Stanton made the opening address, reminding the audience that, while Southern women had put forth every exertion to keep the rebellion alive, Northern women were accused of doing less than their share toward crushing it. The reason was that, like most men, they were confused as to the object of the war. Congress was confused, even the President seemed to be. It was for women, the wives and mothers of the men who were giving their lives in battle, or returning wounded and suffering, to make perfectly plain that the only justification of the war was that it was being waged for freedom.

Susan was even more explicit in declaring that the object of the war was freedom for all, including all women.

"We talk about returning to the 'Union as it was' and the 'Constitution as it is'—about 'restoring our country to peace and prosperity—to the blessed conditions which existed before the war,'" said Susan. "I ask you what sort of peace, what sort of prosperity, have we had? Since the first slave ship sailed up the James River with its human cargo and there, on the soil of the Old Dominion, it was sold to the highest bidder, we have had nothing but war. When that pirate

captain landed on the shores of Africa and there kidnapped the first
negro and fastened the first manacle, the struggle between that
captain and that negro was the commencement of the terrible war in
the midst of which we are to-day. Between the slave and the master
there has been war, and war only. This is but a new form of it.
No, no; we ask for no return of the old conditions. We ask for
something better. . . . By the Constitution as it is, the North has
stood pledged to protect slavery in the States where it existed. We
have been bound, in case of insurrections, to go to the aid, not of
those struggling for liberty, but of the oppressors. It was politicians
who made this pledge at the beginning, and who have renewed it
from year to year. These same men have had control of the churches,
the Sabbath-schools and all religious institutions, and the women have
been a party in complicity with slavery. They have made the large
majority in all the churches throughout the country, and have, without protest . . . accepted pro-slavery preaching from their pulpits;
suffered the words 'slavery a crime' to be expurgated from all the
lessons taught their children. . . . Woman must now assume her
God-given responsibilities and make herself what she was clearly
designed to be, the educator of the race. Let her no longer be the
mere reflector, the echo of the worldly pride and ambition of man.
Had the women of the North studied to know and to teach their sons
the law of justice to the black man, they would not now be called
upon to offer the loved of their households to the bloody Moloch of
war."

And then, in that clear, strong voice which always
filled the largest hall, she read the resolutions, demanding abolition of slavery in the United States by an
amendment to the Constitution; demanding for freed
negroes, men and women alike, equal opportunity with
white people in education, industry and trades, in all
civil and political rights and privileges. The fifth resolution read: "That it is in the same class—favoring
aristocratic interests—that the property, the liberty,
the lives of all slaves, all citizens of African descent,
and *all women* are placed at the mercy of a legislation

in which they are not represented. There never can be true peace in this Republic until the civil and political equality of every subject of the Government shall be practically established."

When it was realized that they were committing themselves to equal rights for women as well as freedom for slaves there was tumult in the assembly. Many delegates protested that the two questions must be considered apart. Susan, "somewhat sharply," as the newspapers reported, maintained in the midst of cries and exclamations, that henceforth the two questions were one. In the new writing of the Constitution universal suffrage must be the demand of all free minded women. "Incidentally," said the *Tribune,* "a man arose somewhere among the back pews, but his voice was speedily lost in the loud rustle of indignant crinolines." It was a women's meeting, and a majority of the women voted for the woman suffrage clause.

A violent rain storm toward evening kept many away from the night meeting in Cooper Institute, but more men were present to hear Susan read an address to President Lincoln which now must be counted among forgotten papers of the Civil War. Nobody living knows whether President Lincoln ever acknowledged it, or whether his secretaries ever permitted it to reach his desk. Just the same it was a statesmanlike paper in which Susan B. Anthony and Elizabeth Cady Stanton collaborated, and its best paragraphs, at any rate, deserve inclusion here:

" . . . We ask not for ourselves or our friends redress of specific grievances or posts of honor or emolument . . but inspired by true patriotism, in this dark hour of our nation's destiny, we come to pledge the loyal women of the Republic to freedom and our country. . . . we come to thank you for your proclamation, in which the Nineteenth Century seems to echo back the Declaration of Seventy-six. Our fathers had a vision of the sublime idea of liberty, equality and fraternity; but they failed to climb the heights which with anointed eyes they saw. . . . To us, their children, belongs the work to build up the living reality of what they conceived and uttered. . . .

"Our special thanks are due to you, that by your proclamation 2,000,000 women are freed from the foulest bondage humanity ever suffered. Slavery for man is bad enough, but the refinements of cruelty must ever fall on the mothers of the oppressed race, defrauded of all the rights of family relation and violated in the most holy instincts of their nature. A mother's life is bound up in that of her child. . . . But the slave-mother in her degradation rejoices not in the future promise of her daughter, for she knows by experience what her sad fate must be. . . .

"By your act, the family, that great conservator of national virtue and strength, has been restored to millions of humble homes around whose altars coming generations shall magnify and bless the name of Abraham Lincoln. By a mere stroke of the pen you have emancipated millions from a condition of wholesale concubinage. We now ask you to finish the work by declaring that nowhere under our national flag shall the motherhood of any race plead in vain for justice and protection. So long as one slave breathes in this Republic, we drag the chain with him. God has so linked the race, man to man, that all must rise or fall together. Our history exemplifies this law. It was not enough that we at the North abolished slavery for ourselves, declared freedom of speech and press, built churches, colleges and free schools, studied the science of morals, government and economy, dignified labor, amassed wealth, whitened the sea with our commerce and commanded the respect of the nations of the earth— so long as the South, by the natural proclivities of slavery, was sapping the very foundations of our national life.

"You are the first President ever borne on the shoulders of freedom into the position you now fill. Your predecessors owed their elevation to the slave oligarchy, and in serving slavery they did but obey their masters. In your election, Northern freemen threw off the yoke, and with you rests the responsibility that our necks shall never bow again.  At no time in the annals of the nation has there been a more auspicious moment to retrieve the one false step of the fathers in their concession to slavery.  The Constitution has been repudiated and the compact broken by the Southern traitors now in arms.  The firing of the first gun on Sumter released the North from all constitutional obligations to slavery.  It left the Government, for the first time in our history, free to carry out the declaration of our Revolutionary fathers, and make us in fact what we have ever claimed to be, a nation of freemen.

"'The Union as it was'—a compromise between barbarism and civilization—can never be restored, for the opposing principles of freedom and slavery cannot exist together.  Liberty is life and every form of government yet tried proves that slavery is death. . . . The war in which we are involved is not the result of party or accident, but a forward step in the progress of the race never to be retraced. . . .

"At this time our greatest need is not men or money, valiant generals or brilliant victories, but a *consistent policy,* based on the principle that 'all governments derive their just powers from the consent of the governed.'  The nation waits for you to say that there is no power under our declaration of rights nor under any laws, human or divine, by which free men can be made slaves; and therefore that your pledge to the slaves is irrevocable, and shall be redeemed.

"If it be true, as has been said, that Northern women lack enthusiasm in this war, the fault rests with those who have confused and confounded its policy.  The pages of history glow with instances of self-sacrifice by women in the hour of their country's danger.  Fear not that the daughters of this Republic will count any sacrifice too great to insure the triumph of freedom.  Let the men who wield the nation's power be wise, brave, and magnanimous, and its women will be prompt to meet the duties of the hour with devotion and heroism. . . .

"On behalf of the Women's Loyal League,
ELIZABETH CADY STANTON, *President.*
SUSAN B. ANTHONY, *Secretary."*

The one mistake the women made in that address was a lauditory mention of the wholly illegal acts of

Frémont and Hunter in emancipating slaves in their
military districts. That was a direct affront to the
President, and it may have prevented the document
from reaching him at all. But Mrs. Stanton could
never forbear a tribute to her hero, Frémont, who, although a little too much on the melodramatic side, was
really a hero. Of the first principles of government,
however, he never had the remotest notion, and as
President he would have been a national calamity.

The Women's Loyal League, which spread rapidly
throughout the North, had for its pledged object, support of Lincoln's Government, "in so far as it makes the
war a war for freedom," and its work was to secure
names, a million names if possible, on petitions to the
House and Senate demanding a Federal Amendment
forever abolishing slavery in the United States. The
entire anti-slavery press of the country commended the
women's project, and men of prominence in and out
of Washington wrote grateful and congratulatory letters. Headquarters were taken in Cooper Institute,
and all during the stifling summer that followed Mrs.
Stanton, Susan and their friends worked ceaselessly,
getting the petitions printed and sent out, writing and
answering thousands of letters, raising money for office
expenses, for printing and postage, for the expenses
of lecturers sent into the field to arouse and encourage
a people grown weary of a war that threatened never to
end. Lucy Stone, Dr. Clemence Lozier, Rebecca Shep-
ard Putnam, Charlotte Wilbour and others gave their
services, but there were clerks and bookkeepers and
messengers to be paid, and very little money to go on
with. A few years before Charles H. Hovey, a rich
merchant of Boston, had died leaving $50,000 to be

spent for anti-slavery agitation and woman's rights. A great deal of the income from the fund was used to support an anti-slavery journal, *The Standard*, but now the committee sent a small donation. Gerrit Smith, Jessie Benton Frémont, a few business firms of New York, made individual contributions; Henry Ward Beecher gave a Sunday morning collection to the fund; signers of the petition throughout the country sent in $3,000. When there was no more money Susan arranged a lecture course, persuading George William Curtis, Hon. William D. Kelley, Wendell Phillips, Frederick Douglass and others to contribute their services for half their usual fees. Susan herself did the work of three people, on a salary of $12 a week, which would have been less than the price of subsistence had not Mrs. Stanton lodged her in her own guest room. Thirteen cents a day bought Susan's luncheon, two rolls, a glass of milk, and when possible a dish of strawberries or other fruit. The work went forward well advertised, for the League strongly supported Lincoln's first draft, the women no more than the men of the country dreaming of the plot which was even then ripening to destroy it.

Reading newspaper accounts of the Civil War, day by day, it is baffling to understand why few efforts or none were put forth in the North to stay the poisonous propaganda of sedition which went on in all the cities, in recruiting stations and even in the army. While in the South the faintest suspicion of disloyalty was instantly suppressed, sometimes with frightful cruelty, in the North, Confederate agents and "Copperheads" seem to have gone about their business without interference. The draft went into operation the second week in

July, 1863, and although some rumors of disaffection were circulated the papers made light of them. On July 11 there was held in Union Square a huge meeting at which, from four stands, men poured forth such traitorous and obscene doctrine, such insult and abuse of the President and the Administration, that during the World War would have sent every speaker to Federal prison or to internment camps. Ostensibly the meeting was a protest against the arrest, court martial and imprisonment of the notorious Vallandigham in Dayton, Ohio. General Burnside was one of the few army leaders who fully realized the danger of propaganda among homesick and discouraged soldiers, and in his department he would have none of it. Vallandigham, although professing to be a Union man, had from the beginning of the war opposed emancipation, and in fact every move of the Administration. In the spring he made a series of defeatist speeches, closely resembling those made by our German sympathizers, alias pacifists, internationalists and Socialists in 1917. Seeing that a not inconsiderable group was forming around this dangerous man, Burnside, as commander of the Department of the Ohio, published an order against his future activities, proclaiming that "treason expressed or implied will not be tolerated by this Department." Vallandigham made one more speech in which he denounced the war as "wicked, cruel and unnecessary, not waged for the purpose of the preservation of the Union, its objects not to free black men but to enslave white men; a war to crush out freedom and erect a despotism." He appealed to the torn emotions of men and women who mourned soldiers dead in battle, declaring that Lincoln could honorably have ended the war months before by accepting the mediation of France. France, which at that moment was establishing a European empire in Mexico!

Very properly Burnside arrested the man, had him tried and sentenced to confinement in a fortress. That sentence Lincoln had changed to deportation to a neutral country. Yet there in Union Square, New York, Lincoln's leniency was attacked as an abominable denial of the right of free speech. "The South," declared one orator, "can never be conquered by Abraham Lincoln or any other damned black Republican!" Cries from the crowd, "Hang him! Hang him!" "Loyalty to Lincoln," shrieked another Copperhead, "is treason! We'll fight for the Constitution but not for niggers or the draft."

Not a newspaper seriously censured the police for permitting this meeting to continue, and in fact, as events proved, the New York police force was not then organized to break up meetings or to control mobs. The draft in every ward of the city progressed quietly until the morning of July 13. At ten o'clock on that morning, in the headquarters at Third Avenue and 46th Street, the wheel was turning and men's names were being called out in the presence of a good-natured crowd of about three hundred. Suddenly a pistol shot exploded in the street, and at the same instant a shower of bricks, paving stones and other missiles shattered the windows of the draft office, and the doors were battered in to admit such a rabble as few New Yorkers knew existed in the city. Where that rabble came from, who organized or led it, was a complete mystery. Out of the fetid tenements and mean streets of the lower East Side, from Five Points and the dens of the Bowery it streamed, ragged, dirty, alien, crazed with fury and the lust for blood. Before a revolver could be drawn the rabble swept over the provost marshal and his aids and the spectators, and with rocks and stones wrecked the room. The soldier clerk caught the draft wheel in his arms and fled upstairs. The officers in charge, uniforms in ribbons, managed to escape alive through a back entrance. A score of dead and wounded men were left on the floor, while a man with a can of turpentine and a torch set fire to the building. When the police arrived they were beaten back by sheer force of numbers. When the fire engines clattered up they were set upon and smashed. By three o'clock in the afternoon the greater part of the city was helpless in the hands of the mob.

A block from the Stanton home stood a large orphan asylum for colored children, and this became the object of immediate attack. Over the heads of the screaming children, with great difficulty rescued from death, the building was fired and sacked, as were half a dozen surrounding houses. Hastily gathering the Stanton children together Susan contrived their escape over the roof. Mrs. Stanton, as she writes in her journal, trying to compose a speech to the mob, in case it broke in, saw with horror from her window one of her older sons captured by a group of ruffians. Neil Stanton, though but a boy, had cool wit enough not to resist. Instead he invited his captors to the nearest saloon for drinks, and thus saved his own life. Mrs. Stanton rejoiced, although she deplored his "departure from principle," and that night the whole family left the house for suburban quarters.

For five days that mob, its numbers swelled by a

horde of criminals, pimps, prostitutes, held the city almost unchecked, pursuing and murdering hundreds of citizens, hunting down and hanging helpless negroes, looting, sacking, burning, destroying. Strangely the rioters, except the professional criminals, had little in the way of firearms, their strength lying in numbers and ferocity, and most of their cruelest murders were done with clubs, workmen's tools, hatchets and kitchen knives. The police were utterly overwhelmed, the fire department defenseless, yet neither the Democratic Mayor nor Governor would consent to declare martial law. Instead Governor Seymour sent a committee to Washington to beg President Lincoln to stop the draft, declaring that his own Irish immigrant servants were likely to burn his house if it continued. Perhaps that idea appealed to Lincoln as not altogether undesirable. At all events he refused to make any such infamous surrender to a mob, and the draft was not stopped. Troops were dispatched, not only to New York but to Philadelphia, Boston and other cities where uprisings were threatened, and after a period of terror such as only France and Russia have seen in their revolutions, order was restored. The ringleaders were never apprehended, but from that time on "free speech" such as the Union Square disloyalists had uttered, was suppressed in a manner which no doubt would be deplored by the radical weeklies of to-day. At the same time the New York Common Council voted an appropriation of $2,500,000 to purchase exemptions for poor men with families. They were not wholly to be blamed for dreading the draft. Most of them were Irish and Germans, too lately landed to know anything about slavery or the Union. They had fled oppression at home, and were too ready to believe Americans who told them that they were about to be killed for a race of black men. If nothing else good came out of the draft riots at least there was a beginning not only of a better housing movement in the city slums, better schools for immigrant children, but of organized charitable and social relief.

The riots had the effect also of speeding up the work of the Women's Loyal League, the petitions receiving thousands of names in the weeks following. The man who helped most in the work was Senator Charles Sumner, many sacks of petitions being sent to his Washington office and sent out under his frank. Another man who helped generously was the Socialist, Robert Dale Owen, at that time a most loyal Unionist, and President Lincoln's appointed chairman in New York of the Freedmen's Inquiry Commission. Susan and Mrs. Stanton gratefully accepted his many services, little knowing how later their association with Owen would be used against them.

On February 9, 1864, the first consignment of signed petitions bearing over a hundred thousand names, were carried into the Senate Chamber and presented in an eloquent speech by Charles Sumner. By August of the same year the number of names on the women's petitions had increased to nearly 400,000. Sumner, accepting them, told the Senate's presiding officer that the sacks were so heavy, the rolls so numerous, that they could not be sent forward to his desk, but he impressed on the whole Senate that those hundreds of thousands of names meant nothing less than an imperative order from the people for the rapid acceptance, by more than the requisite two-thirds majority, of the pending

amendment abolishing slavery. The Senate did pass
the bill, the House later concurring, and in the late
winter the Thirteenth Amendment went to the Legislatures of the loyal States and was ratified.

Not once did Senator Sumner or any member of
Congress, speaking for the amendment, acknowledge
the great services of the women in arousing public
opinion in its behalf. Now that the work was done
they quietly disbanded and turned to less spectacular
war work. When the business affairs of the League
were wound up there was a deficit in the treasury of
$4.72. But no member of Congress offered to pay it.
Susan B, Anthony, out of her own lean purse, paid it.

# CHAPTER XIV

## "IT IS THE NEGRO'S HOUR"

IN 1864 the Abolitionists, women as well as men, were still so distrustful of Lincoln that they worked for the nomination of Frémont. Elizabeth Cady Stanton was of this number, but Susan B. Anthony was not. Great as was her impatience with Lincoln's slow decisions she agreed with him that it was poor policy to "swap horses while crossing a stream." It was really this homely aphorism which elected Lincoln, for in the extreme confusion of the campaign it was about the only thing the ordinary voter could understand. In April, 1865, six weeks after the second inauguration, five days after Lee's surrender at Appomattox, came the greatest calamity that ever befell the American people, the assassination of Abraham Lincoln. Not until then did the radicals perceive how shortsighted and vain had been their opposition of this man, the only one with vision, tolerance, humanity and common sense in right proportions to take the country through the agonies of reconstruction. Lincoln's plans for reconstruction were outlined before the collapse of Confederate arms. His Cabinet knew them. Congress knew them. Even Vice-President Johnson knew them. Yet Lincoln's plans could not be carried out, because there was no broadminded, simple, kindly and conciliating executive to deal with the conquered but still rebellious South. What might not have been, if Abraham Lincoln had lived to call into his counsels such men as Robert E. Lee, Wade Hampton, Joseph E. Johnston, to discover some basis whereby the economic losses as well as the wounded pride of the South could be ameliorated and restored? Lincoln had said: "Get them to plowing once, to gathering in their own crops, eating popcorn at their own firesides, and you can't get them to shoulder a musket again for fifty years." Literally this had been spoken of the rank and file, but in principle it applied to the aristocratic minority as well, and Lee had agreed with what Lincoln said.

Had Lincoln lived it is hardly possible that the most ghastly mistake of reconstruction, the premature enfranchisement of two million illiterate negroes, would have been permitted. He knew, and had often expressed his opinion, that the most serious problem facing the Republic was that of white Americans and slave-born blacks living together on the continent. The negroes bore no resemblance to other immigrants, or indeed to any other people in the world. It may truly be said that the American negro is the only human being whom God did not create. The slave trader and the slave owner created him. Therefore, after the sin of slavery was wiped out it was the plain duty of the American people to recreate the negro in the likeness of civilized man. How Lincoln would have moved to do it can never be known, but it is unbelievable that he would have begun by placing a ballot in his hand. The vindictive Thaddeus Stevens, and the dogmatic Charles Sumner, Lincoln would have had to fight on the question, but he would have had back of him a majority in Congress and certainly the best press of the country.  But Lincoln was slain, and in his place was elevated a man ill-bred, ill-educated, obstinate, and so little appreciative even of his Vice-Presidential dignity that he was drunk when he took the oath of office. In the resultant violent quarrels between President Johnson and his Congress the South was thrown into years of utter anarchy, and two entirely unenforceable amendments were added to the Constitution of the United States.  As one more deplorable consequence, Susan B. Anthony's dream of a new dispensation for women was postponed for over half a century.

Thaddeus Stevens was chiefly responsible for the Fourteenth Amendment, which gave full civil rights to negroes, and was intended to give them the vote as well.  Stevens soon enlisted in his support men in Congress who cared little for the negro but who were violently opposed to President Johnson.  He was warmly supported by the Abolitionists, of course. Their minds had for so long concentrated on the negro's wrongs that they were quite ready to believe that the Civil War could not be liquidated nor any permanent peace restored until all Southern leaders were disfranchised and all negroes armed with the ballot.  It was nothing to them that not one per cent of the freed slaves could read the names on a ballot.  To them any negro was "God's image in ebony," and they may have believed that all would be made literate from on high as soon as the amendment went through.  Congress was under no such delusion.  The Republican Party, precariously in power, was in a hurry to enfranchise not only the negro but the large class of small farmers and "poor whites," politically nonexistent before the war. For many years the Southern aristocracy had dominated Congress, especially the Senate. They were men who, like the ruling classes in Great Britain, were born and bred to politics. They were rich, arrogant and powerful, and were aggressive enough besides to push through most measures they deemed beneficial to their civilization. When all other arguments failed they fell back on physical force. They carried revolvers and bowie knives, and were forever challenging Northern members to duels. In 1856 Representative Preston Brooks beat Charles Sumner almost to death with a gutta-percha stick, several chivalrous Southrons standing by to prevent the Massachusetts Senator from defending himself. Now, while all the machinery was in their hands, the Northern men were ready to adopt any and all measures which would forever dethrone this dangerous power, and to ensure democratic constitutions in all of the new States coming into the Union.

Susan B. Anthony and Elizabeth Cady Stanton were in favor of giving the ballot to negroes, but their approach to the subject was more statesmanlike than that of Congress or the men in the Abolition ranks. Susan's contention was that the Civil War gave Congress power to restate the Constitution in terms clearly intended by the Fathers of the Republic, and to make the nation in fact as well as in theory a political democracy. The secession of the South, the war and the Union victory wiped out all previous measures of compromise, and now at last there was room for a Government by consent of the governed—all of the governed, not a caste either of sex or color. Early in 1865 Susan went to Kansas to visit her brother, Daniel R. Anthony, editor of an influential newspaper, and Mayor of Leavenworth. Into Kansas had streamed thousands of ex-slaves, homeless, hungry, and full of gruesome tales of outrages perpetrated on the helpless freedmen of the South. Susan moved among the refugees, assisting in the relief stations and soup kitchens, hospitals and schools, and her soul blazed within her at what she saw and heard. Discounting all propaganda, there is no doubt that the freed negroes suffered frightful wrongs after emancipation. Their first impulse was to get away from the scenes of their bondage, and in packs they wandered over the face of the earth, not knowing whither or why, begging food, stealing from cornfields and smokehouses, living like beasts. Like unclean beasts they were treated, beaten, maimed, mutilated, murdered, their bodies thrown into ponds and mudholes. Of course very few responsible Southerners were guilty of such deeds. The worst crimes were probably committed by "poor whites," returning soldiers and others, a class which despised the negro far more than the slave owners did. As a fact, the slave owners did not exactly despise the negroes. They merely looked on them as mules or other domestic cattle.

As an Abolitionist Susan desired absolute justice for negroes. She knew that the mass of them in the South were little developed, but having known Frederick Douglass, Robert Purvis and other highly intelligent negroes in the North she believed that all of them could be educated, and, since their plight at the present was so desperate, she thought their enfranchisement was imperative—but only as a part of the general program of citizenship for all adult Americans. In an address delivered July 4, 1865, at Ottumwa, Kansas, Susan stated the case of the negro thus:

"In Virginia," said Susan, "the planters have solemnly leagued themselves together to pay only five dollars a month to able field hands, each laborer to furnish his own clothes and pay his own doctor bills. This too, when the same planters use to pay or receive for the hire of these same laborers the sum of fifteen dollars and upward. In South Carolina General Rufus Saxton reports that the old planters are actually driving the freedmen to work in the fields in chain gangs, and that the woods are strewn with the bodies of negroes shot dead in their efforts to escape the cruel tortures. . . .

"Tennessee, the President's own State, of the loyalty of whose citizens we have heard much, has adopted a free constitution, and under it has framed a new code of anti-negro laws; and we can hardly expect any rebel State to do better, for these new free State law-makers are the persecuted loyal men of Tennessee who have been outraged in their homes, hunted to the caves and mountains, or for a time driven out of the State altogether by the seccessionists. One of these new free State laws says, the testimony of no free colored person shall be received in court against any white person. By this enactment the meanest white man may enter the home of the bravest black soldier, or wealthiest colored citizen, may murder his sons, ravish his wife and daughters, pillage and burn his house, commit any and every possible crime against him and his, and yet, if no human eye but his own, or that of his family, or his colored friends witness the barbarisms, the father, the husband, the landholder, outraged beyond measure, has no possible legal redress in the courts of Tennessee.

"Then again, in case a free colored person is imprisoned and unable to pay his jail fees, he may be apprenticed out to labor until the sum be paid. And yet again, the courts may apprentice colored children as they see proper. The law does not even say friendless or orphaned children. Is not that slavery under a new form? Thus to leave those devoted black men's lives, liberties and property to be protected by white men, whose loyalty to the Government is because it is a means to secure power for themselves, not from any love of republican principles, is to doom them to all the ignominies and cruelties of slavery itself."

Susan was careful to point out that in none of the Northern States, outside of New England, were colored

persons citizens, and she emphasized the fact that nowhere in the world were women, the most intelligent,
allowed a single measure of self-government.  She said:

"We have never from the beginning had any genuine republican
form of government in any State in the Union, for in no State have
'the people' ever been permitted to elect their representatives.  Even
in Massachusetts and Vermont, the States nearest republican, only
one half the people, the male inhabitants, are allowed to vote.  In
other States it is only 'all free, white male persons,' and in others
still, all 'free, white, male inhabitants owning so many slaves or so
much property.'  It is not true therefore that *the people* have
ever exercised the right to prescribe the qualifications of voters or
officers. . . . That this superior 'white male' class may not even be
trusted to legislate even for their own mothers, wives, sisters and
daughters, the cruel statutes of nearly all the States, both slave and
free, give ample proof.  In scarcely a State has a married woman the
legal right to the control of her person, to the earnings of her hand
and brain, to the guardianship of her children, to sue or be sued, or
to testify in the courts, and by these laws women have suffered wrongs
and outrages second only to those of chattel slavery itself.  If this be
true, that this so-called superior class cannot legislate justice even
to those nearest and dearest in their own hearts and homes, is it not
a crime to place a separate race, one hated and despised, wholly at
the will of the governing class?"

Daniel R. Anthony and other Kansas Republicans
were delighted with Susan's speech and begged her to
repeat it before many audiences.  Only they entreated
her to leave out everything in it except what related to
negro suffrage.  She should not confuse the issues, they
said.  To which Susan replied that it was they who
confused the issues, and that in her speeches she proposed to talk, not party politics but straight republicanism.  During this time letters were pouring in on Susan
begging her to return to the East, because Garrison,
satisfied with the achievement of complete abolition,

was trying to disband the Anti-Slavery Society. Exhausted by his thirty-two years of heartbreaking labor Garrison indeed seemed to have no more fight in him. Wendell Phillips wrote to Susan: "Come back. There is work for you here." Parker Pillsbury, Lydia Mott, Mrs. Stanton and Douglass all wrote, but Susan was reluctant to leave Kansas. What finally decided her to leave hurriedly was the text of the proposed Fourteenth Amendment, as she read it one morning in her brother's newspaper. This provided, in its first article, that all *persons* born or naturalized in the United States, were citizens, that representatives should be apportioned among the several States according to their respective numbers, counting the whole number of *persons* in each State, excluding Indians not taxed. But by the second article, if the right to vote in any State were denied to any of the *male* citizens, except for participation in rebellion or other crime, the basis of representation would then be reduced in proportion which the number of such *male* citizens bore to the whole number of *male* citizens, twenty-one years of age, in the State.

For the first time the word male was mentioned in the Constitution, which, in its original form had contained not a syllable limiting the qualifications of voters, as to sex, race, social or financial status. If the word male were now written into the Constitution it would mean that by the fundamental law of the Republic, the political rights of half the population, the woman half, would be denied. The most any State could grant would be partial suffrage. To Susan, chief among the women who had toiled so unselfishly to lift the curse of negro slavery from the land, this new affirmation of women's subjected status came as a stunning blow. Not

only in the Women's Loyal League had Northern
women rendered devoted service to the Union. In
the Sanitary Commission, in military hospitals, in first
aid stations under fire, in war work of every description
back of the lines, they had worked faithfully and well.
Even, in some cases, in the planning of campaigns and
in the secret service women had distinguished themselves. They had been the first to go into the South as
teachers in negro schools. And now, for their sole reward, they found that, as Elizabeth Cady Stanton expressed it, they had "boosted the negro over their own
heads." The male negro, as a matter of fact, for when
Susan returned hastily from Kansas she saw that the
old Abolitionists were so enraptured at the prospect of
getting the ballot into the hands of more men that they
had lost all interest in the women's claims. They had
not even noticed the second article of the proposed
Fourteenth Amendment.

"But do you not see," said Susan to Wendell Phillips
and other members of the Hovey Committee, preparing
to spend the whole income of the fund on the freed
slaves, "that if we succeed in striking out the word
male, the amendment virtually enfranchises not only
the negroes, but all American citizens, including
women? Why? Because, rather than have their representation in Congress cut down, men will be willing
to have women vote."

Perhaps they saw, perhaps not. At all events they
reluctantly gave Susan, out of the Hovey bequest, $500
with which to defray expenses of petitions to Congress,
and also to the New York Legislature which was about
to hold a convention for the revision of the State Constitution. Susan and Mrs. Stanton planned to effect

a union of the Anti-Slavery Society, Wendell Phillips being its new President, and their Women's Rights Society, under the name of the Equal Rights Association, to work for the citizenship of women as well as negro men. This had the approval of practically all the Boston intellectuals, Emerson, Channing, Alcott, Sanborn and Whittier; it was supported in New York by Horace Greeley, Henry Ward Beecher, Theodore Tilton, William Cullen Bryant, George William Curtis; it even had friends in Congress, including Sumner and Thaddeus Stevens, Chairman of the Joint Committee of Fifteen on Reconstruction. But Wendell Phillips, to the women's dismay, was distinctly cool, if not hostile to the idea. He did not see how the Anti-Slavery Society could deal with the two ideas, he said, and as for fusing the organizations, that could only be done by amending the Constitution after a three months advance notice. The month was January, therefore there was ample time in which to give the required notice, and Susan asked Aaron Powell, one of the women's trusted friends to do it. He agreed, but when the Anti-Slavery Society met for its annual convention in May it was found that Mr. Powell had not fulfilled his promise, and, therefore, no notice having been given, Wendell Phillips calmly announced that a coalition of the two societies was impossible under the constitution.

More was to come. The Women's Rights Convention met on May 10, and Susan proposed resolutions changing the name of their organization to the American Equal Rights Association. In her speech she elucidated the terms of the Fourteenth Amendment, showed what an extraordinary opportunity Congress now pos-

sessed to establish in the United States the democracy
which was the unfulfilled dream of the founders of the
Republic. The women did not wish to stand in the
negro's way, she declared. On the contrary, they
wanted votes for negroes, all of them, instead of the
male half only. And she said:

"Of what good is negro suffrage as proposed, to the negro woman?
Before the war she had man for her master, it is true, but at
least he was an educated white man. If the ballot is given now to
negro men the woman will be in a far worse situation than before,
for she will still have man for her master, ignorant and irresponsible.
She will simply be plunged into a worse slavery than she ever knew
before. . . ."

As a result of the war, said Susan, the whole question
of suffrage had reverted back to the United States
Constitution, and the duty of Congress, at that hour,
was to declare what should be the basis of representation in a republican form of government.

"There is, there can be, but one true basis, that taxation and representation must be inseparable; hence our demand must now go
beyond woman—it must extend to the farthest limits of the principle of the 'consent of the governed'. . . . We therefore wish to
broaden our woman's rights platform and make it in name what it
has ever been in spirit, a human rights platform. As women we can
no longer claim for ourselves what we do not for others, nor can
we work in two separate movements to get the ballot for the two
disfranchised classes, negroes and women, since to do so must be at
double cost of time, energy and money. . . ."

The resolution to change the name and the object of
the society was unanimously adopted. In the course
of the day's proceedings both Henry Ward Beecher
and Wendell Phillips made flattering speeches, but
Susan, with sinking heart, perceived that both men
cleverly evaded the real point at issue. Nevertheless

Tilton, Frederick Douglass and Robert Purvis, with
Mrs. Stanton, accepted election as vice-presidents of
the new organization. Lucretia Mott was made President, Susan first secretary and Henry B. Blackwell,
Lucy Stone's husband, recording secretary. Yet a few
days later when Susan and Mrs. Stanton met Wendell
Phillips and Theodore Tilton to discuss plans for immediate work, Phillips had the effrontery to propose
that the Equal Rights Association should drop all plans
for woman suffrage and work only for the negro. Let
the Fourteenth Amendment go through as written, he
suggested. This was the negro's hour, and if anything
was done to interfere with his claims, the sacred hour
might be lost. It was the negro's hour in New York
State also, said Phillips. Therefore it was the women's
patriotic duty to petition for the removal of the word
"white" in the revised constitution, leaving the word
"male" alone. Otherwise they would probably accomplish nothing.

Hardly able to contain her indignation Susan turned
to Tilton, who in the columns of the *Independent* had
so ardently advocated woman's rights, and demanded
tensely: "And what is your opinion of this?"

"Well," said Tilton a little uneasily, "I too believe
that this is the negro's hour, and I think you ought to
canvass the State in his behalf. In the next Constitutional Convention you will be in a better position to
ask votes for yourselves."

"Twenty years from now!" cried Susan.

"Oh, perhaps not as long as that, but—"

Susan's gaze turned to Mrs. Stanton, but she, as if
hypnotized by the arguments of these men whom above
all others she admired, sat smiling and apparently ac-

quiescent. Walking closer to the group Susan thrust out her arm at full length.

"Look at this," she said, "all of you. And hear me swear that I will cut off this right arm of mine before I will ever work for or demand the ballot for the negro and not the woman."

She walked out of the room hearing, as she passed through the door, Tilton's smooth voice: "Why, whatever is the matter with Susan?  I never before knew her to be so unreasonable or so rude."

Susan waited a few hours until she felt herself to be thoroughly under control, and then she went to the Stanton home.  There she found Elizabeth walking up and down her long drawing-room, wringing her hands and weeping.  Whatever reproaches Susan had ready for her best friend were never spoken, for as she entered Elizabeth threw herself into those strong arms, crying: "Oh, Susan! What is the matter with me?  What got into me this afternoon?  I feel absolutely scourged from the crown of my head to the soles of my feet."

She, too, as soon as she left the magnetic presence of Phillips and Tilton, realized the insult of their proposal, that millions of white women wait for their citizenship until a horde of black men, barely emerged from semi-barbarism, were made their civil and political superiors.  The wonder is that Elizabeth Cady Stanton or any of the women ever did trust men like Phillips and Tilton.  There was, at the time, a glamour surrounding Wendell Phillips which in perspective seems wholly specious.  He was an epitome of aristocratic Boston, to be sure, but aside from his abolitionism he appears about as substantial as a cream puff.  To execute a *volte face* on any other subject than that of the negro was no trouble at all to Phillips. He was a man without a spark of humor, and sometimes it would seem, without any warmth of heart. As for Theodore Tilton, the oscillations of his mind and conscience equaled in eccentricity those of his bosom friend and later foe, Henry Ward Beecher. Brilliant, deeply religious, in a sense highly idealistic, Tilton nevertheless was ready at times to sell his pen and his convictions. But Elizabeth and Susan had yet to find that out.

The two women sat down and faced their situation. Their best men had betrayed them. Congress had ignored their existence. Many of their own women associates had been caught in the current hysteria and were echoing the parrot cry: "This is the negro's hour." Susan B. Anthony and Elizabeth Cady Stanton, Lucy Stone and Lucretia Mott, with a handful more of level-headed women were left to carry on the struggle for democracy in a republic. But this handful, at any rate, would die before it surrendered.

# CHAPTER XV

## ANOTHER RICHMOND IN THE FIELD

THROUGH the spring and summer of 1866 a small squad of women had the work of a battalion on their hands. In Congress the Fourteenth Amendment was being hurried to a final vote, and there was also being sponsored a bill giving votes to negroes in the District of Columbia. The women therefore expended all their energies in rolling up petitions asking for the exclusion of the word "male" from the amendment, and for the inclusion of women in the District of Columbia franchise bill. They had good reason for expecting the dominant Republican Party to grant their petitions, for from the very formation of the party it had been supported, not only by women abolitionists, but by so many Northern and Western women of liberal views that Elizabeth Cady Stanton was actually conspicuous for having remained a Democrat. Susan and other woman's rights leaders believed that the Republicans would see in them future party strength, but from the standpoint of practical politics their reasoning fell short of one important consideration. What the Republicans were seeking at the moment was geographical extension of their power, and this they sought in the South among negroes and yeoman whites, who as voters would outnumber the old oligarchy. They did not particularly need the votes of Northern women, so they could be pushed aside for the present. Said Charles

Sumner, in one of the Senate debates: "That question (woman suffrage) I leave untouched, contenting myself with the remark that it is obviously the great question of the future—at least one of the great questions—which will easily be settled whenever the women in any proportions insist that it shall be settled."

This was fairly brazen even for a politician, considering that no negroes had asked for the vote, while women's petitions from East and West were daily pouring into both House and Senate. Some of the petitions were casually presented, but many were simply dropped into waste-baskets by men whose own constituents had forwarded them. One long petition from Massachusetts had for its sponsor and first signer Lydia Maria Child, a woman who in the middle 1830's had sacrificed a promising literary career to become an editorial drudge on the Anti-Slavery *Standard,* and who occupied in popular esteem a position hardly second to that of Lucretia Mott. Sumner presented it, saying that he did so under protest, as he considered Mrs. Child's action "most inopportune." Other Republicans declared piously that they favored woman suffrage and would vote for it as a separate measure, but not now, while the real issue was votes for negroes. Still the women went on piling up names, rushing in petitions, to the endless harassment of the Republicans and the boundless delight of the minority group of Democrats. Alarmed at the unexpected success of Susan and Mrs. Stanton in enrolling so many woman suffrage advocates, men as well as women, Garrison, Phillips, Greeley, Gerrit Smith, Higginson, Curtis, even Frederick Douglass, did everything they could privately to encourage Congress to ignore the women.

The defection of Frederick Douglass was particularly despicable, since he owed almost all his success in life to women. After his escape from slavery in Maryland it was a Baltimore woman who started a subscription to buy his freedom, and when he wished to establish an anti-slavery newspaper it was English women sympathizers with abolition who furnished his presses. Yet Douglass with callous ingratitude, now fought for his own enfranchisement at the expense of women's freedom. To the credit of another intellectual negro, Robert Purvis, it should be remembered that he refused to do this, saying that he was ashamed to vote before his own wife and daughter. Three other men stood by the women, these three being the Rev. Samuel J. May, Stephen S. Foster and Parker Pillsbury, editor-in-chief of the *Standard*. When that paper, supported by the Hovey Fund, which bequest, now that emancipation had been achieved, really belonged to the woman's rights group, refused any longer to carry Susan's announcements or notices of meetings except at full advertising rates, Pillsbury resigned his position in disgust.

Before the close of the 39th Congress, in July, 1866, the Fourteenth Amendment was passed in Congress— the word male included. Susan and Mrs. Stanton dauntlessly then prepared to turn their guns on the New York State Convention soon to meet for revision of the Constitution. Susan organized a corps of speakers—it was always Susan who did the organizing work—and during the first months of 1867 they held a series of meetings and conventions all over the State. In some cities they had enthusiastic receptions, large audiences, the majority present signing petitions that both "white" and "male" should be left out of the revised constitution. In other places the women met hostility, or what was worse, small and indifferent audiences. In general the newspapers were opposed to their crusade, although many gave the speakers, especially Susan, flattering notices. Other women, they said, made speeches, but Susan B. Anthony advanced arguments. Early in January Susan went alone to Albany to persuade Charles J. Folger, Chairman of the Senate Judiciary Committee, to arrange a hearing at which, before a joint session of Senate and House committees, Mrs. Stanton should present their case. Susan had armed herself before her arrival with all the legal arguments, prepared for her no doubt by some very astute lawyer. She pointed out to Mr. Folger the fact that when a new constitution was taking form, the State was resolved into its original elements, and that those in charge of the matter had no right in law to exclude from the reconstruction any class of the people. Senator Folger granted the soundness of Susan's contention, and he arranged the hearing. On January 13th Elizabeth Cady Stanton, before a crowded Assembly Chamber, made one of the greatest speeches of her career in favor of universal and impartial suffrage in New York State. It was, as usual, the "product of our joint brains," and it was based on the legal plea presented first to Senator Folger. Unless women's interests were given full consideration in the convention, Mrs. Stanton said, the new constitution could not rightfully be presented for ratification to the voters of the State as a representative document. A number of legislators took part in the debate which followed, but of the arguments which they advanced in

*Susan B. Anthony*

SUSAN AT FORTY-EIGHT
When She Was Working for Revision of the New York State Constitution

favor of giving negro men, but not white women the ballot, Parker Pillsbury said scornfully: "Any and all of them Susan could have extinguished with her thimble."

It may seem strange that many of the men who had fought the women on the Fourteenth Amendment supported them in their effort to have woman suffrage written into the Constitution of the State of New York. Still, when you think of it, there were not very many negroes in New York, and either political party, within those borders could have annexed the woman vote to its advantage. At least so seemed to reason George William Curtis, the distinguished editor of the *Evening Post;* Henry Ward Beecher, whose principal financial backers, Henry Bowen and Robert Bonner, were Republicans; Gerrit Smith and other up-State Republican leaders. But Horace Greeley, almost the original woman's rights advocate among editors, and now chairman in the Convention of the committee on suffrage, revealed himself as a bitter and uncompromising opponent. At a committee hearing in June, at which both Susan and Mrs. Stanton appeared, there occurred that classic and oft-quoted passage at arms between Susan and Horace.

"Miss Anthony," drawled Greeley, in that acid voice dreaded by his enemies, "you are aware that the ballot and the bullet go together. If you vote are you also prepared to fight?"

"Certainly, Mr. Greeley," flashed Susan, in her most acid tones. "Just as you fought in the late war—at the point of a goose-quill."

His pink moon face with its fringe of whiskers and white hair, aflame with anger, Greeley repeated that for his part he stood on the fact that the best woman he knew did not want to vote. Whereupon up rose George William Curtis and said: "Mr. Chairman, I hold in my hand a petition signed by *Mrs. Horace Greeley* and three hundred other women of Westchester, asking that the word 'male' be stricken out of the constitution." The laughter and applause that rocked the committee room made Greeley a life enemy of the women. A few days later his committee handed in a report to the Constitutional Convention recommending that the word male be retained, thus robbing women of all hope of legislative consideration for decades to come.

Such was the result, as far as American women were concerned, of the bloodiest civil war in history, fought, as the Gettysburg Speech forever reminds us, "that Government of the people, for the people and by the people shall not perish from this earth."

In this succession of bitter disappointments Susan lost something of her youthful idealistic optimism, and much of her faith in men. She learned that women had no ally in any political party, and very few friends in even the most altruistic organization of men. She made up her mind that henceforth women must depend on themselves alone, and, this being the case, they were justified in using whatever means of progress they judged right and proper at any given hour. This became Susan's policy, and in some very queer and regrettable mistakes it involved her in the course of her career. It resulted, two years later, in a split in the woman suffrage ranks, Susan and Mrs. Stanton representing the radical group, Lucy Stone and Julia Ward Howe the conservatives.

An event which occurred shortly after the adoption of the Fourteenth Amendment, and the refusal of the New York Constitutional Convention to grant woman suffrage, precipitated this division in the ranks, which lasted quite twenty years. While the leaders were in the thick of the New York struggle, word came from Kansas that amendments to their constitution for both woman and negro suffrage were about to be submitted to popular vote. Republicans who favored both amendments telegraphed Susan begging her to go to Kansas, but as this was impossible she persuaded the Blackwells, Lucy Stone and Henry B., to go in her place. Lucy, who had been resting on her laurels ever since her unconventional marriage twelve years before, went rather reluctantly, the more enthusiastic Mr. Blackwell leaving his business in Boston to accompany her. They traveled and spoke for two months, finding, exactly as Mrs. Stanton had prophesied, that the women had "boosted the negro over their own heads," for everywhere they went in Kansas it was the negro, still unenfranchised, who most strongly opposed woman suffrage. In this course they were encouraged by vitrolic editorials in the *New York Tribune* and disapproving silence on the subject in the *Independent,* both of which journals circulated widely in Kansas. In May Lucy and Henry returned to the East with no very heartening reports. The woman suffrage amendment had been submitted by a Republican Legislature, sponsored by a Republican Governor and supported by most of the Republican newspapers of the State. But alarmed by the opposition of the pro-negro voters, the Republican State Committee had decided to kill the measure. The party, they argued, was sure to get the negro vote, whereas nobody knew what women would do with the ballot. If they voted as their husbands did the Democratic vote would be doubled, and that prospect no good Republican could do aught but view with alarm.

To get woman suffrage even in one sparsely settled Western State stirred Susan's ambition to fever heat, but although Mrs. Stanton agreed to go with her into the fight there was no money available for expenses or even for literature and tracts. The last of the year's income from the Jackson fund, about $1,500, had gone to pay the expenses of Lucy Stone and her husband, and there was nothing left in the Hovey fund—or at least so Wendell Phillips decreed. The unbeatable Susan set out to collect the $2,000 necessary for the campaign, and of course she collected it. From sewing machine companies, drygoods stores, from Madame Demorest's "Fine Millinery and Patterns," from a number of other Broadway firms she got advertisements for the fly leaves of new literature she was having printed on pure faith. From several wealthy friends of the cause she got contributions from fifty to two hundred dollars. From her own small savings account she drew every possible dollar, and in late August she and Elizabeth started for Kansas, into hardships and discouragements which made their anti-slavery campaigns in wintry New York look like a Roman holiday. The little stark prairie town of Lawrence became their headquarters, and from this comfortless metropolis they traveled hundreds of miles to meetings, in lumber wagons, in rocking buggies, in any sort of vehicles, fording muddy streams, plowing through mud and dust, or crossing unbroken prairie; sleeping in cabins,

eating sour bread, canned and dried meat badly prepared, drinking alkaline water, and every night waging
a hopeless fight with that curse of the prairies, bedbugs.

"It is now ten A. M.," writes Susan in one of her letters home, "and
Mrs. Stanton is trying to sleep, as we have not slept a wink for
several nights, but even in broad daylight our tormentors are so
active that it is impossible. We find them in our bonnets, and this
morning I think we picked a thousand out of the ruffles of our
dresses."

The pair of martyrs was joined about this time by the
celebrated Hutchinson family of singers, a quartet ex-
ceedingly popular in the late sixties and indeed well
into the eighties. With them came the Rev. Olympia
Brown of Massachusetts, and although these added at-
tractions helped to draw audiences it did not blind
Susan and Mrs. Stanton to the fact that the amendment
could not win over the now thoroughly organized Republican opposition. Their only hope, and that a forlorn one, was to gain enough Democratic votes to turn
the tide. As they were racking their brains to discover
some means of special appeal to the Democrats, in
Kansas represented mostly by Irish immigrants, they
received from Omaha a telegram from George Francis
Train, a prominent Irish Democrat, offering to join
them and "win every Democratic vote in the State."
Neither Susan nor Mrs. Stanton had ever seen this individual, whose name was a synonym for reckless
wealth and eccentricity, but in their desperate need of
assistance they telegraphed him to come on. George
Francis Train came on, and into a fine Irish bog of adventure he led them, not only in Kansas, but during the
two years following in New York. Mr. Train arrived
elegantly attired in the latest thing the well dressed man

was wearing in 1867, and almost at his first encounter with a prairie wagon and a prairie bedbug he was ready to fly back to the luxuries of Omaha. But Susan would not let him off his bargain. One leading Democrat, Mark W. Reynolds, editor of the party newspaper in Lawrence, had already deserted her, going off without notice on a buffalo hunt, and it would not do to allow a second one to escape. "The next meeting," said Susan, firmly, "is announced for Olathe to-morrow night. I shall take Mr. Reynolds' place. At one o'clock I shall send a carriage to your hotel. You can do as you please about going. If you decline I shall go there and to all the other meetings alone."

"Miss Anthony," said Train with a low obeisance, "you know how to make a man ashamed."

To at least twenty towns and rural centers the cavalcade swept on, Train by his persuasive eloquence and wild Irish humor proving an immense attraction. He might actually have carried the entire Democratic minority, thus securing the amendment, but for the fact that Susan did not know, and could not find out, exactly where the Irish settlements in Kansas were located. Railroads were few, railroad connections uncertain, and the time was very short. Besides, Susan had not only her full share of speaking to do, she had to manage the entire campaign, see to the halls, the lighting— candles and smoky kerosene lamps—the advertising, the newspaper notices, tickets and ushers, and practically all the advance correspondence. In this sort of work Mrs. Stanton was never of the slightest use. Her powers of physical endurance were less than Susan's, and of managerial ability she possessed no trace. Extremely fastidious in her person, Elizabeth literally could not go on a platform and speak unless she had beforehand bathed, slept for an hour, and dressed as for a drawing-room function. Mr. Train was of the same temperament. No matter what mudholes their wagons had dragged through, or what jerkwater train had conveyed them to their place of meeting, George Francis had to retire long enough to change into full evening dress with white waistcoat and fresh lavender kid gloves before he would consent to face an audience. Poor Susan never had any opportunity to bathe and change before a meeting. Arrived at a town it was her duty to rush to the hall, consult with committees, interview newspaper editors, look up absentee janitors, get everything in order for the meeting, and then, often without a moment left to wash her hands or eat a bite of dinner, go straight to the platform. For her reward she would read afterwards in the newspapers that Mrs. Stanton was a beautiful and attractive woman, but that Susan B. Anthony was a homely old maid.

The person who got the longest notices—not all of them entirely complimentary—was George Francis Train. Just then at the height of his fame as a financial wizard, a millionaire, a traveler in mythical lands of the Far East, a friend of royalty in Europe, and above all a sartorial miracle, Kansas came miles to see him. Ranchers and cowboys, buffalo hunters and gamblers, in high boots and ten gallon hats, chaps and spurs and flannel shirts, came to hoot and remained to wonder. Women and girls came to giggle and admire. But George Francis Train was no mere tailor's dummy. He gave them the worth of their money not only by displaying raiment the like of which the frontier had never beheld, but by speeches full of political dyna-

mite, and by all the dramatic touches he could contrive
to add to the program. One of Susan's meetings was
invaded early by a Republican orator who took the
platform uninvited to deliver an anti-suffrage speech.
In addition he warned the audience against Train.
Just as he was shouting: "This man Train is an infernal traitor and a vile copperhead," the audience
burst into unaccountable cheers and laughter. Turning hastily the Republican intruder was amazed to see
a little behind him the redoubtable George Francis,
resplendent in evening clothes and lavender kid gloves,
bowing and smiling as if the platform was entirely his
own.

In the whole question of woman's rights, and especially in the courage and genius of Susan B. Anthony
and Mrs. Stanton, Train professed the deepest interest.
One day on the train he asked Susan why she did not
establish an equal rights newspaper. Susan replied
that this was her dearest wish, but that she had no
money for such an enterprise and no possible hope of
getting any.

"How about your friends, Beecher, Tilton, Wendell
Phillips and the rich Boston liberals?" asked Train.
"Have you suggested such a paper to them?"

"Ah!" said Susan with a wry smile. "You forget
that with them this is the negro's hour. They have
neither money nor sympathy to lavish on women any
more."

"Dear, dear," said Train musingly. "Well, I think
I shall have to give you the money myself."

That was the end of the conversation and Susan
thought no more about it. At that night's meeting
Train was late. Adorning himself a little more than

usual, Susan thought contemptuously, for the elegant Mr. Train was getting slightly on her nerves. She made her speech, lengthening it a little until she saw him enter at the back of the platform. Then she sat down and Train advanced, to the usual applause. To the blank astonishment of the women Train held up his hand for silence and said impressively:

"Ladies and gentlemen, I have an announcement to make. When Miss Anthony gets back to New York she is going to start a woman suffrage paper. Its name is to be the *Revolution;* its motto, 'Men, their rights, and nothing more; Women, their rights, and nothing less.' This paper is to be a weekly, price two dollars a year; its editors, Elizabeth Cady Stanton and Parker Pillsbury; its proprietor, Susan B. Anthony. Let everybody subscribe for it."

After the meeting, which yielded quite a number of pledges to subscribe for the new paper, Train assured the women that he meant every word of his careless promise to finance their journalistic enterprise. He could afford a hundred thousand dollars or so without the slightest inconvenience. The name suggested, the *Revolution,* he was sure they would approve, and surely they could ask no better editorial associate than the nationally known Parker Pillsbury. There was a preceptible length of string tied to Mr. Train's generous offer. He wanted to make a lecture tour across the country—oh, yes, a woman suffrage lecture tour— and he wanted to make it in company with Susan and Mrs. Stanton. If they would consent to this, at the end of the Kansas campaign, he would pay all expenses, and at the close of the season in New York he would give them money enough to establish the paper.

Thereafter, he promised, he would be its financial supporter until it reached a paying basis.

The two women were a little dazed. They knew that Train was an eccentric, that many of their conservative women members would find him in some ways objectionable because he inspired a certain amount of ridicule wherever he appeared. Wendell Phillips, the utterly correct Charles Sumner and other Bostonians, would doubtless shudder. But at the very mention of their names Susan's wrath boiled over. What had Phillips and Sumner, or any of their erstwhile men supporters, Greeley, Curtis, Beecher, Tilton, Powell, Gerrit Smith, done for equal rights when the test came? In Congress and out, when the great opportunity, the Fourteenth Amendment was in their hands, they had knifed the women like so many brigands. Even those who had supported them in New York State had placed the negro's claims ahead of all others. But here was a man, not a reformer, to be sure, but one who had come forward at a critical moment and proved his devotion to the cause by enduring the horrors of the Kansas campaign. Now he offered them a fortune to establish a weekly paper which might be built up to equal in influence and power the Anti-Slavery *Standard* and the *Independent*. No doubt Train was queer, but his private life and public honesty nobody had ever called into question. Elizabeth trembled a little, but decided to leave it all to Susan's judgment. Susan herself waited until after election day, which they all spent together in Leavenworth. The returns revealed that both the negro suffrage and woman suffrage amendments had been defeated, but woman suffrage had received, out of a total of 30,000 votes cast, 9,070. Considering that this was the first time the question had ever been submitted to any State electorate the result was truly encouraging. Of course Susan and Mrs. Stanton could not be sure how many votes George Francis Train had won for them, but it was at least significant that in Leavenworth County, the stronghold of the Democrats, a large majority for woman suffrage was recorded. Susan decided to accept Mr. Train's offer, including the lecture tour eastward.

It was something of a circus or vaudeville, that equal rights lecture tour in most large cities between Leavenworth and New York, with the curious combination of Elizabeth, Susan and George Francis on one platform. But huge audiences, enormous publicity and considerable money rewarded them in almost every city they visited. Also the women enjoyed, for the first time in any of their campaigns, every luxury money could provide. Train did the thing *en prince,* the most expensive hotels, the choicest food, the handsomest carriages, servants in constant attention, flowers, suppers, receptions. Elizabeth basked in it all as in summer sunshine, and tired Susan found in it infinite comfort and relief. After Kansas, after hot winds, dust, bad roads, dirty and unkempt hotels, unspeakable food, and oh! the bedbugs, this was heaven.

As soon as they reached New York Train said to Susan: "Now, Miss Anthony, get on with the *Revolution* as quickly as you can. Just as a beginning of things, here is a trifle of money, $3,000. And remember, I can easily spare $100,000."

Susan wasted no time in getting on with the *Revolution.*

# CHAPTER XVI

## THE "REVOLUTION"

SUSAN'S paper, which may be said to have been born of a Kansas cyclone, was destined from beginning to end to live a life of storm. The Kansas campaign and the woman's rights lecture tour with George Francis Train had stirred up in the Equal Rights Association a furious scandal, for Train was a Democrat, and he was anything in the world but a negrophile. The men in the association were all Republicans, and while the women's faith had been somewhat shaken by the terms of the Fourteenth Amendment, they too adhered to the party as their only hope. To both men and women therefore this unholy alliance of Susan and Mrs. Stanton, hitherto the suffragists' pillars of cloud by day, of fire by night, was almost as shocking as Daniel Webster's repudiation of the Missouri Compromise. A woman's rights paper had long been desired, and Mrs. Stanton and Lucy Stone had been spoken of as its probable editors, but no one in the ranks of the orthodox had offered to supply the funds. And now a paper had materialized—but with Democrats backing it! And with what a name—the *Revolution!* A worse combination of circumstances could hardly be imagined. In spite of this chorus of disapproval subscriptions to the paper rolled in, for Susan, with her usual energy took care of that. She went to Washington and got a good many subscriptions in Congress, and next she invaded the White House and secured President Johnson's name. Susan's description of the White House in 1867 indicates that our democracy has at least assumed considerable dignity since reconstruction days. Crossing a long corridor crowded with henchmen and office seekers, all chewing tobacco and squirting the juice over carpets and furniture, she walked right into the President's private office. Making a mental note, the while, that in Queen Victoria's anterooms, or those of any female ruler, things would present quite another appearance.

"I don't want to subscribe to any more papers," said Johnson gruffly. "Look at that table over there—just piled up with mail I haven't had time to open. Besides, I never read papers."

"You'll read this one," said Susan confidently. "It's going to tell you any number of things your Congress never did."

The President of the United States burst forth in comments on the Legislative Branch of the Government of the United States which Susan decided it were best not to hand down to posterity. He finished very red in the face, but evidently with relieved feelings. "Here's your two dollars," he said.

The first issue of the *Revolution* appeared on January 8, 1868, and at the sight of it the conservatives threw up their hands in horror. Not that it did not present a handsome appearance as far as paper and typography were concerned, and not that it was not well written, for Parker Pillsbury and Elizabeth Cady Stanton were among the most forceful writers of their day. But only about two thirds of the paper was devoted to equal rights. The rest of it was given over to

Democratic propaganda for greenback currency and to the dubious financial schemes of George Francis Train. Innocent as babes in such matters, Susan and Mrs. Stanton had agreed with Train and his friend, David M. Melliss, one of the editors of the New York *World,* that in return for their financial backing they should have limited space in which to express their opinions on current political and financial affairs. This would in no wise affect the general editorial policy, Train assured them, and it would make men read the paper. It certainly did, for the Melliss contributions were written in a style only recently achieved by the most sensational of our modern tabloids. Under shrieking headlines and subheads Melliss and Train hurled compliments and curses, distributed according to their own convictions, on most of the Washington and Wall Street stock-jobbing cutthroats of the day: Fisk, Gould, Daniel Drew, Oakes Ames, Oakey Hall, Abel Corbin, Grant's brother-in-law, and Sidney Dillon, head of the notorious Crédit Mobilier, a scheme introduced from France by George Francis Train, but relinquished by him into the hands of sublime rascals. The *Revolution's* financial pages, moreover, urged the public to buy the shares. Wall Street read the pages and roared. The Equal Rights Association read them and wept. If they had understood more fully they woud have wept much harder.

A little of George Francis Train's biography must be included here, for his malign influence haunted Susan and Mrs. Stanton long after he passed out of their lives. Train was the son of an Irish gentleman and a woman member of one of New England's oldest families. In 1831, when George was a babe of three, the family removed from Boston to New Orleans where within a year a yellow fever outbreak killed all of them except the boy. Just before the father succumbed he secured passage for the child on a northbound freightship, this pathetic card being sewed to his clothes:

"This is my little son, George Francis Train, consigned on board the ship *Henry,* to John D. Clark, Jr., Dock Square, Boston, to be sent to his Grandmother Pickering, in Waltham, ten miles from Boston. Take care of the little fellow, as he is the only one left of eleven of us in the house, including the servants. I will come as soon as I can arrange my business."

The sailors on the *Henry,* delighted with the brightness of the child, took care of him after their fashion, incidentally teaching him a choice lot of profanity. The elder Train was buried in a yellow-fever trench long before the boat reached Boston, but Grandmother Pickering took George in and educated him, and at fifteen an uncle gave him a place in his shipping office in Boston. Both recognized in the boy a genius, which Train undoubtedly was, either one "to madness near allied," or else that not uncommon type whose brain develops uncannily young and declines early in a confusion of loose wheels. Before he was twenty George had annexed a third interest in his uncle's business, and when the California gold rush was at its height he was building and operating a fleet of forty crack ships to San Francisco. The Australian gold discoveries coming next, George went to Melbourne where he established a shipping and commercial house, in one year cleaning up over $100,000. He traveled in India and the Far East, making money wherever he halted, and by the time he returned to Europe, in the '50's, he was almost as celebrated as Marco Polo. In Paris Napoleon III and Eugénie received him intimately, and perhaps Eugénie taught him how to dress, for when he crossed to England tailors and haberdashers hailed him as a reincarnation of Beau Brummel. In England Train made a fortune by introducing street railways, two of which he built in London, and a third between Liverpool and Birkenhead. Already he was growing erratic, for as a sideline to business he began dabbling in radical politics, the nearest thing that then existed to anarchism—in France represented by the Marseilles commune.

When the Civil War broke out Train was somehow in the United States, supporting the Union but not emancipation. Most of the time he was in the West promoting the Union Pacific Railroad, and organizing for its benefit the American Crédit Mobilier, a French idea of a joint stock corporation for the general purpose of financing corporations. Train lived in Omaha where for two generations afterward tales of his wild eccentricities, his mad extravagance and his exaggerated deference to women were remembered. When he began to pile up another fortune in Omaha real estate Train lost all interest in managing the Crédit Mobilier, which, as has been said, then fell into the hands of the corruptionists, and a few years later figured in the Union Pacific scandals and the expulsion from Congress of James Brooks and Oakes Ames. By the time he joined Susan and Mrs. Stanton in Kansas, ready to invest $100,000 in a woman's rights paper, Train's brilliant mind was slipping into near-insanity. That is, his dramatic and unstable temperament was again athirst for the excitement of radical "causes," the more revolutionary and disturbing the better. On the very day the *Revolution* appeared he abruptly announced that he was sailing for England to get subscribers, and the very best literary talent as contributors. He gave Susan all the money he happened to have in his pockets, $600, and assured her that he and Melliss would continue their financial support. Susan was aghast, and while she retained a measure of confidence in Train, she told Mrs. Stanton that they would probably soon have the whole burden of the paper on their own shoulders. Her instinct proved correct, for Train did not go to England for subscribers and contributors. He went instead to Dublin to lend aid to the Fenians, was arrested within a week, tried and sentenced to prison for life. Later this was commuted to deportation. As long as he could command any funds he sent money to Susan, along with lurid screeds about English prisons and the sacred cause of the Fenians, a part of which Pillsbury and Mrs. Stanton felt bound to publish. Mr. Melliss tried to keep his financial engagements with the paper, but at the end of the year he defaulted altogether, and the sensational column happily lapsed. But not its memory. Not with the Equal Rights Association. All the really good work for woman's rights contributed by Parker Pillsbury and Elizabeth Cady Stanton; all the able articles and stories by women writers such as Olive Logan, Eleanor Kirk, Dr. Clemence Lozier; sparkling foreign correspondence; news of women, their rapid advance in business and the professions, in their recently opened colleges and schools of art and design, were forgotten in the one dreadful fact that the paper had dallied with the heresies of the Democrats, the hated Copperheads of the war. Besides, Mrs. Stanton, and of course Susan, for she and Elizabeth were one, had advocated divorce, and had taken the part of women involved in serious breaches of decorum. In those evangelical days this was equivalent to defending the hideous doctrine of free love. A whispering campaign began—it was but a question of time before the respectables would have to separate themselves from these radicals and apostates.

The first explosion came in May, 1868, at the second anniversary meeting of the Equal Rights Association in Cooper Institute, New York. Lucretia Mott, whose husband had recently died, could not be present, and it therefore became Mrs. Stanton's duty to preside. Knowing that disagreeable scenes were ahead the easy-going Elizabeth made up her mind to stay away, but in this she reckoned without Susan, who, when the day came simply took her by the arm and marched her to the hall. Thomas Wentworth Higginson was on hand, and as the convention was about due to open he approached Susan, saying suavely: "Now Miss Anthony, we want everything nice and peaceable, do we not? Well then, we'll have Lucy Stone open the meeting."

"Indeed!" exclaimed Susan. "When Mrs. Stanton is first Vice President? That would not only be an insult to her but a clear violation of parliamentary rules. I shall not allow it." And as officers and speakers advanced to the platform Susan gave Mrs. Stanton a smart push forward into the President's chair, from which the fluttered Elizabeth, getting herself together, called the convention to order with her usual grace and dignity.

The convention, however, soon became little more

LUCY STONE
Pioneer in Modern Marriage

than an anti-woman-suffrage meeting. The men accused most of the women members of putting their own interests ahead of those of the negro, and Susan and Mrs. Stanton were charged with having used the movement to advance the Democratic politics of George Francis Train. Theodore Tilton even expressed his opinion that Susan and Mrs. Stanton, with their friend Train were responsible for the loss of the negro suffrage amendment in Kansas. At this Lucy Stone and Olympia Brown, who had also campaigned in Kansas, were obliged to rise to the defense. It was the treachery of the Republican Party, they declared, which had lost the negro his vote in the West. Whereupon Tilton offered a sarcastic resolution that "as Susan B. Anthony, through various published writings in the *Revolution,* had given the world to understand that the hope of the woman's rights cause rested more largely with the Democratic Party than with any other portion of the people, therefore she be requested to attend the approaching Democratic National Convention in New York City, for the purpose of fulfilling this cheerful hope of securing in the Democratic platform a recognition of woman's rights to the elective franchise." With equal sarcasm and with more brevity of style, Susan replied that if such was the wish of the convention she would gladly comply, hoping to demonstrate that the Democrats would at least be no more unfriendly than the Republicans had shown themselves. Against strong Republican opposition, and with the aid of Mr. Train, they had recently secured in Kansas over 9,000 votes for woman suffrage. Had Mr. Tilton and the *Independent* anything as good to show for their labors?

Frederick Douglass broke in with an arrogant speech, in effect an order from the Anti-Slavery Society, for the women to cease all their efforts for the ballot until it was securely in the hands of negro men. He quoted a pearl of wisdom from Wendell Phillips: "One idea enough for a generation, in the order of their importance. First negro suffrage, then temperance, then the eight-hour movement, then woman suffrage." He quoted further from Horace Greeley, Charles Sumner, Gerrit Smith, in support of this theory. Elizabeth Cady Stanton left the chair to reply in a flaming speech, elaborated later in the *Revolution*.

"Three generations hence woman suffrage will be in order," cried Mrs. Stanton. "What an insult to the women who had labored thirty years for the emancipation of the slave, now when he is their political equal, to propose to lift him above their heads! Gerrit Smith says . . . 'This is the time to settle the rights of races; unless we do justice to the negro we shall bring down on ourselves another bloody revolution, another four years of war, but we have nothing to fear from woman, for she will not avenge herself.' Woman not avenge herself? Look at your asylums for the deaf, the dumb, the blind, the insane, and there behold the results of this wholesale desecration of the mothers of the race! Woman not avenge herself? Go into the streets of your cities at the midnight hour, and there behold those whom God intended to be queens of the moral universe giving your sons their first lessons in infamy and vice!"

The Equal Rights Association had its knife out for Susan B. Anthony and Elizabeth Cady Stanton, but those two were prepared to put up a good fight first in the pages of the *Revolution*. The first thing they did was to demonstrate beyond question that neither political party offered the slightest hope to women. Nobody else would have dared approach the conventions,

knowing the situation in both, and with what contempt
and scorn both would receive a delegation of women.
The Republican Convention was meeting in Chicago
to nominate Grant and to these men a memorial was
sent, signed by Susan, Mrs. Stanton, Mary Cheney
Greeley, Horace Greeley's wife, Elizabeth Smith
Miller, Gerrit Smith's daughter, and Abby Hopper
Gibbons, daughter of Isaac Hopper, one of the most
famous of the old Abolitionists. The memorial was
not even acknowledged, and of course it received no
consideration in the resolutions committee.

The Democratic Convention met in New York in
July, to nominate Horatio Seymour and to dedicate
Tammany Hall. Susan, with a few other women, went
in person to this convention, and gaining the platform
handed her memorial to Horatio Seymour, who
directed the secretary to read it to the delegates. What
followed may best be told in the letter sent to the
*Chicago Republican* by its correspondent in the convention.

"The name of Miss Anthony was greeted with a yell such as
Milton might imagine to arise from a conclave of the damned. 'She
asked to plead the cause of her sex; to demand the enfranchisement
of the women of America—the only class without a vote, and their
only disability the unsurmountable one of sex.' As these last significant words, with more than significant accent and modulation, came
from the lips of the knightly, the courtly Horatio, a bestial roar of
laughter, swelling now into an almost Niagara chorus, now sub-
siding into comparative silence, and again without further provoca-
tion rising into infernal sublimity, shook the walls of Tammany.
Sex—the sex of woman—was the subject of this infernal scorn; and
the great Democratic gathering, with yells and shrieks and deafening
howls, consigned the memorial of Susan B. Anthony to the committee on resolutions."

Burning with shame and indignation—but not for themselves—the women left the hall, the echoes of that lewd laughter following them beyond the doors. Susan determined to try one more convention of men, this time the National Labor Union Congress which met in New York in September, 1868. The *Revolution* had devoted a great deal of space to working women and their interests. In twenty years many more trades had opened to women and girls, but in none of them were opportunities for advancement offered, and in all trades women's wage scales were much lower than the men's. Susan B. Anthony was one of the first women who attempted to raise the condition of women workers, and to organize them in trade unions. She got together representative workers in a number of trades, urging them to acquire more and more skill until the men would be obliged to recognize them as equals in the crafts. "I do not demand equal pay for any woman," she told them, "save only those who do equal work in value." Just as in former years the women in the State Teachers' Association had depended on Susan to be their champion, so now these helpless and submerged trade workers looked to her for leadership. Before the great Labor Union Congress, forerunner of the American Federation of Labor, assembled in New York, Susan held a large meeting of working women—typesetters, printers, bookbinders, dressmakers, milliners, seamstresses, embroidery workers, machine operators in various factories, down to rag sorters in junk shops—and organized the Working Woman's Association, with the object of appealing to the Labor Union Congress to admit women to industry on equal terms with men, and to aid them in becoming citizens. The meeting unanimously elected Susan as their representative, and by the courtesy of the President, J. C. C. Whaley, a master workman in the iron mills of Pennsylvania, she was accepted as a fraternal delegate.

After her speech, which was received by these workingmen a thousand times more respectfully than by the Republican or the Democratic politicians, a committee on female labor was appointed, with Susan as chairman. Their resolutions for an eight-hour day, better opportunities and equal pay for women, and a pledge for labor union support of woman suffrage, was accepted, all, that is, except the woman suffrage clause. That far even organized labor was not prepared to go. Especially as it was now threatened with the competition of freed and enfranchised negroes.

In all of this, in the sudden cleavage between tried friends and comrades, the benefits forgot by men like Douglass, the rejection on all sides of ideals of the past, we see the psychological reaction which invariably follows a great war. After superhuman efforts, after the necessity of burying the individual in the mass, there comes a period when the mental and spiritual energies of the people seem completely dead. In the sublimity of war the fighting man abnegates even his primal right to life, and those outside the conflict, yes, the meanest, feel themselves for an hour lifted up into the embrace of an idea. But the aftermath of war is cynicism and cowardice. The soldier returns to a life of anti-climax. He cannot function in a world so tame, and groping in a maze where he vainly seeks the self he has lost, he leaves to far less worthy men the task of rebuilding civilization. But they too are exhausted, bewildered, nerve-wracked. They cannot rebuild on the old foundations, nor can they at once formulate plans for the emerging future. They grasp at any straw that floats, at anything that offers a guarantee of stability. Usually this takes the shape of some panacea that symbolizes peace, peace that can never come on this whirling globe, the very life of which is mutation. After every war a panacea. After the Napoleonic wars it was the Holy Alliance. After the World War it was the League of Nations. After the Civil War it was the freedom of the negro. Once that subject class was made citizen, and above all once the class which had subjected it was shorn of all power, the Republic, its statesmen believed, would rise again in majesty. In the forties and fifties the freedom of the negro was a noble ideal. After the Civil War it became a political expedient.

# CHAPTER XVII

## DROPPING THE PILOT

WITH that naïve confidence of Americans that the deepest-seated opinions and prejudices can be altered by statute, Congress had assumed that the Fourteenth Amendment would automatically enfranchise the negro, but to the annoyance of Charles Sumner and other enthusiasts it did nothing of the kind. Few of the Northern States moved to delete the word white from their constitutions, and two Western Territories, seeking admission as States, adopted constitutions definitely including the word white. Therefore in February, 1869, Senator William Stewart of Nevada introduced the Fifteenth Federal Amendment, providing that the right to vote should not be denied or abridged . . . on account of race, color, or previous condition of servitude. This law Congress believed to be burglar-proof, although cool-headed men, Senator Oliver P. Morton of Indiana, for one, warned the Senate that it could never be enforced. Sooner or later Northern bayonets would be withdrawn from late Confederate territory, the Southern States would return to the Union, take control of their own legislatures and pass educational and property qualification laws which would simply nullify the Federal law. The warning was unheeded and the Fifteenth Amendment was pushed quickly through both houses of Congress.

In the pages of the *Revolution* Susan B. Anthony

and Elizabeth Cady Stanton issued a warning even graver than that of Senator Morton. With prophetic intuition those women clearly forecast the evil effects of a law which bestowed the suffrage on negro men while denying it to white women. The worst effect, they prophesied, would be on the psychology of the negro himself.

"The proposed amendment for 'manhood suffrage,' " they declared, "not only arouses woman's prejudice against the negro, but on the other hand his contempt and hostility towards her. . . . Just as the Democratic cry of a 'white man's government' created the antagonism between the Irishman and the negro, which culminated in the New York riots of 1863, so the Republican cry of 'manhood suffrage' creates an antagonism between black men and all women, which will culminate in fearful outrages on womanhood, especially in the Southern States. . . . The negro will be the victim for generations to come of the prejudice engendered by making this a white man's government. . . . Just so with woman, while the enfranchisement of all men hastens the day for justice to her, it makes her degradation more complete in the transition state. It is to escape the added tyranny, persecution, insults, horrors which will surely be visited upon her in the establishment of an aristocracy of sex in this Republic, that we raise our indignant protest against this wholesale desecration of woman in the pending amendment."

How extraordinarily far-seeing these two women were, when no man in Congress, and hardly a man or woman in the Equal Rights Association, agreed with them, is written in the bloody annals of race wars, rapes and lynchings in the Southern States for the past fifty years. That editorial, with its "deadly insult" to the negro brought down anathema on all the editors of the *Revolution*. Liberal newspapers called attention to the fact that during the war women in small towns and remote plantations had lived alone, surrounded by negroes, without a single recorded case of insult or attack. That was true, said Susan, but before emancipation the negroes had been brought up in almost superstitious respect for white people, especially white women, who were as far above them as the planets. Since the collapse of the Confederacy much respect for white men had disappeared. What savage instincts would now be awakened in revengeful ex-slaves when they were taught that the law made them the civil and political superiors of their former mistresses?

Well aware that this editorial, and the whole policy of the *Revolution* would be brought up against them in the approaching May convention of the Equal Rights Association, Susan and Mrs. Stanton still went ahead with arrangements for it, Susan, as chairman of the business committee, arranging for half rates on the railroads, which ensured the attendance of many Western delegates. Mrs. Stanton presided, although it soon developed that the Massachusetts delegation presented a solid bloc against her. After the usual program of speeches and addresses by distinguished guests, Stephen S. Foster, who in pre-war days had campaigned under Susan's leadership, arose and said that in his opinion persons who had prevented harmony in the association should retire from prominent positions. "I object," said Mr. Foster, "to certain women, on the grounds that they have repudiated the principles of this association and have advocated Mr. George Francis Train's theory of educated suffrage. One of these women is the presiding officer, and another is Miss Anthony. I suggest that they retire and that we nominate officers who can receive the respect of both parties. As it is now organized the Massachusetts Abolition Society can no longer coöperate with the Equal Rights Association."

The proposal to expel Elizabeth Cady Stanton, who had organized the first equal rights society in the world, and Susan B. Anthony, who had done more than any individual alive to keep the question before the public, was so shocking to the Western delegates that Mr. Foster's motion was voted down. But Susan and Elizabeth saw the handwriting on the wall and understood that this association, which they had been so active in founding, had convened with the set purpose of throwing them out. The men of the old abolition crowd took over the program and hardly a woman was allowed to speak. Attack after attack was launched against Susan, her demand for the inclusion of Women in the Fifteenth Amendment being denounced with particular venom by Frederick Douglass.

"I must say," said Douglass, "I do not see how any one can pretend that there is the same urgency in giving the ballot to the women as to the negro. With us it is a matter of life and death, at least in fifteen States of the Union. When women, because they are women, are dragged from their homes and hung upon lampposts; when their children are torn from their arms, and their brains dashed out upon the pavements; when they are in danger of having their homes burned over their heads; when their children are not allowed to enter schools; then they will have an urgency to obtain the ballot equal to black men."

A voice from the audience asked: "Is not this equally true about black women, and do they not also need the protection of the ballot?"

"Yes, yes, yes," returned Douglass irritably, "it is true of the black woman, not because she is a woman but because she is black. Julia Ward Howe, in her great speech delivered at the convention in

Boston last year, said: 'I am willing that the negro should get the ballot before me.' Woman! Why, she has ten thousand modes of grappling with her difficulties, the negro but one."

Douglass after that speech had little trouble in forcing through a resolution "gratefully accepting the pending Fifteenth Amendment," and "earnestly soliciting the State legislatures to pass it without delay." Practically alone in opposition, since Mrs. Stanton, as chairman, could do little speaking, Susan protested against the endorsement by that body of another measure of manhood suffrage.

"The question of precedence," she said, "has no place on an equal rights platform. The only reason it ever forced itself here was because the old anti-slavery school insisted that women should stand back and wait until another class of men should be enfranchised. In answer we say: 'if you will not give the whole loaf of justice to the entire people, if you are determined to extend the suffrage piece by piece, then give it first to women, to the most intelligent and capable of them, at least. If intelligence, justice and morality are to have precedence in the government, let the question of women be brought up first, and that of the negro last."

And turning squarely to Douglass she said:

"If Mr. Douglass had noticed who applauded when he said, 'black men first and women afterwards,' he would have seen that it was only the men. When he tells us that the case of black men is so perilous, I tell him that outraged as they are by the hateful prejudice against color he himself would not to-day exchange his sex and color with Elizabeth Cady Stanton."

Susan's memory flashed back fifteen years to another reform organization, the Woman's State Temperance Society, founded by Mrs. Stanton and herself, and taken out of their hands by men, and she thought desperately that with a few good allies she might, even in this hostile assembly, play the same game against their enemies. Seeking in the cold faces surrounding her a single friendly countenance, her eyes lighted on the ageing and semi-invalid Ernestine Rose. A few sentences exchanged between them, and Ernestine gained the floor just long enough to throw Susan's extemporaneously constructed bomb.

Said Ernestine: "Madame Chairman and delegates, now that Congress has passed a measure guaranteeing impartial man suffrage, one half of the object of the Equal Rights Association has been achieved. I therefore move that the name of this society be changed to the National Woman Suffrage Association."

The Massachusetts delegation was on its feet instantly, protesting that the motion was out of order until the ballot was secure in the possession of black men, that three months' notice was required for any change in the constitution, and that woman suffrage was not now a question before the house. Mrs. Stanton was obliged to rule against the motion at that time, but Susan, grimly smiling, knew that her *coup d'état* required only one more move to make it a *de facto* success. At the conclusion of the convention she called together a meeting of women delegates from nineteen States and organized informally the first National Woman Suffrage Association. Since few of the States had suffrage organizations it was necessary to wait until the following spring before securing accredited delegates to a convention, but a constitution was drawn up and officers elected. Elizabeth Cady Stanton was chosen president; Anna Dickinson, then in the zenith of her fame as an orator, headed a long list of vice presidents; Mrs. Greeley and Laura Curtis Bullard, a popular writer, were made secretaries; Elizabeth Smith Miller, treasurer; Susan, Ernestine Rose and Charlotte Wilbour the executive board. The avowed object of the new association was a sixteenth amendment to the Constitution giving the ballot to women.

A few months later, in response to a circular signed by Lucy Stone, Julia Ward Howe, Caroline M. Severance, Thomas Wentworth Higginson and George H. Vibbert, stern Boston conservatives, a convention met in Cleveland and organized the American Woman Suffrage Association, with Henry Ward Beecher as President, Henry B. Blackwell and Amanda Way as Secretaries, and Lucy Stone as chairman of the executive committee. Their object, thinly concealed, was opposition to everything Susan's organization furthered, and above all, to form a right wing in the suffrage forces, faithful through everything to the Republican Party.

This split in the suffrage forces caused consternation in the ranks of equal rights advocates, and several attempts were made to unite the two associations. Lucy Stone, who had developed an unreasoning animus toward her former beloved friends, Susan and Elizabeth, wrote that the American Woman Suffrage Association would receive the other society, provided it agreed to remain a purely local branch, auxiliary to her association, but these terms could not, of course, be accepted. Mrs. Stanton wrote: "I will do all I can for union. If I am a stumbling-block, I will gladly resign my office. Having fought the world for twenty years, I do not wish to turn and fight those who have so long stood together through good and evil report. I should be glad to have all united, with Mr. Beecher or Lucretia Mott for our general. I am willing to work with any or all, or to get out entirely, that there may be an organization which shall be respected at home and abroad."

But the Boston contingent knew well that any organization with Susan B. Anthony in it would soon have her for its supreme leader, and they declined all overtures. They could not forgive Susan for having scuttled the Equal Rights Association, for scuttled it was by her first move for an independent woman suffrage movement. In May, 1870, it held a last board meeting, Lucy Stone and Henry Blackwell alone voting that the society be dissolved. All the others voted to transfer its books and accounts to the National Woman Suffrage Association, under the new name of the Union Woman Suffrage Association. Mrs. Stanton refusing to serve longer, Theodore Tilton was elected President, while Susan, as usual, retained control of the executive board. For twenty years the two suffrage societies worked separately, Susan concentrating on a federal amendment, Lucy Stone's group in the field of polite propaganda. Within a few years the Union's name was changed back to the National Woman Suffrage Association, and Mrs. Stanton again became its president.

The truth is that the leaders of the two groups represented fundamentally different schools of thought. Lucy Stone and Julia Ward Howe on every subject except abolition of slavery, were as puritanically conservative as Plymouth Rock. Susan and Mrs. Stanton in their whole social outlook were radicals. The evangelical thou-shalt-not which in this generation expresses itself in church boards of temperance and morals, in fights against the teaching of evolution, against the use of the mildest wine, and for the standardization of all conduct according to middle-class conventions, in Susan's generation had for its chief taboos divorce and any public discussion of sex questions. Respectable women were not supposed to think about sex at all, yet it is difficult to see how they could avoid thinking about it most of the time. Practically every social custom of the day reminded them that woman's sex was as dangerous on the public highways as a cartload of dynamite. Few hotels would admit a woman traveling alone, no high-class restaurant would serve her a meal, and any lady venturing to attend a theater unaccompanied by a gentleman simply invited insult from the first loafer she encountered. Naturally, no pure woman dared associate herself in thought or deed with one whom the charitable called an "erring sister," but to whom inwardly they applied a term too indecent to use except when quoting Holy Writ. The greatest offense of Susan B. Anthony and Elizabeth Cady Stanton was that they broke the big taboo. As far back as the 1850's Mrs. Stanton had wrought confusion in woman's rights meetings by advocating, in addition to the one permissible Scriptural cause, divorce for drunkenness, with custody of the children to the mother, and birth control for drunkards' wives. In 1860 she came near driving Wendell Phillips from the equal rights movement by introducing resolutions for more liberal divorce laws.

No sooner had the *Revolution* begun its spectacular career than Susan and Elizabeth, backed up by Parker Pillsbury, another radical, embarked on the dangerous course of defending "erring sisters," who, they insisted, were usually victims of a damnable double standard of morals. There was the Hester Vaughn case, rather pitifully like that of George Eliot's "Hetty" or Walter Scott's "Effie Deans." Hester Vaughn was a young Englishwoman who had followed her husband to America, only to find him bigamously married to another woman. Having no money with which to obtain legal redress she went to work as a servant in Philadelphia. Seduced by her employer she was turned into the streets penniless. Her child was born on the bare floor of an attic, and when, four days later, they were discovered, Hester was unconscious from hunger and cold and the baby was dead. A jury decided that she had killed her child, and the girl was sentenced to be hanged. The *Revolution* took up the case, Susan's Working Woman's Society agitated it, Eleanor Kirk and Dr. Clemence Lozier visited Hester in prison, and finally Mrs. Stanton and Elizabeth Smith Miller went to the Governor of Pennsylvania and induced him to pardon the girl and send her back to England.

This was bad enough, but the worst was yet to come. The McFarland-Richardson murder case was in 1869-70 what the Thaw murder of Stanford White was to 1906 and on. Albert D. Richardson, a well-known journalist on the staff of the *New York Tribune,* was fatally shot by Daniel McFarland, another prominent citizen, with whose divorced wife Richardson was alleged to be on terms of tender intimacy. Two days before Richardson died Henry Ward Beecher married him to Mrs. McFarland, rather a commendable act, one would say, but an act that nearly cost him his pulpit. Certainly it created great public sympathy for the murderer, who was promptly acquitted on the ground of insanity, or the unwritten law, or else just masculine approval of a red-blooded man's vengeance on another male who had "broken up the home." In-sanity was the defense, yet the court took that woman's child away from her and gave it to a man who had been pronounced of unsound mind.  As for Mrs. Mc-Farland, or Mrs. Richardson, by the verdict of the court and of all respectable society there was no room for her except in a brothel.  Yet what did the *Revolution* do but take up her defense also!  With all the fire and eloquence of her pen Elizabeth demanded through the paper that McFarland be placed in a lunatic asylum and that the boy be given back to the mother.  A mass meeting of women was called, three thousand invita-tions being sent out by Susan and Elizabeth, both of whom addressed the gathering, not only on the Mc-Farland case but on the whole subject of sex subjection, under the double standard of morals.  Press and pub-lic suffered convulsions of horror over the affair, and the meeting resulted in no relief for the unhappy woman.

Instead it resulted in the failure of Susan's most cherished enterprise, the *Revolution*.  For a year the paper had limped along without even the precarious support of George Francis Train, and although sub-scriptions came in regularly until, at the beginning of 1870, they reached 3,000, the advertisers held off. From the first the editors had refused to accept cer-tain advertisements which were printed daily in the newspapers, and even in such pious weeklies as the *Christian Union* and the *Independent*.  Patent medicines and worse. Susan tramped Broadway soliciting mercantile advertisement, but she got few because, as some merchants said, the daily papers served their needs, and, as others averred, the *Revolution* was too radical. In those days moral considerations entered into everything. Friends helped a little. Mary Anthony, now principal of a school in Rochester, loaned all her small savings; cousin Anson Lapham went on Susan's note for $1,400; Paulina Wright Davis, Anna Dickinson and Elizabeth Phelps made gifts from $500 to $1,000; Susan, whenever she gave a lecture, turned in her fee, but still the paper ate up money far in excess of receipts. Daniel R. Anthony suggested a stock company, in which he agreed to take as many shares as he could afford, and this scheme was actually about to be realized when the paper suspended. Isabella Beecher Hooker was interested to such a degree that she persuaded her sister, Harriet Beecher Stowe, to go into it, the two women to join the staff as associate editors. Anything Hattie Stowe engaged in, anything she wrote, carried a tremendous prestige, and her new novel, which she promised to publish serially in the *Revolution,* would unquestionably have saved its life. But Catherine Beecher, the godly elder sister, anti-suffrage to the core, got hold of Hattie, with the result that Isabella wrote a reluctant letter saying that, as Beechers, they would have to ask a few concessions. The name of the paper, for example, could it not be changed to something a little less aggressive? No, said Elizabeth firmly, it could not.

"The establishment of woman on her rightful throne," wrote Mrs. Stanton, "is the greatest of revolutions. It is no child's play. You and I know the conflict of the last twenty years; the ridicule, the persecution, denunciation, detraction, the unmixed bitterness of our cup during the last two, when even good friends have crucified us. We have so much hope and pluck that only the Good Father knows what we have suffered.   A journal called The Rosebud might answer for those who come with kid gloves and perfumes to lay immortelle wreaths on the monument which in sweat and tears we have hewn and built; but for us and that great blacksmith of ours who forges such red-hot thunderbolts for pharisees, hypocrites and sinners, there is no name but the "Revolution."   There is no other like it, never was and never will be."

Isabella was obliged to agree with her and negotiations were resumed, only to be brought to an abrupt close by the furore caused when Susan and Elizabeth called the mass meeting in behalf of the woman victim of the Richardson-McFarland tragedy.  The Beecher family were in bad on that case anyhow, and they could not afford to get in any deeper.  So Hattie withdrew and Isabella, with genuine regret, followed her.  Mrs. Stanton, at this time, was offered a flattering contract by a lecture bureau, and she felt that she could hardly afford to go on indefinitely without a salary.  Parker Pillsbury also, who had drawn a very small income as editor, can hardly be blamed for accepting a better paid job.  Susan alone, who had never taken anything from the paper except the barest price of subsistence, could not endure the thought of giving it up.  Yet in the end she was obliged to yield.  For a consideration of one dollar she surrendered the *Revolution* to Laura Curtis Bullard, who turned it into a genteel ladies' magazine which lasted another year and then faded into oblivion.

There was an appalling debt of $10,000, which Susan as proprietor was forced to assume, for Mrs. Stanton, for some reason did not feel obligated to pay a single penny of it. Yet it was not the debt, staggering as it was to a woman who had never had any money, that bowed Susan's head and for a space well-nigh broke her heart. It was the thought that at this crucial moment, when at least half the woman suffragists had turned against her, the paper, her most direct avenue of influence, must also pass out of her hands.

"If I could only die, and thereby fail honorably," she wrote despairingly to her mother, "I would say amen. But to live and fail—it is too terrible to bear."

Yet as soon as the thing actually happened her stoic nature reasserted itself. "I feel a great calm sadness," she said, "like that of a mother binding out a dear child whom she cannot any longer support."

Without an hour's loss of time she set herself to the task—a matter of years—of paying the debts of the *Revolution*. The Lyceum was at the height of its popularity in the seventies, and lectures were in great demand. Susan, who never had believed herself a first-class speaker, was offered a contract that winter which took her as far west as Chicago, Milwaukee, Kansas City, Cincinnati and St. Louis, each lecture paying her from $75 to $150. At that rate, with the economy she knew so well how to practice, the debt could be substantially reduced with each season. Besides, in every city she appeared, she made converts and friends. In St. Louis she was the guest of Francis Minor, a lawyer of high standing in the profession, and his wife, Virginia Minor, an active suffrage worker. Mr. Minor told Susan that he had made a close study of the Fourteenth Amendment, and in his opinion it might be construed as giving women the ballot without any further legislation.. The amendment plainly stated that all *persons* born or naturalized in the United States were citizens thereof, and that no State should make or enforce any law abridging the privileges or immunities of citizens of the United States. Women's right to vote under that amendment hinged on the meaning of the word persons. Were women persons?

Instantly Susan declared her intention of putting that question to the test. The Supreme Court, in the Dred Scott case, had ruled that a negro was not a person, and now Congress, by special action, had declared that he was. She asked nothing better than to become the Dred Scott of the woman movement, to force Congress, then local election boards and State courts, and finally the Supreme Court of the United States, to make an open decision as to whether or not a woman was a person. If all of them ruled that their own mothers, wives, sisters and daughters were lower in the human scale than recently freed African slaves, in a word, a mere sub-species of the human race, the end of the long struggle was in sight. For a flaming brand of resentment would be kindled in women's hearts that no time and no flood would ever extinguish.

# CHAPTER XVIII

## ENTER VICTORIA WOODHULL

FRANCIS MINOR was not the only legal authority who thought that the Fourteenth Amendment might confer on women the rights and privileges guaranteed by the Constitution to all American citizens. The question was discussed pro and con in legal journals and received serious consideration in the editorial columns of the daily newspapers. The American Woman Suffrage Association, on the advice of its first president, Henry Ward Beecher, ignored it. Beecher just then was in no frame of mind to engage in woman suffrage politics, for in late 1870 his troubles with Theodore Tilton were boiling to the top, and he was desperately staving off the hideous scandal which, a little later, was to burst on a horrified country and shake the Congregational Church to its foundations. As yet nothing had been made public, and although a good many people—one of them being Susan B. Anthony—were in full possession of the facts, the Beecher clan were in blissful ignorance of the approaching calamity.

Isabella Beecher Hooker, now that Susan and Mrs. Stanton were temporarily deposed, herself undertook the leadership of the National Woman Suffrage Association, and in January, 1871, she arranged in Washington for a convention purely political in character, and for which she assumed full financial responsibility.

*Isabella Beecher Hooker*

**ISABELLA BEECHER HOOKER**
At the Time of the Fight for a Ruling on the XIVth Amendment

She did this against the opposition of her brother, who could not exactly explain the nature of his objections, and much against the wishes of Harriet Beecher Stowe, who in all matters sided with her adored Henry. There was between those two a bond of natures equally steeped in emotionalism and sentimentality. Isabella was of another type, possessing a cool intellectuality which correctly appraised the qualities of her famous brother, by whom she was never strongly influenced. She admired his eloquent sermons, but while she laughed and applauded with the rest of the congregation, the swimming bath of tears into which he loved to plunge his audiences offended her taste. Isabella was, after all, only a half-sister of Henry and Harriet, being a child of old Lyman's second marriage to Harriet Porter, an aristocrat to the tip of her fingers, cousin to the Cabots and Lowells of New England, the Kings and the Van Rensselaers of New York, and the Pinckneys and Allstons of South Carolina. There was a good deal more Porter than Beecher in Isabella's composition, though no doubt, could she have foreseen the direful consequences which were to follow her excursion into practical politics, she would have acted like a Beecher and remained within the protecting fold of Plymouth Church. But all unaware of gathering clouds she went about her preparations with perfect confidence that the distinguished men she invited as speakers would one and all accept. To her dismay they one and all sent regrets. Even Theodore Tilton, in whose little Brooklyn house she and Susan and Elizabeth were more intimately at home than any other friends—except, of course, their pastor. Wendell Phillips, Robert Collyer, George William Curtis, and worse than all, Mrs.

Stanton, made excuses. Susan was far away on a lecture tour, working herself to a shadow to get herself out of that mire of debt. Isabella wrote to Susan, begging her to intercede with Mrs. Stanton, and to the best of her ability Susan did. She wrote Elizabeth one of those scathing letters which usually brought her to time. The letter ended:

> "To my mind there never was such a suicidal letting go as has been yours in the last two years. . . . I am teetotally discouraged, and shall make no more attempts to hold you up to what I know is not only the best for our cause, but equally so for yourself. How I have agonized over my utter failure to make you feel and see the importance of holding the helm of our ship to the end of the storm. How you can excuse yourself is more than I can understand."

When she read that Elizabeth quailed, but she held to her determination not to go to Washington. She hated conventions anyhow, and in her wounded pride she thought it not a bad idea to let another captain hold the helm until the passengers suffered a brief spell of *mal de mer*. She wrote a letter, to be read from the platform, and sent besides $100 toward defraying the expenses. Susan, on the other hand, canceled half a dozen lectures, went to Washington, and by her extraordinary powers of organization, rescued Mrs. Hooker's convention from disaster. While she did not share Isabella's optimistic hope that this one demonstration would force Congressional action, she welcomed it as a first step toward getting a ruling on women's status under the Fourteenth Amendment. What was her astonishment, and Isabella's, just before the convention opened, to learn that a memorial on the subject was about to be presented to the House Judiciary Committee by Victoria Woodhull, not only a

rank outsider in suffrage circles, but a lady quite dé-
classée in any society which called itself polite.

Victoria Woodhull and her sister, Tennie C. Claflin,
may be said to have represented in their two persons all
the scandals of the 1870's. The dominating figure was
Victoria, one of the most amazing women who ever
crossed the orbit of these skies. Like a comet she appeared, and like a comet she passed, but while she
tarried she spread as much death and destruction as
in the Middle Ages was expected of those baleful va-
grants of illimitable space. The first we really know
about Victoria is that after pursuing with great profit
in Indianapolis the profession of spiritualist and mental
healer, something occurred to cause her to leave the
place with despatch. Victoria claimed as her leading
"control" no less a shade than that of Demosthenes, and
in Pittsburgh—of all unlikely places—the Athenian
sage appeared to her with orders to move on to New
York where in Great Jones Street she and Tennie
would find an elegant house ready for their occupancy,
and in a street farther downtown influential friends to
help them on to fame and fortune. The sisters took
possession of the house—or a house—in Great Jones
Street, and they opened in Broad Street a brokerage
office where, under the guidance of the spirits and the
patronage of Cornelius Vanderbilt and other financial
magnates they proceeded to make a great deal of money.
That they attracted a prodigious amount of attention
also need hardly be said. Ladies in the financial district
of the New York of their day naturally would, especially ladies who, under the ægis of "Corneel" Vanderbilt, had made in one year half a million dollars in
Harlem Railroad. The New York *World* of Febru-

ary 7, 1870, thus describes the daily sensation they created:

"Outside on the walk throughout the day is an assemblage of men, who look anxiously in at the windows, peer curiously in through the doors, and utter expressions of surprise and pleasure if they can but catch a glimpse of one of the members of the firm. A clarence remains in front of the door the greater part of the day, and as the ladies frequently have occasion to drive here and there in pursuit of their business, these hangers-on and morbid curiosity seekers have ample opportunity to gratify their sight-seeing propensities. Inside the office door a doorkeeper has been placed who excludes all those who have no real business with the firm. On the door of the private office is a card on which is written:

'All Gentlemen
Will state their business
and then
retire at once.' "

From which it will be seen that Victoria and Tennie C., despite their sinister reputation, were no mere ladies of the evening, no frail butterflies who wore the diamonds, drank the wines and drove behind the fast horses of the money kings and grafting politicians of "The Dreadful Decade." Such as, for example, Miss Josie Mansfield, in rivalry for whose smiles Mr. Edward Stokes spilled the blood of Mr. Jim Fisk on the stairway of the Broadway Central Hotel. Woodhull and Claflin wanted no diamonds, no wine suppers and no fast horses. What they wanted was inside information on the stock market, and they got it. What price, if any, they paid "Corneel" and the other stock manipulators, was never certainly known, but still in such cases it is always a pleasure to believe the worst.

Neither Susan nor Isabella had ever laid eyes on Victoria. All they knew of her was that she and her sister published a sensational newspaper, *Woodhull and Claflin's Weekly,* which nice people—females—did not read, and which advocated suffrage, birth control, spiritualism, and Victoria Woodhull for President. The sisters defended and supposedly practiced "free love," and though no one knew exactly what that meant the very name was enough to frighten Isabella half to death.  Susan was less disturbed.  She said that since this woman had been given a hearing before a committee of Congress she thought they had better attend it and find out what she had to say.  Senator Pomeroy, in whose house Mrs. Hooker was staying, agreed with this view.  "My dear Mrs. Hooker," he said, "men could never work in a political party if they stopped to investigate each member's antecedents and associates. If you are going into this fight, you must accept every help that offers."

Accordingly, on the morning of January 11, Susan, Isabella and Paulina Wright Davis, escorted by Judge A. G. Riddle, M.C., appeared at the hearing in the House Judiciary committee room, where they beheld in Victoria Woodhull no painted Jezebel, but a quiet, well mannered and extremely pretty woman, wearing a dark gown, cut short, that is to her shoe tops, and on her cropped brown curls a severe little Alpine hat. A reformed dress, Susan admitted, much handsomer than the bloomers which through one miserable year, she had worn.  In a clear, musical voice Victoria read her memorial, to which the committee listened with profound respect, and the women with equally profound pleasure.  For that memorial was by all odds the strongest, most logical, most lawyer-like argument for women's enfranchisement under existing Constitutional provisions that had yet been presented. It read like a legal brief, which indeed it was, for although Victoria claimed that it was written for her by Demosthenes, the weight of evidence indicates that its author was the Hon. Benjamin F. Butler of Massachusetts, a known admirer of Mrs. Woodhull. After finishing her speech Victoria smilingly yielded the floor to Susan and Mrs. Hooker, both of whom made pleas for the question to be brought to debate in the House. The committee paid them the compliment of close attention and at the end seemed actually favorable to their plea.

What was there to do, after all that, but to invite Victoria Woodhull to the convention? "The New York sensation" as the Washington press described her, accepted the invitation, sharing the platform with Senator Nye of Nevada, Senator Warner of Alabama, Senator Wilson of Massachusetts, Frederick Douglass, Lillie Devereux Blake, Josephine Griffing, and other notables. With becoming modesty, even diffidence, Victoria read her memorial to an impressed audience which, to a man, if not to a woman, decided that here was a much misunderstood woman. Said the *Philadelphia Press* correspondent:

"Mrs. Woodhull sat sphynx-like during the convention. General Grant himself might learn a lesson of silence from the pale, sad face of this unflinching woman. . . . She reminds one of the forces of nature behind the storm, or a small splinter of the indestructible; and if her veins were opened they would be found to contain ice. . . ."

The purpose of the convention, said Susan, following Mrs. Woodhull's masterly paper, was to get from Congress a ruling on the intent of the Fourteenth Amendment. Already it had been established that for purposes of taxation women were persons. They were persons in the sense that they were held responsible for their acts under the laws of the country. Now they presented to the Legislative branch of the Government the following resolution:

" . . . That the Congress of the United States be earnestly requested to pass an act declaratory of the true meaning and extent of the said Fourteenth Article."

The resolutions further stated that "it is the duty of American women in the several States to apply for registration at the proper times and places, and in all cases where they fail to secure it, to see that suits be instituted in the courts having jurisdiction, and that their rights to the franchise shall secure general and judicial recognition."

This was taking a woman suffrage meeting far beyond anything yet contemplated, but the resolutions were unanimously adopted. Women were committed to a test of the question as to whether or not they were people. If Congress failed to pass the declaratory act and if the elections boards refused to recognize women as citizens under the Constitution, then, said Susan, there would be nothing to do but agitate for a Sixteenth Amendment which would do for women what the Fifteenth had done for negroes. As a spur to Congress, to prove that there was a demand on the part of women for the ballot, Mrs. Hooker had prepared a large book, containing a "Declaration and Pledge of the Women of America," which within a few months, with 80,000 signatures, was presented to Congress. If Victoria Woodhull's name did not literally lead all the rest it was at least conspicuously displayed. Mrs. Hooker, Mrs. Stanton, Paulina Wright Davis and Matilda Joslyn Gage, among other leaders, had fallen quite violently in love with Victoria, who, in spite of a few vagaries, they felt was an acquisition to the cause, and a much maligned and misunderstood person into the bargain. Isabella thought that if she could only be persuaded to give up her peculiar ideas on the divorce question the last objection to her would vanish. Accordingly the austere Catherine Beecher was induced to call on Mrs. Woodhull and show her how wickedly wrong those ideas were, but Catherine, as Isabella was forced to report, got such a black eye from the redoubtable Victoria that she fled in horror. Nevertheless, and in spite of a flood of letters from all over the country protesting against association with The Woodhull and her sister, Tennie Claflin, Mrs. Hooker and a few other leaders persisted in their championship. In a public letter Mrs. Stanton said:

"When the men who make laws for us in Washington can stand forth and declare themselves pure and unspotted from all the sins mentioned in the Decalogue, then we will demand that every woman who makes a Constitutional argument on our platform shall be as chaste as Diana. . . .

We have had women enough sacrificed to this sentimental, hypocritical prating about purity. . . . This is one of man's most effective engines for our division and subjugation. He creates the public sentiment, builds the gallows, and then makes us hangmen for our sex. Women have crucified the Mary Wollstonecrafts, the Fanny Wrights, the George Sands, the Fanny Kembles, of all ages; and now men mock us with the fact, and say we are ever cruel to each other. Let us end this ignoble record and henceforth stand by womanhood. If Victoria Woodhull must be crucified, let men drive the spikes and plait the crown of thorns."

A very noble sentiment and a brave resolve, but it was too bad that it began with Victoria Woodhull who, as it turned out, was better able to take care of herself

than the women were able to take care of the National
Woman Suffrage Association.   In fact Victoria, at that
moment, was laying her plans, not to avoid crucifixion,
but to bend the association to her incredible ambitions.
Even Susan, although she felt a vague distrust of Mrs.
Woodhull, could not know that.   She was off again,
immediately after the Washington convention, lecturing in the West, working, as Parker Pillsbury expressed
it, like a whole plantation of slaves, not only to earn
money to cancel the debts of the *Revolution,* but to advance the view, now shared by a substantial minority
in Congress, that women had a legal right to vote under
the Fourteenth Amendment.   True, the House Judiciary Committee had tendered a report that, in its
opinion, Congress had no power to pass a declaratory
act, but Benjamin F. Butler of Massachusetts and William Loughridge of Iowa had given a minority report
which strongly favored the resolution.   It was as much
as Susan had expected, and she began to look ahead to
a piece of militant action which she had been planning
ever since her conversation in St. Louis with Francis
Minor.   Susan was so occupied with her lectures and
her plans that she had hardly time to notice that in
Washington and New York Mrs. Stanton and Mrs.
Hooker, furious with the House Judiciary Committee,
were nursing a wild scheme for a third party in the
Presidential election of 1872, nothing less than a labor
and woman suffrage party, "with one hundred aristocratic Democrats pledged to the work," declared Mrs.
Hooker.   Also Victoria Woodhull.

Susan, as a fact, had more on her mind than the
Fourteenth Amendment, although of this she had said
nothing to a living being except Elizabeth Cady Stan-

ton.   About the time of the Washington convention
Susan had dropped into the Tilton home in Brooklyn
on one of her frequent visits, to find little Mrs. Tilton,
usually so *exalté* in her domestic happiness and her religion, in a misery of tears and despair.   Safe in Susan's
comforting arms she poured out a terrible story. . . .
Susan at first doubted her own ears. . . . She had
known that almost next to her God poor little "Lib"
idolized the pastor of Plymouth Church, who had married her to Theodore, his closest friend, had baptized
her children, and conducted the funeral of baby Paul.
Susan remembered the funeral, the house full of sunshine and flowers, the white casket, Beecher standing
over it, his rich voice uttering words of hope and joy,
while Theodore with bowed head listened and Lib's
rapt eyes gazed at the speaker, too entranced for tears.
And then the god had become clay, the preacher had
turned tempter, and Lib, the loving and devoted wife,
had yielded.   She had confessed all to Theodore, she
told Susan, and Theodore had forgiven.   At least for
a time.   But Lib was to learn that there are things that
no man forgives.   At first he had agreed with her that
it was better for them to endure their little private hell
of suffering than to drag the miserable affair into the
light of publicity.   Better for them to nurse their
wrongs together in pain and remorse than to create a
horrible scandal which would not only destroy Beecher
but Plymouth Church as well.

Lib was equal to it, but not Theodore.   Man-like he
could not keep off the subject.   He was forever demanding the story over again, accusing the wretched
woman of concealing essential details, accusing her of
falsehood when she swore that it was all a thing of the

past. Frightful scenes were becoming frequent—one
of them had scarcely ended when Susan arrived that
day. Theodore had flung out of the house with fearful threats on his lips. She was afraid for her life—
perhaps still more for Beecher's life. Would Susan
stay with her until Theodore came home? Susan
would and did. At ten o'clock she put little Lib to bed
promising that she should rest undisturbed until morning. Theodore came in raging, determined to see his
wife, threatening—he did not know exactly what—
Susan told him brusquely not to be an idiot. Lib was
asleep and she should stay asleep. There was a storm
of words, a brief, undignified struggle on the stairs,
but Susan reached the bedroom door first. Planting
herself against it she told the half crazed man that if
he got into that room it would be only after he had hurt
her, badly.

"Leave my home at once, and never dare enter it
again," shouted Tilton.

"Your home, forsooth," retorted Susan. "As far as
I know it is your wife's home also, and I will enter it
as often as she wants me." And in front of that bedroom door she remained until daylight, never leaving
the house until she saw a kind of a reconciliation affected between the unhappy pair. Before she left
Theodore told her that except in those intervals of extreme anguish he realized that he must keep the thing
a secret. To draw Beecher down would be a satisfaction, sometimes he thought it even a public duty. But
his wife, his children, his own career, all these had to
be taken into consideration. Yes, he would keep silence,
and he would loyally try to torture Lib no more.

This story Susan confided to Mrs. Stanton, not as a

matter of gossip, for Susan never gossiped, but as a
necessity.  Not one person involved in the ghastly mess
was a private individual.  Beecher was Beecher, far
and away the most celebrated clergyman in America, a
power, not only in religious circles but in the whole social and political life of the country.  Theodore Tilton
was one of the foremost journalists and editors of his
generation.  Besides, he was a member of their association, had been its president.  It was impossible for
Susan to go away without telling Mrs. Stanton the facts,
for in spite of Theodore's promises, there was great
danger that a terrible scandal might be unloosed.  Mrs.
Stanton, of course, swore to keep her lips sealed, but
the trouble with Elizabeth was that never in her life
had she been able to keep her lips sealed about anything.  The very candor of her nature, her impetuosity,
her bursts of indignation, especially against men,
forbade her to keep secrets.  Still, in this case, Susan
had to trust her, arguing that after all there was no one
she was likely to tell the story to unless it was Henry
Stanton, who would never under any circumstances
divulge it.  How could she dream that the person who
very soon became Elizabeth's confidant was the impossible Victoria Woodhull?  How it happened Elizabeth
herself could never explain, except that all this time
Catherine Beecher was viciously attacking the Woodhull and Claflin "free lovers," and more than once in
his sermons Henry Ward had used the women as horrible examples of vice, along with card playing, thea-
ter-going, dancing and other Sodom and Gomorrah
elements rampant in the community.  Victoria was beginning to chafe under the attacks of the Beecher
family, and once or twice she hinted to Elizabeth that

if she were pushed just a little farther she might have some things to say about that whited sepulcher over there in Brooklyn, that pious sensualist who loved rare wines, carried loose jewels in his pockets and kissed his women parishioners when he paid them clerical calls. She understood that kind of man.  It is more than probable that in the course of some such conversation, Elizabeth burst forth and said:  "You are perfectly right.  *I* could tell you—"

No sooner had she told than remorse overwhelmed her.  But remorse, alas, is but a synonym for too late. From that moment Elizabeth Cady Stanton was in the power of a woman relentless, ambitious, implacable and as unscrupulous as Satan himself.  She never threatened, never made demands, never uttered a word that suggested blackmail.  She simply took hold of the National Woman Suffrage Association and used it to gratify her magnificent ego, perhaps the most perfect ego in existence except that of Henry Ward Beecher. When the woman suffrage convention of 1871 met in Apollo Hall, New York, Victoria was about the most conspicuous woman on the platform.  True, she sat between Mrs. Stanton and Lucretia Mott in frozen dignity, and her speech, a splendid constitutional argument for immediate enfranchisement, was delivered with the passionless logic of a lawyer in a court of justice.  The very sight of her, so staunch and brave in the face of ferocious attacks against her character, the women thought, was an object lesson against that double standard of morals that forgave a man anything, even degradation, but forgave a woman nothing, even an innocent unconventionality.  Even Susan felt this, and it inspired her to one of the best speeches she had ever made before a convention.

"We can well believe," said one of the newspapers, "that in any movement for the enfranchisement of women, like MacGregor, wherever Susan B. Anthony sits will be the head of the table."

But most of the papers called it "The Woodhull Convention."

# CHAPTER XIX

## THE TERRIBLE YEAR

On the last day of 1871 Susan notes in her diary:

". . . Left Medicine Bow at noon, went through deep snow cuts ten feet in length. . . . Reached Laramie at ten P. M. Thus closes 1871, a year full of hard work, six months east, six months west of the Rocky Mountains; 171 lectures, 13,000 miles of travel; gross receipts, $4,318, paid on debts $2,271. Nothing ahead but to plod on."

She is writing in the comparative comfort of the private car of Senator Sargent of California, journeying eastward to Washington. The Sargents have picked her up, half dead of cold and exposure, after a six-horse sleigh had carried her through a blizzard from Virginia City, Nevada, to the main line of the railroad. Before that she has lectured in twenty towns between San Francisco and the mining regions of Montana and Nevada to as many people as can manage to plow their way through the deep snows. The Sargent special car seems like heaven, although in those days the hardships of cross-continental travel are many even for United States Senators. Diners are unknown, and during the twelve days between Ogden and Chicago they subsist on cold food from lunch baskets, with tea brewed on a coal stove which uncertainly heats the car. At frequent intervals the train makes long halts while men shovel tons of snow and ice from the tracks. Susan has plenty of time to brood on experiences past, and troubles that face her in the East. If she gave her diary chapter headings she might well call 1871, "The Terrible Year." It has been full of tumult, full of apparent failure, for that $4,318 has been wrested from audiences mostly hostile, sometimes abusive and even threatening.

The echo of that "Woodhull Convention." From the beginning of a joint lecture tour undertaken with Mrs. Stanton shortly after the convention, Susan seems to head directly into trouble. In Salt Lake she speaks in the new meeting hall of the Liberal Mormons, in revolt against the despotism of Brigham Young. Among the younger members there is even a beginning reaction against polygamy, and to these young men and women she talks so kindly, so tactfully, so tolerantly, that many shed tears. She tells them that she understands what suffering is involved in the breaking up of plural families. Her heart aches for the men, the women and the children, and cries, "God help you all." But this is only a part of the world revolution in the status of women, the inevitable end of their subjection to sex. The solution of it all is economic independence of women. In marriage this means the recognition of the wife as full partner of her husband, her earnings her own property, until the law makes joint earnings joint property. Every unmarried woman must be fitted for self-support, that never, in any circumstances need she sell her body in marriage or out. In a monogamous or in a polygamous community the problem is the same. Here religious conviction partially sustains the woman who must share her husband with other women. In other States women, powerless to earn bread for themselves or their children, suffer the same degradation in secret shame and misery. That is the only difference.

Susan is ignorant even of the dogmatic political economy of her time. She does not know how industry and the trades are to be made over to admit women, those child-like women who listen to her, mystified, repelled, yet strangely thrilled. Hoopskirts have gone out of fashion, but the "new" women are quite as helpless in their "Dolly Vardens" and long ruffled trains heavy with the filth of the streets. A "Dolly Varden" is a bustled polonaise, or overdress, tied back so tightly as to hamper normal locomotion, drawn in so tightly that the waist measures twenty inches at most. On their heads the women wear pounds of false hair, braided, puffed and curled, and on top of that ridiculous little hats. Impossible to imagine them doing useful work, yet here is Susan telling them that wage earning is woman's only permanent insurance against prostitution or polygamy, legal or illegal. Work is hard to find, but not so hard as when she began life. Women's colleges are opening, Vassar, Holyoke. Coeducational universities exist in half a dozen States. Girls are learning a revived art called shorthand, and a clumsy machine has been invented that prints letters three times as quickly as they can be written with a pen. It is a presage of the new time coming. But first of all they must have the ballot, that card of admission to a free human race. Susan knows little of economics, but she knows more, foresees more than all the learned professors and savants whose text-books and heavy tomes mislead students and clutter up the shelves of libraries.

Naturally this rouses fierce antagonism. In advance of her the newspapers publish large headlines: "Susan B. Anthony defends Polygamy;" "Suffragists advocate free love." "It is a mistake to call Miss Anthony a reformer," writes one editor. "She is a revolutionist, aiming at nothing less than the breaking up of the very foundations of society, and the overthrow of every social institution organized for the protection of the sanctity of the altar, the family circle and the legitimacy of our offspring. . . ."

In San Francisco Susan and Mrs. Stanton found the whole coast in the throes of a sensational crime, the shooting of A. P. Crittenden by his discarded sweetheart, Laura Fair. The unhappy woman in the case being without a defender in the world Susan and Elizabeth visited her in jail, hoping, as Susan said, for the sake of womanhood, to hear from her lips some mitigating circumstance. That night the hall was packed with Crittenden's resentful supporters. Susan's speech, on "The Power of the Ballot," contained her usual attack on the theory that women were so well protected by men that they needed no political safeguards. All her speeches being more or less extemporaneous she used illustrations uppermost in her mind. Thus after telling of a foundling asylum in New York where in the first year the sisters received 1,300 new-born babies whose mothers, in disgrace and destitution, had been forced to abandon them, she said: "If all men had protected all women as they would have their own wives and daughters, you would have no Laura Fair in your jail to-night."

A perfect bedlam of boos and hisses interrupted her, but since in abolition days Susan had faced much worse, she simply waited until the noise died down, and more impressively than before repeated: "You would have no Laura Fair in your jail to-night." Again the storm of hisses, and again, as soon as they subsided, Susan repeated the words. This time some of the Dolly Vardens paid her courage the tribute of timid applause, and Susan closed by saying: "I declare to you that women must not depend upon the protection of men, but must be taught to protect themselves, and there I take my stand."

It was the end of the meeting, the end of any further meetings as far as Susan was concerned. So many towns telegraphed to cancel engagements that she gave up trying to speak in California until the Fair hysteria was over. Mrs. Stanton, although she loyally defended Susan in newspaper interviews, was welcomed in a number of places, where she spoke with her usual success. In August she went home, and Susan, by invitation of Abigail Scott Dunniway, the leading suffragist of Oregon, turned her face to the Northwest. She had varying success, in some places crowds and generous fees, in others every hall closed against her and the newspapers filled with vitrolic denunciations. In Victoria, B.C., she raised a frightful dust by alluding to the law which in that province still gave men a legal right to beat their wives. Sometimes she was so troubled by fears that she would not be able to meet the notes due at the end of the year that she could not do herself justice on the platform, and that was hardest of all to bear. Yet she wrote cheerfully: "If meetings pay me so as to give me hope of adding to my $350 in the San Francisco bank (my share of Mrs. Stanton's and my lectures, which we divide equally), making it reach $2,000 or even $1,000 by December 1st, I shall plod away." There were, in those dreary months of plodding away, through unheard-of discomforts and hardships of travel in a new country, a few bright spots. In Salem, Oregon, the judges of the Supreme Court heard her lecture, afterward calling on her in a body. In Olympia, Washington, she was invited to address the Legislature on the women's interpretation of the Fourteenth Amendment. Finally, like balm to her wounds, came an invitation, signed by a number of prominent citizens of San Francisco, begging her to return for a series of lectures. She was well received, audiences were attentive, and a not inconsiderable sum was added to the bank account slowly piling up against that mountain of debt.

In Washington she addressed the Senate Judiciary Committee, making a last appeal to the Republican Party to repudiate, by a declaratory act, the sex distinctions which since the war had been written into the Constitution. She appealed to their own self-interest, told them that now, if ever, was their chance to add hundreds of thousands of women voters to their rolls. In Wyoming Territory in 1869 the tiny legislature, partly for a joke, partly to advertise themselves, had passed a woman suffrage bill, fully expecting the Governor to veto it. To their dismay he returned it with his signature and a message of congratulation that Wyoming should be the first community to do justice to its women. That Governor, years before, had heard Susan B. Anthony speak and had ever since been a disciple. Susan did not mention this to the committee, but she told them that before the Wyoming women voted no Republican had been elected to any office in the Territory, whereas since, one Republican had been sent to Congress and seven to the Legislature. Remembering that Abraham Lincoln had freed the slave and that his party had passed the Thirteenth Amendment, most women believed the Republicans to represent ideals of freedom, and she asked them how they could be so stupid as to refuse this wholesale acquisition to their party's strength. Nevertheless they returned an adverse report, and Susan began to lay plans for a militant test of the Fourteenth Amendment.

She needed more money first, so she plodded on in another western lecture tour, for in spite of newspaper attacks people kept calling for her. Although she shocked every community she had a genius for making people think, and invariably she left behind her the nucleus of a woman suffrage group. This journey was full of torment, for in Washington she had learned that Victoria Woodhull's influence on Mrs. Stanton and Isabella Hooker was as strong as ever, and the women were laying plans for a third party, to which Isabella stubbornly insisted the Democrats would rally. Susan stormed and raged, and between lectures she wrote warning and indignant letters:

"I tell you that I feel utterly disheartened—not that our cause is going to die and be defeated—but as to my place and work. Mrs. Woodhull has the advantage of us because she has her paper, but she persistently means to run our craft into her port and none other. If she were influenced by *women* 'spirits,' either in the body or out, in the direction she steers, I might consent to be a mere sail-hoister for her, but as it is, she is wholly owned by *men* spirits and I spurn the control of the whole lot of them."

Her name, she repeatedly told them, must not be used in connection with any third party movement, but what was her horror one spring day in Illinois to be handed a copy of *Woodhull and Claflin's Weekly,* containing the following notice:

"The undersigned citizens of the United States, responding to the invitation of the National Woman Suffrage Association, propose to hold a convention at Steinway Hall, in the city of New York, the 9th and 10th of May. We believe that the time has come for the formation of a new political party whose principles shall meet the issues of the hour and represent equal rights for all. As women of the country are to take part for the first time in political action, we propose that the initiative steps shall be taken by them. This convention will declare the platform of the People's Party, and consider the nominations of candidates for President and Vice-President of the United States, who shall be the best possible exponents of political and industrial reform.

"ELIZABETH CADY STANTON,　　SUSAN B. ANTHONY,
ISABELLA B. HOOKER,　　　　 MATILDA JOSLYN GAGE."

Pausing just long enough to send a telegram ordering her name removed from the atrocious thing, Susan flew back to New York. She reached there the 6th of May and at once descended in wrath on the infatuated Elizabeth in Tenafly, New Jersey. Finding it impossible to influence her Susan took steps to prevent the Woodhull contingent from appearing in Steinway Hall, which fortunately had been rented in the name of Susan B. Anthony, with a clause stating that the place had been secured solely for a woman suffrage convention. Thus when the morning session opened Mrs. Stanton was obliged to say that they would have to abandon their plan for nominating candidates, but, she said: "We propose to take the initiatory steps for a convention such as we have never had before. To-day we are combined with the Liberal Reformers, the Prohibitionists, and the Internationalists—with all classes of men who will help us roll back the constitutional doors, that we may enter and enjoy the rights that belong to every free citizen of the United States."

The hall was packed with strangers, a weird collection of men and women, the like of which had never before invaded a woman suffrage convention, and it required all Susan's iron resolution, all her peremptory challenges to keep the business of the day in hand. Toward the close of the evening session a side door opened to admit Victoria Woodhull, who glided gracefully to the platform and uninvited began to speak. But Susan was all set for Victoria Woodhull, and before a sentence was completed she planted herself squarely in front of the intruder, declaring that she was not a member of the association, had no place on the program, and that the chairman must rule her out of order. Mrs. Stanton, completely beaten, threw up her hands and Susan and Victoria were left to fight it out. Victoria managed to shout a motion that the convention adjourn to meet the following morning in Apollo Hall. Some ally in the audience shrieked a second to the motion, but Susan's strong voice rose above the din:

"No motion has been made and none seconded," she proclaimed. "Nothing that this person has said will be recorded in the minutes. The convention will now adjourn, to meet to-morrow at eleven o'clock, *in this hall.*"

Rushing to the door she ordered the janitor to turn out the lights, and in a babel of cries and protests the evening ended. The next morning Elizabeth took the chair, but gave notice that she would not again serve as an officer of the association. Susan was unanimously chosen president, and through one more session conducted the program, and took the sinking ship, as it were, into drydock for repairs.

That same day Apollo Hall was crowded with Victoria Woodhull's tatterdemalion followers, and "The National Radical Reformer's Party" was organized, "to obtain the human rights of all mankind." The platform, an extraordinary mélange of socialist, communist, populist, spiritualist ideas, contained such generously inclusive planks as the initiative and referendum, unlimited free speech, expanded currency, free trade, woman suffrage, Government guaranteed employment for all, and a brand new Federal Constitution. Amid wild acclaims Victoria Woodhull was nominated for President, and Frederick Douglass (who was not there) for Vice-President. If he declined the honor the executive committee was directed to name some other colored man.

"I come from the west," shouted one "delegate," "and I nominate Spotted Tail. An Injun is better than a nigger any day."

Mrs. Stanton and Mrs. Hooker, completely disillusioned, sought Susan's forgiveness for their little spree. Elizabeth declared herself through with political parties for all time, but Isabella, accepting Susan's leadership of the demoralized National Woman Suffrage Association, was ready to follow her into a final trial of Republican good faith.

In that year of Grant's second nomination the Republicans included in their platform a cautious pronouncement for woman suffrage. The party was badly split, the scandals of the past four years, especially those growing out of Grant's weakness in appointing to lucrative offices a host of grafting relations, resulting in the Cincinnati Convention of Liberal Republicans, with Horace Greeley nominated for President, B. Gratz Brown for Vice-President. The Republicans were panic stricken, for some of their best men stampeded to the Liberals, and since Greeley had not only denounced the miserable carpet-bag régime in the conquered South, but had offered bail for Jefferson Davis himself, they feared that he would get an avalanche of ex-Confederate votes.  This explains why in the Philadelphia convention this sop was thrown to the women:

"The Republican Party is mindful of its obligations to the loyal women of America, for their noble devotion to the cause of freedom; their admission to wider fields of usefulness is received with satisfaction; and the honest demands of any class of citizens for equal rights should be treated with respectful consideration."

It was not much more than a splinter, but neither the Liberals nor the Democrats conceded anything at all, and the further fact that Grant had appointed a large number of women to small post-masterships rallied the suffragists to the Republican standard.  The Vice-Presidential nominee, Senator Henry Wilson, was a sincere suffragist, and through his insistence Susan was swept into the campaign.  The National Committee and the New York State Committee gave her $1,000 to be spent in meetings throughout New York, which they thought Greeley, with the aid of the *Tribune,* might carry.  But Susan, although her meetings were immensely popular, very soon became a thorn in the side of the politicians.  She absolutely refused to denounce Greeley as a Copperhead, or to emphasize his white "stovepipe" hat, his queer wrinkled trousers or his unkempt chin whiskers as campaign issues.  Instead she put forward the suffrage "splinter" as an earnest of Republican ideals, which was no end embarrassing.  Besides, Greeley proved a poor candidate, his platform was weak, and the *Tribune,* after he relinquished his editorial control, hardly supported him at all. In fact, even before Greeley's death, which followed fast on his defeat, the paper virtually belonged to Whitelaw Reid. Before the campaign was half over the Republicans dropped the women and forgot all about their suffrage promises.

On one of the last days of registration in Rochester Susan gathered her two sisters, Guelma McLean and Hannah Mosher, with a dozen other women residents of their ward, marched through a crowd of gaping men in a barber shop, and demanded that they be registered as voters. The election board offering a few faint objections, Susan read them the Fourteenth Amendment and the article in the State Constitution regarding the election oath. As neither document contained any sex qualifications Susan warned the men that if they refused she would swear out warrants for their arrest, standing the whole cost of the suits herself. Inspired by this audacious example about forty more women went out the next day and registered, but on election day only the fifteen from the eighth ward were permitted to cast their ballots. Every paper in the country carried sensational stories, most of them demanding that those women, especially Susan B. Anthony, be severely punished. About two weeks after the election a United States deputy marshal called at the Anthony home and in manifest embarrassment, informed Susan that she was under arrest for illegal voting. She would have to appear at the District Attorney's office immediately, but he supposed she could be trusted to go alone.

"Oh, dear no," said Susan. "I much prefer to be taken, handcuffed if possible."

The marshal firmly declined to furnish handcuffs,

but he escorted the most popular woman in Rochester to the District Attorney's office and in a dingy room where, in former years, fugitive slaves were examined before being returned to their masters, she and the other women were formally arraigned. Bail was fixed at $500, which Susan refused to furnish, but on a writ of habeas corpus she was freed. While the lawyers were discussing the trial date she remarked pleasantly that she couldn't conveniently be tried before December 10th, as she had quite a number of lecture engagements to fill.

"But you are under arrest," expostulated the District Attorney.

"Just the same," said Susan, "don't fix that trial before December 10th, for I can't afford to lose any lecture dates."

That very day she started out through the county with a new lecture, "Is it a Crime for a Citizen of the United States to Vote?" At the close of every meeting the audience voted that it was not, and so worried did the authorities become lest no proper jury could be secured either in or around Rochester that an order was obtained removing the case to the United States Circuit Court at Canandaigua. Into Canandaigua and environs went Susan, speaking every night to crowds of men many of whom came forward to assure her that if they were called to the jury they would acquit her. As it turned out no jury was allowed to do this.

# CHAPTER XX

## THE UNITED STATES VS. SUSAN B. ANTHONY

". . . Without having a lawful right to vote in said election district the said Susan B. Anthony, being then and there a person of the female sex, as she, the said Susan B. Anthony, then and there well knew contrary of the statute of the United States of America in such cases made and provided, and against the peace of the United States of America, . . . did knowingly, wrongfully and unlawfully vote . . ."

UNDER a lengthy indictment of which the above paragraph is at least intelligible, Susan B. Anthony, in June, 1872, went to trial in a case as famous as that of the slave, Dred Scott, in 1856. In both cases the law, as such, was set aside to serve deeply ingrained prejudice and a state of mind which seems as remote from the present as the Crusades. The indictment charged Susan with having voted in defiance of a statute of the United States, made and provided, while, as a matter of fact there was no such statute. The original Constitution claimed little power over the election laws of the separate States. It provided that United States Senators must be elected by the legislatures, but it left members of the lower house of Congress, the legislatures themselves and all State officials to be chosen or appointed by the citizens, all of them or special classes only, as the various States preferred. Not until after the Civil War did Congress attempt to define the word citizen. In the Fourteenth Amendment a citizen was described as any person born or naturalized in the United States, which seems fairly comprehensive. Persons of both sexes were counted citizens in all their responsibilities to the States, and the amendment was passed especially to confer the vote on one class previously not counted as persons, *i. e.,* negroes. The trial of Susan B. Anthony as a fraudulent voter was, therefore, a crucial test of the amendment, and in no sense involved a criminal charge, as we see it now. Had she been pronounced not guilty she would have walked out of the courtroom not only free but a voter. For in 1872 it had not occurred to any one that a single article of the Constitution could be ignored. Since then we have seen the Fourteenth and even the Fifteenth Amendments deliberately set aside, for the latter, the Supreme Court has decided, does not, in spite of its specific intent, confer on any negro in the United States a right, under the Constitution, to vote. If logic holds good no woman, and indeed no man, has a right to vote, except under legislative statute. Yet the revered Supreme Court has held that all men over twenty-one, and all women of legal age, are now legally enfranchised. It is puzzling.

The case of the United States vs. Susan B. Anthony was tried before Associate-Justice Ward Hunt, United States District Attorney Richard Crowley prosecuting, and two eminent lawyers, Hon. Henry R. Selden and John Van Voorhis, defending. The courtroom was thronged, many lawyers being in attendance, among them a son of ex-President Fillmore and Judge Hall of Buffalo. A strong effort was made to have Judge Hall try the case with Judge Hunt, because with only one judge on the bench an appeal to the Supreme Court could not be taken. But Judge Hunt, acting throughout on the advice of the bitterly anti-suffrage Roscoe Conkling, refused. From the outset of the trial this judge showed himself prejudiced, ill-tempered, overbearing and determined on a verdict of guilty. He allowed Judge Selden to go into the witness box and testify that he had advised Susan to vote, believing that the Fourteenth Amendment gave her full power to do so. But Judge Hunt would not allow Susan to testify in her own behalf, ruling that she was not a competent witness. After this he admitted all the testimony taken in her first examination before the commissioner and the district attorney, although her counsel protested vigorously against the version of her statements as recorded by the local officer. Judge Selden spoke three hours, giving a masterly presentation of the rights and privileges of citizens of the United States as implied in the Constitution and stated in the Fourteenth Amendment. In conclusion he said:

"Miss Anthony believed and was advised that she had a right to vote. She may also have been advised, as was clearly the fact, that the question as to her right could not be brought before the courts for trial without her voting or offering to vote, and if either was criminal the one was as much so as the other. Therefore she stands now arraigned as a criminal, for taking the only step by which it was possible to bring the great constitutional question as to her right before the tribunals of the country for adjudication. If for thus acting, in the most perfect good faith, with motives as pure and impulses as noble as any which can find place in your honor's breast in the administration of justice, she is by the laws of her country to be condemned as a criminal, she must abide the consequences. Her condemnation, however, under such circumstances, would only add another most weighty reason to those which I have already advanced, to show that women need the aid of the ballot for their protection."

As soon as the district attorney finished his speech Judge Hunt, without leaving the bench, read an opinion, *written in advance of the trial,* to the effect that the Fourteenth Amendment was "a protection, not to all our rights, but to our rights as citizens of the United States only, that is, the rights existing or belonging to that condition or capacity." And then he ordered the jury to bring in a verdict of guilty. Judge Selden was on his feet at once objecting that the Court had no right, in a criminal case, to do more than charge a jury, afterwards permitting it to bring in its own verdict. He demanded that the jury at least be polled. But Judge Hunt refused both pleas and summarily discharged the jury. They went out dazed, without having been allowed to say a word, several men protesting outside that they had intended to vote in favor of the defendant. The next day Judge Hunt refused a motion for a new trial, and ordering Susan to stand up asked her:

"Has the prisoner anything to say why sentence shall not be pronounced?"

Susan had plenty to say. Her natural rights, her civil rights, her political rights, her judicial rights, had all alike been ignored. She had, in the first place, been denied a trial before her peers, and "under such circumstances a commoner of England, tried before a jury of lords, would have far less cause to complain than have I, a woman, tried before a jury of men." But even before this jury she had been refused her right to testify in her own defense; she had been refused the right of trial by jury, guaranteed in the Constitution, and never denied in a criminal case, except to slaves.

"But yesterday," said Susan, "the same man-made forms of law declared it a crime punishable with $1,000 fine and six months imprisonment to give a cup of cold water, a crust of bread or a night's shelter to a panting fugitive tracking his way to Canada; and every man or woman in whose veins coursed a drop of human sympathy violated that wicked law, reckless of consequences, and was justified in so doing. And then the slaves who got their freedom had to take it over or under or through the unjust forms of law, precisely as now must women take it to get their right to a voice in this government; and I have taken mine, and mean to take it at every opportunity."

The whole speech was interrupted by orders from the Court to cease talking and sit down, but Susan persisted, and at the close of her speech said: "Failing to get this justice—failing even to get a trial by a jury *not* my peers, I ask not leniency at your hands, but rather the full rigor of the law."

The affronted Judge Hunt then sentenced Susan to pay a fine of $100 and the full costs of the prosecution. She said: "May it please your honor, I will never pay a dollar of your unjust penalty." And she never did.

From one end of the country to the other the newspapers denounced the trial as a travesty of justice. It was a new thing in the United States for any white person to be denied a jury trial or the right to testify in his own behalf. The New York *Sun* said that if Judge Hunt's assumption of power in Susan B. Anthony's case were established as a legal principle, then any judge might, on his own *ipse dixit,* and without the intervention of a jury, fine, imprison or hang any man, woman or child in the United States, and the *Sun* added that Judge Hunt's impeachment and removal was a public duty. Many other newspapers, even those opposed to woman suffrage, made the same demand. Judge Hunt was especially scored for his evasion in imposing on Susan a fine without the alternative of prison. Had she gone to prison and been freed on a writ of habeas corpus she could have taken the case through the higher courts, where a different verdict might have been rendered. In the trial of the three inspectors of election, arrested for receiving the ballots of Susan and fourteen other women in the eighth ward of Rochester, Judge Hunt refused to allow Mr. Van Voorhis, their counsel, to address the jury, but he did not again take it upon himself to order a verdict. He said: "You can decide it here or go out." The verdict was guilty, and the inspectors were fined $25 each and the costs, which they refused to pay. They were imprisoned, but after a week, during which time the women of Rochester served them luxurious meals in their cells, President Grant pardoned them all. In Susan's case her counsel took the only step possible, and acting on an old precedent appealed to Congress to remit her fine "and declare that trial by jury does and shall exist in this country." The Senate Judiciary Committee reported adversely, with the astonishing statement that they were not satisfied that the ruling of the judge was as represented in the petition. The House Judiciary's report said: "Congress cannot be converted into a national court of review for any and all criminal convictions where it shall be alleged that the judge has committed an error." It also said that there was no reason for further action in the case since President Grant had already pardoned the criminal. The pardon had been granted the election inspectors, Susan having refused to ask leniency for herself. But the Congressional committees were only too anxious to evade the real point at issue, for had they remitted

Susan's sentence it would have amounted to an admission of the illegality of the action of Judge Hunt and would have furnished a precedent for other women to test, by voting, the intent of the Fourteenth Amendment.

They did it anyhow in several places, and the case of Virginia Minor of St. Louis, was conducted by her husband through all the courts up to the Supreme Court of the United States, where a decision was handed down, March 19, 1875, by Chief Justice Waite, that while women were persons and citizens, still the National Constitution did not define the privileges and immunities of citizens. The National Constitution did not confer the right of suffrage on any one, the States alone regulating that power. The Fourteenth and Fifteenth Amendments forbade discrimination on account of color or race, but not on account of sex.

Very curiously, as Ida Husted Harper, in her detailed account of the trial and final result, points out, Judge Waite's decision directly contradicts that one handed down in the Dred Scott case. Said Chief Justice Taney in his opinion in that *cause célèbre:* "The words 'people of the United States' and 'citizens' are synonymous terms and mean the same thing; they describe the political body who, according to our republican institutions, form the sovereignty and hold the power, and conduct the government through their representatives. They are what we familiarly call the sovereign people, and every citizen is one of this people, and a constituent member of this sovereignty."

Judge Taney, however, had ruled that Dred Scott, because of race and color, was less than a human being. Judge Waite ruled that women, because of sex, were

less than human. The indignation caused by Susan's
trial and the ultimate verdict was terrific, and from all
over the United States people sent her sums of money
from a few pennies to hundreds of dollars to enable
her to pay the costs. She received more than enough,
the residue, needless to say, being turned into the treasury of the National Woman Suffrage Association to
begin the fight for a sixteenth amendment for woman
suffrage. Not for years, however, did the women succeed in persuading any member of Congress to introduce their bill. As one of her firmest friends in Congress, Hon. A. G. Riddle, wrote Susan in 1874, it was
a question of "the never-seen, ever-felt law of caste
which has always walled women around, and which few
have the courage to step over." The politicians would
never in a hundred years take the question up. "The
Republicans want no new issues or disturbing elements.
The Democrats are certain that the Republicans are
about to dissolve; and they want to hold on as they are.
Both think this thing may, perhaps will, come, but now
is not the time; and with both there never will a 'now'."

Garrison, Wendell Phillips, Benjamin F. Butler and
other friends whom Susan consulted agreed with this
view, but in 1876 she thought she might introduce an
entering wedge in the shape of petitions for the amendment, and having secured in twenty-six States over
10,000 names, Susan, in another piece of militancy, went
to the Capitol and with several aides boldly walked
into the Representative Chamber and handed the petitions to Congressmen of those States. The History of
Woman Suffrage says that Susan, "on finding herself
suddenly whisked into those sacred enclosures, amid a
crowd of stalwart men, spittoons and scrap baskets,"

made a laughing apology to her friend and champion, Representative Hoar, to which he responded: "I hope yet to see you on this floor, in your own right, and in business hours, too." The women also invaded the Senate, where they were treated with great courtesy. Their petitions, however, were treated as a colossal joke, and in the Senate were referred to the Committee on Public Lands. In both Houses they were at least read, which was all the women hoped for.

Susan's trial, and the decision of the United States Supreme Court that the Constitution bestows the ballot on no citizen, marks the climax of the woman movement in the Nineteenth Century. In the quarter of a century since 1848 it had advanced with spectacular swiftness, on the crest of a great wave of idealism which after the Civil War receded and sullenly died. Out of the wreck of war a new United States emerged, in all material ways more splendid than the old, but spiritually and intellectually distinctly inferior. The age of big business began, ruthless competition without the slightest regard to decent standards of ethics; exploitation of immigrant labor; barefaced buying and selling of legislative measures; plundering of the common domain, especially in railroad building and public works. The production of rich literature, American in character, almost ceased. People seemed to have lost interest in ideas and to have thought only for wealth and the display of wealth. After a great conflict, with destruction on a large scale of property as well as life, this always happens, just as a glorious forest, destroyed by fire, is replaced for a time by a jungle of worthless and unsightly vines and brush. It is nature's way of recovering breath.

Had the woman movement attained a little more momentum by 1865, when all idealism suffered a fatal slump, there is every reason to believe that universal suffrage would have been attained, with what results we can, of course, only conjecture. It may be argued that the women of that period were ill-fitted to vote, but they were presumably as well fitted as the men who received the franchise at the close of the Revolutionary War, and in 1865, and later they were a thousand times better fitted than the immigrants who, from the 1870's on began to pour into the United States until their number reached the appalling figure of one million a year. These ignorant peasants from the slums and ghettos of Europe, the fields where they plowed and reaped with tools as primitive as ancient Egypt, were seized upon by the political rings in all our cities, naturalized before many of them could speak the English language or remotely comprehended American ideals, and voted like sheep in municipal and State elections. Had women, at the close of the Civil War, been given the ballot one result at least would have followed, the American vote would have held its own against those untaught aliens, and we should have avoided some of the reeking scandal and debauch of municipal politics which has lowered us in the eyes of every intelligent European observer, and in our own self-respect.

The woman movement halted, but in the economic expansion of the United States, the growth of business, the increase of machinery, opportunities of women in wage earning doubled and trebled. In the Civil War dearth of man-power drew them into Government employment, and the vast army of women civil servants appeared, never to lose their hold. The telegraph companies also began to employ women. When the telephone came into use a very short experiment revealed that only women were fitted for operators in central exchanges. The typewriter also proved a woman's machine. In the trades, in shops and department stores, in a hundred avenues of trade a demand for women workers increasingly appeared. At first the tendency of women to leave domestic for professional work was overlooked by economists, or when noticed was regarded as a disturbing, but temporary manifestation.

Susan B. Anthony believed no such superficial nonsense. From her early womanhood she had perceived that men, even with the best intentions, were powerless to protect women whom the laws did not protect. She early perceived that wage earning outside the home was a necessity for the family as well as for individual women, and that no theories of economists could alter that fact. It was a habit of hers to read the want advertisements in the *New York Herald,* observing that more than half of them came from women. She often went out in the early morning to watch the stream of women and girls, careworn, scantily clad, their poor lunch boxes under their arms, going to work, always for wages half or less than those paid to men. In the opening of women's colleges, schools of arts and crafts, and even the few trade classes then in existence, she saw that the subsistence problem underlay the whole question of women's status, and that no edict of professors or fulminations from the pulpit could stay the steady advance of women into wealth producing. This advance she divined as an absolute guarantee of women's political freedom, as it had been in the case of men. It was necessary to hasten the day of women's enfranchisement, for the ballot would put an end to arbitrary inequalities of wages and opportunities. She saw how, in history, the extension of the franchise, from nobles to commons, from merchants and traders to craftsmen and laborers, had weakened the barriers of caste, and to a great extent overthown them. The extension of the ballot to women would break down the strongest caste barrier of all, that of sex. The delusion of grandeur on the part of men, the delusion of inferiority on the part of women, would gradually disappear, and with these many other delusions that held back the higher evolution of society.

Susan had allied herself with the woman's rights movement at thirty-three, believing that through the ballot women could obtain specific reforms, such as temperance and the right to function in other reforms of special interest to the home. At fifty-three woman suffrage was to her no mere means to moral reforms, no highway to class justice. It had grown into an entire social philosophy. Against the economists, against the Constitutional law of the land, as interpreted by a Supreme Court decision, against two powerful political parties, against the mass mind of a whole people, she set herself to imparting that social philosophy. To change the mind of a nation was more than a life-time task, yet Susan undertook it with a confidence that no amount of ridicule, abuse, contumely, falsehood, not even the branding of herself as a criminal could halt for a single hour. She knew she could do it. Strangely, even her enemies unwillingly believed it. She had become a personage, a power, by some looked up to as a prophet, by others, opposed to the changes she propounded, a public menace. An opinion editorially expressed in the St. Louis *Globe-Democrat* in the early '70's reflects the general impression she created everywhere:

Miss Anthony is one of the most remarkable women of the Nineteenth Century—remarkable for the purity of her life, the earnestness with which she promulgates her peculiar views, and the indomitable courage with which she bears defeat and misfortune. No longer in the bloom of youth—if she ever had any bloom—hard-featured, guileless, cold as an icicle, fluent and philosophical, she wields to-day tenfold more influence than all the beautiful and brilliant female lecturers that ever flaunted upon the platform as preachers of social impossibilities."

"Cold as an icicle," however, describes Susan about as accurately as it does Savonarola, Galileo or Francis of Assisi. No woman, no man ever deliberately chose a life of poverty, chastity and obedience to an ideal unless he was the reverse of cold. The passionate nature alone dares to seek truth, and only those in whom the blood runs hot and strong ever deem it worth while to preach the truth to unbelievers.

# PART III

*"There have been others also, just as true and devoted to the cause—I wish I could name every one—but with such women consecrating their lives, FAILURE IS IMPOSSIBLE."*

SUSAN B. ANTHONY'S *last public speech, at the celebration in Washington of her 86th birthday, February 15, 1906.*

# CHAPTER XXI

## BEECHER, TILTON AND SOCIAL PURITY

ONE encounter with Susan was enough for Victoria Woodhull, and as soon as she realized the impossibility of using the woman suffrage movement for her mysterious ends, she turned to her most ambitious project, the destruction of the Beecher family. Not that Victoria can rightly claim the credit, or the discredit, of revealing the Beecher-Tilton secret to the world, for it would have exploded in time without her intervention. For nearly four years the nauseating thing had rotted and crawled beneath the surface of the hymn-singing, tear-shedding, sermon-shouting smug religiosity which gave Brooklyn its proud title of the City of Churches. Poor Lib Tilton's story was already known to a score of Brooklyn's social and religious leaders, for after Susan had gone off on another of her interminable lecture tours, Lib sobbed it out to her mother, Mrs. Nathan B. Morse, which at this present would be equivalent to confiding it to a microphone or to a rural party-line telephone. Not that Mrs. Morse broadcast it indiscriminately—it was too good for that. She used it principally to browbeat and blackmail Theodore Tilton, and to poison the mind against him of Henry C. Bowen, founder and principal bond holder of Plymouth Church, owner of the *Independent* and the Brooklyn *Union,* and Theodore's employer. Bowen, although as pious as any other good Brooklynite, was hand in glove with political corruptionists and was getting richer than ever at it. According to Paxton Hibben, Beecher's most complete biographer, Bowen's particular crony was Grant's friend, Thomas Murphy, Collector of the Port of New York, and Bowen shared with him the rich graft of the "general order business" of the Custom House.

Bowen had his own grudge against Henry Ward Beecher, a black one enough, if we believe the story of his first wife's deathbed confession. Like Theodore Tilton, Bowen had decided that it was good policy and good business religion to lock the door on his skeleton. But there sat those two men together in the office of the *Independent,* often seeing Beecher, oftener speaking of him, and finally the two began to unload in confidence the burden of their common hate. As usual they ended by hating each other. Tilton probably thought that had Bowen accused Beecher in time the tragedy of little Lib would have been forestalled. Bowen thought that he now owned Tilton, body and soul, and could force him to back up in the columns of the *Independent* the grafting politicians who were contributing so importantly to his income. At this Tilton balked. Then came Mrs. Morse, accusing Tilton of brutally abusing his wife, of consorting with "free lovers" like Victoria Woodhull, Mrs. Stanton and Susan B. Anthony, which gave Bowen exactly the excuse he was looking for to break his five years' contract with Tilton. Thrown out of a job which paid him extremely well in honors as well as money, Theodore's mind became a breeding ground for revenge. Especially when Bowen, with Beecher's assent, had Tilton expelled from Plymouth Church, which he had not entered since the night of his wife's confession in 1869.

Another agent of Mrs. Morse, Bessie Turner, a maid in the Tilton household, slipped the story of Theodore's alleged infidelities, and the only too true story of his frequent ill-tempers, to Mrs. Beecher. Infuriated, Theodore himself started in to talk, and to write that series of letters which figured so fragrantly in the trial in 1875. From the evidence in a case triple plated with perjury, the relations between Beecher and Mrs. Tilton lasted about a year and a half. Then after Beecher tired of his supine victim she sat alone in mingled remorse and hope, praying God to forgive her sin—and send her elderly lover back to her. He never came, but she saw him, spoke to him sometimes, in Sunday-school and in her club for poor mothers, and every Sunday morning and evening she sat under the spell of that sixty-year-old Lothario, hearing him preach love, love, and more love, imagining that he was talking over the heads of his congregation to her. It is the marvel of the ages on what an attenuated diet a starved sex love can exist, especially during that emotional second blooming that afflicts nearly every life. No, the Beecher-Tilton scandal could never have been kept a secret, but just the same it was Victoria Woodhull's brief association with the National Woman Suffrage Association that fired the spark. Like a certain bullet-shot at Sarajevo.

What Victoria learned from Elizabeth Cady Stanton she supplemented with details from Theodore Tilton himself. Just what his relations were with the lady brokeress can not be known. In Paxton's "Beecher" he is represented as trying to keep her from reprisals against Henry Ward and Catherine Beecher, who habitually alluded to Woodhull and Claflin as "the two prostitutes." He certainly visited her, and he prostituted his own pen by writing a "whitewashing" biography of her, full of extravagant and utterly insincere flattery. Whatever their relations, they were abruptly severed when Theodore hotly resented her scandalous imputations against Susan B. Anthony, and refused to support her preposterous candidacy for President. So Victoria, partly to get even with Theodore and with the suffragists, and partly to stab the whole Beecher family to death, told the Beecher-Tilton story, with embroidery, on a Boston lecture platform and published it in full in *Woodhull and Claflin's Weekly*. The sensation it created was without any parallel before or since. Within a few hours of publication that issue of the *Weekly* was not only sold out, but used copies were being resold for as high as forty dollars apiece. Almost at once the sisters were arrested for sending obscene reading matter through the United States mail, but in line with the hypocrisy of the times, the warrant was sworn out, not for what had been published about Beecher, but for a libel on another man inserted for good measure in the Beecher story. George Francis Train, bobbing up again, in Victoria's defense, of course, published selected stories from the Bible which he truly declared were more obscene than anything she had written, and he also was arrested. All three were sent to the Tombs, but after languishing there for six months, during which time no suits were brought against them by the pastor of Plymouth Church, the Woodhull-Claflin indictments were dismissed. General Benjamin F. Tracy, United States District Attorney, and a pillar of Beecher's Church, saw to that little matter.

Up to this time neither Susan nor Mrs. Stanton (after her one lapse of discretion) had breathed a word of what they knew. Susan often visited the Tilton home, doing what she could to heal the increasing estrangement between husband and wife. But now Isabella Hooker rushed to them for sympathy and help. Henry's feeble denials, or rather his shallow evasions, were guilt-clothed in Isabella's eyes, and very naturally all three women took up the defense of Mrs. Tilton. In a letter to Isabella Susan wrote:

"For a cultivated man at whose feet the whole world of men as well as of women sits in love and reverence, whose moral, intellectual, social resources are without limit—for such a man, so blest, so overflowing with soul-food—for him to ask or accept the body of one or a dozen of his reverent and revering devotees—I tell you *he is the sinner.*"

Isabella's solution of the whole trouble, and in this Susan earnestly agreed, was for Henry to come out in open confession before his assembled congregation. Or to let her confess for him by reading from the pulpit of Plymouth Church his own written statement of the case. She knew perfectly well with what drama, what Greek tragedy draperies he would be able to clothe such a story, and with what tears of love and forgiveness it would be received. Henry himself would spout tears like a geyser, and the end would be an old-fashioned love-feast of hymns, prayers, sobs, handclasps and kisses. A few might leave the church, but for every one who left a score would come in. But Henry Ward Beecher had no bowels for such a test of his own power. It seemed safer to let the clerk of Plymouth Church,

"Tearful Tommy" Shearman, jackal of Jim Fisk and Jay Gould, the *New York Times* called him, assure the press that Tilton's mind had long been unhinged, and that Mrs. Tilton was an hysterical woman, subject to "mediumistic fits." Safer also to let a whole crew of unscrupulous lawyers and politicians, together with his lecture manager, his publishers and others whose social and financial fortunes were bound up with his own, to lie and counter-attack him out of the mess.

General Tracy cynically told Theodore that he was beaten before he began to fight, because no man would ever forgive him for condoning his wife's infidelity, and in the 1870's this was probably true. But Lib would have forgiven anything the scandal mongers raked up against him, and she never would have left him for the Beecher camp had he only shown himself compassionate to her. But that too, perhaps, was impossible in the '70's. So, even after Beecher, and his friends, had thrown on her the onus of being an unsuccessful tempter of a great man's virtue, she suddenly left her husband, her home and her children, to take her stand in defense of the man she always called "my pastor." It was after this, after the famous "investigation" made by Plymouth congregation, in which, by a miracle of casuistry, Beecher was found innocent but Lib Tilton guilty, that Elizabeth Cady Stanton wrote for the *Chicago Tribune* a series of articles on the case which, as examples of interpretive reporting, must ever be admired. Of Mrs. Tilton she wrote:

"Bewildered, racked, tormented, tempest-tossed in the midst of misery and wretchedness, in her last act on leaving home, and in her statement before the Committee, a touch of grand womanhood is revealed, after all; in the face of law, gospel, conventionalism, ready

A photograph taken of
Elizabeth Cady Stanton
about 1875.

H. ROCHER.

CHICAGO.

ELIZABETH CADY STANTON AT SIXTY

to leave her home forever, she says: 'Theodore the end has come; I will never take another step by your side.' And to her brother, in announcing her decision, she said: 'I have always been treated as a nonentity—a plaything—to be used or let alone at will; but it has always seemed to me that I was *a party* not a little concerned.'

"Thus leaving her husband, children, home, she went forth to vindicate the man she loved. . . . With what withering cruelty, then, his words must have fallen on her heart: 'She thrust her affections on me, unsought—' though a mutual confession of love is revealed in the course of the investigation, and recognized in the verdict. . . ."

She scored Beecher unmercifully for calling the suffragists who foregathered in the Tilton home "human hyenas," "free lovers," and other pleasant names, and representing his sister Isabella as weak-minded and insane. Was it their fault that the suffragists had discovered the truth and was it to their discredit that they had seen through his hypocrisies? No, declared Elizabeth, the discredit lay elsewhere, and she proceeded to tell where.

"You ask if it is possible for Mr. Beecher to maintain his position in the face of the facts. His position will be maintained *for* him, as he is the soul and center of three powerful religious rings, as he tells you himself in his statement; (1) Plymouth Church; (2) The *Christian Union;* (3) 'The Life of Christ.' The church property is not taxed, its bonds in the hands of the wealthy members of that organization are valuable, and the bondholders, alive to their financial interests, stand around Mr. Beecher, a faithful, protective band, not loving truth and justice less, but their own pockets more. They are shrewd enough to know that in Mr. Beecher's downfall their bonds must be of little value.

"Next, the *Christian Union.* . . . Another circle of suffering stockholders would be brought to grief.

"As to 'The Life of Christ,' in the words of one of the fold, that would indeed be blown 'higher than a kite' were the author proved an unworthy shepherd. I have heard that he was paid $20,000 for that work before he put pen to paper. Then he ground out one volume which the English market refused to touch until the second was forthcoming; and thus the whole investment hangs by the eyelids until Mr. Beecher is whitewashed and sees fit to finish his work. . . . Under such circumstances justice for Mr. Beecher is impossible. . . . They who try to see Theodore Tilton vindicated do but maintain the claims of common justice for those who have not the money to buy it."

It did Elizabeth Cady Stanton a world of good to unburden herself thus in the public prints. Particularly as she lived to see her version of the case accepted by practically the whole community, and her prophecy of the outcome, as far as Beecher was concerned, fulfilled. He alone, the chief culprit, outrode the storm. Theodore Tilton went to France, a life-exile. Elizabeth Tilton, dropped from membership in Plymouth Church, tried a little school, then did seamstress work, and finally died in the home of one of her daughters. But all this came later.

Susan's temperament, unlike Mrs. Stanton's, demanded no expression in the Beecher-Tilton affair. It became known at the beginning that she had been Lib Tilton's first confidant, and in every newspaper office in New York, and in every city and town where she appeared, reporters were detailed to "interview Susan B. Anthony. Get the story out of her. Make her talk." She never left her hotel, never took a train or descended from one, never went to or from a lecture hall, never showed herself in public anywhere, without a train of reporters, detectives, sleuths from the law offices of both sides trailing her. Her conversations were listened to by eavesdroppers, her mail was tampered with, her friends were approached with bribes, she herself was offered fabulous sums to write what she knew. Letters and telegrams from strangers, as well as from lawyers in the case, suggested to her that her own character would suffer unless she told. They might as well have tried to interview the Great Sphinx. She was not even flattered when the newspapers said that her slightest word in the matter would be more convincing than a volume of testimony from any one else. "Miss Anthony," said the New York *Sun,* "is a lady whose word will everywhere be believed by those who know anything of her character." And John Hooker, Isabella's husband, voiced the general opinion when he wrote: "A more truthful person does not live."

And so, because every one knew that Susan B. Anthony could not lie, neither side, when Tilton finally sued Henry Ward Beecher for alienation of his wife's affections, dared call her to the witness stand.

The only thing Susan did, as a result of the miserable affair, was to go across the country in 1875 with a new lecture, one on "Social Purity." Perhaps the public thought she was at last prepared to tell something, for the lecture was an immense success financially. The first time she gave it in Chicago, the crowd seeking admission to the Grand Opera House was so great that she could not get inside, except through the engine room at the back of the building. Her lecture manager, Mr. Slayton, and even Elizabeth Cady Stanton, told her that that lecture would finish her career in Chicago, but on the contrary she was invited the next winter to come back and repeat it. So throughout the country, although a large section of the churches berated her, most of the high social lights in each community pointedly staying away, the Social Purity speech attracted throngs, especially of women. The press condemned her for giving it even when they admitted its strength, its delicacy of expression, and its timeliness. For, as one paper said: "Spinsters are presumed to be wholly innocent of the necessary information—are supposed, in truth, to be too pure-minded to contemplate vice in its most repulsive shape, not to say analyze it and dwell oratorically before the world on its nauseous details."

Considering that every metropolitan newspaper had carried the Beecher-Tilton story for two years on the front page, and every small town and country paper had featured it, a spinster to remain wholly ignorant of such matters would not only have had to be extraordinarily "pure-minded," she would have had to be illiterate. Still the great taboo lingered, and Susan's boldness in addressing mixed audiences on a subject of such vital importance to every home in the world was an added excuse for conservative men to urge on their wives that Woman's Place was in the Home, a phrase which at that time was coming into its first popularity.

The Social Purity speech and "Bread and the Ballot," Susan's favorite lecture, proved so profitable during the next seasons that on May 1, 1876, Susan was able to write in her diary: "The day of jubilee has come. I have paid the last dollar of the *Revolution* debt!" Six years to a month since she had taken on her shoulders the burden of a $10,000 obligation, and now she was free. All over the country the press, even that majority section which had fought her ideas, had to admit that in an age of graft and corruption, public and private, this feat of a woman was a reproach to the average business man. Said the Buffalo *Express:*

" 'She has paid her debts like a man,' says an exchange. Like a man? Not so. Not one man in a thousand but who would have 'squealed,' 'laid down,' and settled at ten or twenty cents on the dollar."

And the Rochester *Post-Express:*

"There are a good many men who would have hidden behind their wives' petticoats for a much smaller sum than $10,000. . . . Yet here is an example, in a woman, who our laws say is not fit to exercise the active and defensive principle of citizenship, that puts to shame the lives of nine hundred and ninety-nine in every thousand men."

It was the year of the Centennial, that first world's fair in the United States, our first juvenile, flamboyant demonstration of what we had done in a hundred years to deserve a place among first-class nations of the earth. Centennial stock was sold all over the country to pay for buildings, exhibits, management and entertainments, and women had subscribed to this at least $100,-ooo. Yet in none of the plans, in none of the public entertainments of distinguished guests, nowhere on the program, in fact, was any woman included. It struck Susan that this was a crowning insult which American women could not afford to accept without a mighty protest, and she and Mrs. Stanton and Matilda Joslyn Gage, in conference decided that they would, whether invited or no, take part in the great celebration of July 4, in Independence Square. They first prepared an eloquent document expressive of the failure of government by consent of the governed as long as half the governed were in legal, political and economic subjection, and this they asked permission not to read, but merely to present as part of the day's proceedings. That permission General Joseph R. Hawley, president of the Centennial Commission, brusquely refused. Whereupon the women most successfully presented it any-how. With great effort five platform seats were secured, Susan's a press seat, as reporter for her brother's paper. President Grant being unable to at-tend, acting Vice-President Ferry represented the Gov-ernment, and welcomed the gorgeous procession of visitors of State, the Emperor Dom Pedro of Brazil and Crown Prince Oscar of Sweden heading the list. Following them came Count Rochambeau, descendant of the great French admiral who had fought with the Americans in the Revolution, the Japanese commis-sioners, ambassadors and special envoys from England, Prussia, Austria, Spain, Russia, Turkey and other monarchies. The women had agreed upon their moment, which followed directly after the reading of the Declaration of Independence by Richard Henry Lee of Virginia, grandson of Light Horse Harry Lee of Revolutionary fame. As the applause died down and the band was about to strike up the Brazilian Hymn, the five women rose from their seats at the back of the stage and walked down the aisle toward the presiding officer's throne. The "History of Woman Suffrage" describes what followed:

"The foreign guests, the military and civil officers who filled the space directly around the speaker's stand, courteously made way while Miss Anthony, in fitting words, presented the Declaration. Mr. Ferry's face paled, as bowing low, with no words, he received it. . . . The ladies turned, scattering printed copies as they deliberately passed up the aisle and off the platform. On every side eager hands were stretched; men stood on seats and asked for them, while General Hawley, thus defied and beaten in his audacious denial to women of the right to present their Declaration, shouted, 'Order, order!'

"Going out through the crowd, they made their way to a platform erected for the musicians in front of Independence Hall. Here on this historic ground, under the shadow of Washington's statue, back of them the old bell which had proclaimed 'Liberty to all the land and all the inhabitants thereof,' they took their places, and to a listening, applauding crowd, Miss Anthony read a copy of the Declaration just presented to Mr. Ferry. It was warmly applauded at many points, and again scattering a number of printed copies, the delegation descended from the platform and hastened to the convention of the National Woman Suffrage Association."

For of course there was a suffrage convention in Philadelphia along with the Centennial. The laws of Pennsylvania, even in 1876, forbidding a married woman making a contract, Lucretia Mott, official head of the committee, could not rent the headquarters, which stood open all summer, but Susan, as a spinster, was allowed to do so. Tea, with speeches, was a daily function, and a crowd of strangers, many from Europe, came every afternoon to meet and to listen to the women who had made the militant demonstration of July 4th. For it was Susan B. Anthony, and not her famous disciple, Emmeline Pankhurst, who invented militant suffragism. Susan was always militant, and she would have kept the movement militant had it been possible. The only difference between her militancy and Mrs. Pankhurst's was the attitude of the police, or rather of those who gave orders to the police in the two countries. If a police line had ever tried to stop Susan from presenting a petition to Congress, from entering political conventions, or pushing her question into any limelight, it would have had a fight on its hands. The women who came after Susan B. Anthony made the movement "ladylike," eschewed all publicans and sinners, and relied entirely upon persuasive methods. With their policy Susan had to be patient in her old age, but in youth she would have scorned it. To a group of reformers who adopted prayer as one of their chief weapons against vice Susan once said ironically: "Frederick Douglass used to tell me that when he was a Maryland slave, and a good Methodist, he would go into the farthest corner of the tobacco field and pray God to bring him liberty; but God never answered his prayers until he prayed with his heels."

# CHAPTER XXII

## PLODDING ON

THE disputed elections of 1876 brought the country a threat of civil war, but as soon as Rutherford B. Hayes was inducted into office things settled down to a respectability which, after the scandals of the Grant régime, people found grateful. There was little to talk about, except the cold water dispensation which Mrs. Hayes introduced at state dinners, and which astonished the diplomatic corps almost as much as if she had substituted spinach for the *roti*. Hayes abolished the spoils system, sacred since Andrew Jackson's reign, and his civil service reforms gave many more women positions in the departments. But although Mrs. Hayes was a suffragist the President did nothing to further the sixteenth amendment in Congress. Susan labored with him, of course, as she did with every President and every presidential candidate from Lincoln to Roosevelt, getting little satisfaction from any of them. Yet with each successive administration, the Arthur and Cleveland reigns possibly excepted, she had the encouragement of visible concessions, a rapidly growing acceptance, at any rate, of the changing status of women. And even Grover Cleveland signed the bill, hotly opposed in Congress, for the admission of Utah, with woman suffrage. Susan's correspondence with Garfield, in 1880, illustrates very well the attitude of every President of the United States, since the Civil

War, toward an extension of the franchise which they knew to be inevitable but which each man wanted to hand over to his successors. Soon after the conventions in which Garfield became the Republican, Hancock the Democratic nominee, Susan addressed a letter to each candidate, asking if he as President would recommend to Congress the submission of the amendment prohibiting the disfranchisement of United States citizens on account of sex.

"Neither platform," she wrote, "makes any pledge to secure to the women of the several states a *national guarantee* of their right to a voice in the government on the same terms with men—neither platform makes any pledge to secure political equality to women— hence we are waiting and hoping that one candidate or the other, or both, will declare favorably, and thereby make it possible for women, with self-respect, to work for the success of one or both nominees."

To this letter General Hancock vouchsafed no reply, but Garfield wrote a letter characteristic of his rather weak will powers, so strangely in contrast with his intellectual gifts. General Garfield more or less threw himself on Susan B. Anthony's mercy in regard to his actions independent of the Republican platform. Did she not think it would be a violation of the trust reposed in him to "add to the present contest an issue which they have not authorized?" Personally, although open to the freest discussion, etc., he had not quite reached the conclusion that it would be best for women and for the country. . . . "I may reach it; but whatever time may do to me, that fruit is not yet ripe on the tree. I ask you therefore, for the sake of your own question, do you think it wise to pick my apples now?"

Susan's reply to that letter was such a wise, yet merciless analysis of the rise and decline of the party of her own affiliation that it is rather a pity that so few Republican leaders have ever read it. She spoke of its birth in idealism and its retrograde movement after the death of Lincoln, not only for women but for the negro freed, then deserted by his friends—

"until what we gained by the sword is lost by political surrenders. We need nothing but a Democratic administration to demonstrate to all Israel and the sun the fact, the sad fact, that all is lost by the Republican Party. . . . The first and fatal mistake was in ceding to Rhode Island the right to 'abridge' the suffrage to foreign born men; and to all the States to 'deny' it to women in direct violation of the principle of *national supremacy*. From that time, inch by inch, point by point has been surrendered, until it is only in name that the Republican Party is the party of national supremacy. Grant did not protect the negro's ballot in the presidential election of 1876—Hayes cannot in 1880—nor will Garfield be able to do so in 1884—for the scepter has departed from Judah. . . .

"As for plucking the fruit before it is ripe! Allow me to remind you that very much fruit is never picked; some is nipped in the bud; some is worm-eaten and falls to the ground; some rots on the trees before it ripens; some, too slow in ripening, is bitten by the early frosts of autumn; while some rare, ripe apples hang until frozen and worthless on the leafless boughs. Really, Mr. Garfield, if after passing through the war of the rebellion and sixteen years in Congress; if, after seeing and hearing and repeating that *no class* ever got justice and equality of chances from any government except that it had the power—the ballot—to clutch them for itself; if after all your opportunities for growth and development, you cannot yet see the truth of the great principle of individual self-government; if you have reached only the idea of class government, and that of the most hateful and cruel form—bounded by sex—there must be some radical defect in the ethics of the party of which you are the chosen leader."

What was Susan's exasperation therefore when, after Garfield had written, not a satisfactory letter, but a frank one, and Hancock had not even given them the courtesy of any reply at all, a number of suffragists, taking silence for consent, went out in the campaign to help Hancock's election. Would Susan never be able to teach her followers political sense? Garfield was not yet a suffragist, but he was open to argument. In the last session of Congress he had been one of three who reported in favor of a woman suffrage committee in the House. "Before I shall consent to put my name to any document favoring either candidate, I must see in black and white, in the candidate's own pen tracks, something to warrant such favoring." This had the effect of retiring all except a few Democratic women from the campaign, and it established the policy of the suffragists ever after—to lend no aid or comfort to any political party not definitely pledged to their franchise. The regrettable result was that women lost interest, after 1880, in political questions which before that date many had studied with real intelligence. Thus when in 1920 they went to the polls, full voters, not one American woman in a thousand knew the policies of either party. The consequence has been a noticeable apathy in the women voters of the country, only now beginning to change for the better.

President Garfield died at the hands of a cowardly assassin before Susan could even try to bring him across the narrow line which separated him from her convictions. His successor, Chester A. Arthur, whose nomination as Vice-President had been deplored because of his shady political background, developed into a dignified executive, but his type of mind offered no hope for the women. Hardly one of his administration officials could be called a liberal, and his sister, Mrs. McElroy, who presided over the White House, was a woman of old and very conservative traditions.

Susan's one interview with the President was socially agreeable, but nothing more, the Washington correspondents writing frivolous letters telling how President Arthur had "squeezed Susan B. Anthony's hand."

Susan, Mrs. Stanton and Matilda Joslyn Gage settled down to finish the monumental "History of Woman Suffrage," begun in 1877 as a 500-page pamphlet, extended into one large volume, then two and finally three. They worked without knowing exactly how funds were to be found for printing and distributing the volumes, for no publisher regarded it as a commercial proposition, and only Fowler and Wells, publishers of phrenological and other pseudo-scientific books, would consider it at all. But early in 1882 a miracle happened. Susan received a letter from Wendell Phillips, telling her that by the will of Mrs. Eliza Eddy, daughter of Francis Jackson, old abolitionist and defender of woman's rights, a small fortune was devised in equal parts to her and to Lucy Stone, to be used, absolutely at their discretion, for the advancement of woman suffrage. Susan's share, Phillips informed her, would not be less than $25,000 to $28,000. But some time would have to elapse before she received the money, for while Mrs. Eddy's three living daughters heartily approved the bequest, the husband of a daughter who had died shortly before her mother, was prepared to contest the will. Benjamin F. Butler had been retained by the executors, and there was no question that the will would be upheld. Three years passed before the money actually became available, but Susan waited happily, knowing that now their precious work, the History, was certain to be published. It never occurred to her for a moment that a single penny of the money could be spent to give her, even in her work, an hour's ease, and when, after long litigation, the money was paid into her account, she spent it all on the book, buying out the interests of Mrs. Stanton and Mrs. Gage, and even that of Fowler and Wells. This she did that she might feel at complete liberty to use the History as a means of education, not only in the United States but all over the world. Copies of the first three volumes and the last two written by Susan and Ida Husted Harper, were placed at Susan's expense in more than one thousand libraries in this country and Europe; in the British Museum, in Oxford University, the Bibliothèque Nationale, Paris, in university libraries in Dublin, Edinburgh, Berlin, Helsingfors, Toronto and Melbourne. Members of Congressional committees in charge of woman suffrage bills, statesmen in the United States and England received copies. Wherever Susan thought that extraordinary record of woman's progress in forty years from legal slavery to a status nearly equal to man's, would help to change the minds of legislators or students of public affairs, she sent the History. There is no other, and in spite of prolixity, repetitions, and much material which time has rendered less valuable, the History will always remain an invaluable reference book, the one accessible record of an astounding social revolution.

The writing of the History was a severe drain on Susan's vitality, for while she could endure any hardships of action, indoor work at a desk was torture. As soon as the second volume was in the hands of the printers Mrs. Stanton went to England to visit her daughter, Harriot Stanton Blatch, and a little later, in 1883, Susan, in her sixty-fourth year, took the first vacation of her life and went to Europe. Her lecture trips had been profitable of late years, there were no State campaigns in prospect, and several of the early suffrage leaders abroad had written her that they needed advice and encouragement. When the newspapers announced her sailing a perfect flood of letters, telegrams and gifts descended upon her, total strangers sending expensive dress materials, traveling bags and all the aids to comfort and convenience they thought a woman of her years might need. One New York man sent an anonymous gift of a hundred dollars to be spent toward an India shawl, his unsigned note saying, "I don't believe in woman suffrage, but I do believe in Susan B. Anthony." Susan bought the shawl, a red one, and a garnet velvet gown besides, delighting in her finery almost as she had those first good clothes in Canajoharie. But the aids to comfort for an old woman were in the nature of superfluities, for what Susan, at sixty-three, accomplished on that vacation would stagger the average man of fifty.

With her as traveling companion, interpreter and general courier, went Rachel Foster, daughter of J. Heron Foster, founder of the Pittsburgh *Dispatch,* and one of the modern college women newly come into the woman movement. Together they wandered over the Continent, Susan out-walking, out-climbing, and often quite out-doing her vigorous young companion. There was no railway up Vesuvius in the early eighties, but Susan tramped it to the crater through lava and ashes ankle deep, declaring the climb many times worth while. She climbed every old castle tower and donjon she encountered, and walked miles through Naples, Rome, Pompeii, Paris and German cities. Italy fed her soul with beauty, but the poverty, the beggars, the enslaved peasant women, and especially the neglected children filled her with rage and pain. Once in Rome, being driven to see great sights by a lady of ancient lineage, she had pointed out to her a closed and shuttered palace, one only of five which belonged to a noble family. Susan seemed to be making a mental calculation. Finally she said: "What an orphan asylum it would make. I should think at least seven hundred of these little ragamuffins we have seen to-day could very comfortably be put in there."

In Germany she passed several rainy days writing letters and sending home newspapers which had interviewed her. All her letters were stamped with the usual slogans: "No just government can be formed without the consent of the governed," or "Taxation without representation is tyranny." These, in Bismark's Empire, created a terrible sensation, and the whole batch was returned to her hotel with the official inscription: "Such sentiments cannot pass through the post office in Germany."

In France—does it seem strange?—Susan lingered longest over the tomb of Napoleon. "A very great genius," she said. "Who knows but if he had lived in another age he might not have been our champion?" A sentiment which would have enchanted Madame de Staël!

The last six months were spent in England and Scotland, and there Susan was relieved of the self-reproach of having lived for three months a "purposeless life." In England her progress was filled with homage from women just entering on their own struggle. All the leaders entertained her, Mrs. Peter Taylor, Lydia Becker, Helen Taylor, stepdaughter of John Stuart Mill, Mrs. Jacob Bright, Frances Power Cobbe, Jane Conden, Emily Faithful, Millicent Garrett Fawcett, Priscilla Bright McLaren, Laura Ormiston Chant, Eliza Sanderson, Florence Fenwick Miller, women whose names stand highest in the older suffrage movement. She went to hear Canon Wilberforce speak on temperance, which he said had advanced only because the Lord had willed it, which made Susan smile, and alluded to women as "maiden aunts," and "old grandmothers," which caused her to laugh out loud. She sat behind the grill in the House of Commons and heard Gladstone, who disappointed her, and she went to the theater to see Sarah Bernhardt, who did not. But principally she thrilled at visiting the bleak home of the Brontë sisters, and the cottage of Harriet Martineau. Before she left England she had laid the first plans for an international woman suffrage association, not possible of realization at the time, because English and Scottish women were far apart in their ideas, and the theory of universal suffrage for men or women had taken little root in Great Britain.

Back in Washington one of the correspondents wrote of her:

"She is sixty-three, but looks just the same as twenty years ago. There is perhaps an extra wrinkle in her face, a little more silver in her hair, but her blue eyes are just as bright, her mouth as serious and her step as active as when she was forty. She would attract attention in any crowd. She is of medium height and medium form but her face is wonderfully intellectual, and she moves about like the woman of purpose she is."

Mrs. Stanton was growing very stout, her curls were white as snow, and she could no longer endure the burden of travel. Most of the old guard were invalids or dead. But Susan was in her vigorous middle age. Some one asked her about that time how she managed to keep her energy, and she replied: "Being the leader of an unpopular cause." Toward Elizabeth she was as cantankerously loving and impatient as ever. "It's all nonsense her charging all her ills to her labors for suffrage," stormed Susan, "when she knows and I know that it is her work for women that has kept her young and fresh and happy all these years."

January 26, 1886, was a great day in Susan's life, for then occurred the first vote ever taken in Congress on the woman suffrage amendment. It was seriously debated for several hours, and Susan, sitting with fifty other women in the galleries, was able to contrast it with the first debates in Albany over the married women's wages bill. There was not even a mention of Adam's rib or St. Paul's admonitions to the early churches. But Susan knew that the road beyond stretched very far when President Eliot of Harvard and nearly two hundred New England men of prominence could send on such an occasion a remonstrance against freedom for women. Their petition, with two hundred names, was balanced by women's petitions running into the hundred thousands, but the vote in the Senate stood sixteen to thirty-four against, all the affirmative votes being Republican.

The uneventful eighties, uneventful except for increased immigration, many labor troubles, and the anarchist outbreak in Chicago, closed graciously for the suffragists, for it marked the union, after twenty years of discord and separation of the National and the American Woman Suffrage Associations. The initiative came from the Boston group, largely at the insistence of Henry B. Blackwell—who always did admire Susan extravagantly—and Alice Stone Blackwell, his daughter. Lucy and Susan were appointed a committee to consider a satisfactory base of union, and as Lucy felt unable to travel Susan saw her in Boston. These two with Alice Stone Blackwell and Rachel Foster, held several conferences, and in late December, 1887, Miss Blackwell wrote Susan giving her mother's plan for union. It was just like Lucy, New England conservative to the last.

"Since many members of the National Society regard Mrs. Stone as the cause of the division, and many members of the American regard Mrs. Stanton and Miss Anthony as the cause of it, Mrs. Stone suggests that it would greatly promote a harmonious union for those three ladies to agree in advance that none of them would take the presidency of the united association."

Susan did not want the presidency for herself, but she was firmly set against displacing Elizabeth Cady Stanton. Lucy urged politely that Mrs. Stanton was advanced in age and spent most of her time abroad, and that Susan—if the National Association insisted on electing either—would be more acceptable. But at the final meeting of national delegates preliminary to the first joint convention, Susan said, with deep emotion:

"Don't vote for any human being but Mrs. Stanton. There are other reasons why I wish her elected, but I have these personal ones: when the division was made twenty years ago, it was because our platform was too broad, because Mrs. Stanton was too radical. . . . If we Nationals divide now, and Mrs. Stanton is deposed from the presidency, we virtually degrade her. If you have any love for our old association, which from the beginning has stood like a rock in regard to creeds and politics, demanding that every woman should be allowed to come on our platform to plead for her freedom . . . vote for Mrs. Stanton.

"The National always has allowed the utmost liberty. Anything and everything which stood in the way of progress was likely to get knocked off our platform. I want every one who claims to be a National to continue to stand for this principle. We have come now to another turning-point and, if it is necessary, I will fight forty years more to make our platform free for the Christian to stand upon whether she be a Catholic and counts her beads, or a Protestant of the straightest orthodox creed, just as I have fought for the rights of the infiels the last forty years. These are the principles I want you to maintain, that our platform may be kept as broad as the universe, that upon it may stand the representatives of all creeds and no creeds —Jew or Christian, Protestant or Catholic, Gentile, Mormon, pagan or atheist."

Although it was a bitter dose for the Boston group to swallow, unpalatable also for many of the Nationals, in the end all accepted it. Elizabeth Cady Stanton was elected President of the National American Woman Suffrage Association; Susan, Vice-President-at-large; Lucy Stone, chairman of the executive committee; Alice Stone Blackwell and Rachel Foster, now Mrs. Avery, corresponding and recording secretaries.

The union of the two societies, which never again was interrupted, came shortly after the fortieth anniversary of the first convention at Seneca Falls, an event which Susan intended to make memorable for its own sake, and also by organizing at the congress of the International Council of Women, the International Suffrage Alliance discussed in England in 1883. Few, who had taken part in that first woman's rights meeting or in the second one in Rochester, forty years before, were left alive. Gentle Lucretia Mott had died, very old, in 1880; Martha C. Wright several years before that; Rhoda de Garmo, Amy Post, Samuel J. May, of the Rochester pioneers were gone. Gone also were Garrison, Phillips, Francis Jackson, Bronson Alcott, his much-enduring wife, and their famous daughter Louisa, Lydia Mott, John G. Whittier, Emerson, Daniel Anthony and Lucy Read. Beecher had died the year before, Theodore Tilton was a recluse in Paris. But Frederick Douglass wrote that he would be there if he was alive. And Elizabeth Cady Stanton wrote from England:

"We have jogged along pretty well for forty years or more. Perhaps mid the wreck of thrones and the undoing of so many friendships, sects, parties and families, you and I deserve some credit for sticking together through all adverse winds, and with so few ripples on the surface. When I get back to America I intend to cling to you closer than ever."

And then after that, what did Elizabeth do, a few weeks before the convention, but write again and say that she dreaded the ocean voyage too much and Susan would have to carry on without her! Susan was so furious that she allowed a day and a night to pass without a reply, and then, as she writes in her journal: "I wrote the most terrific letter to Mrs. Stanton; it will start every white hair in her head." It did, for ten days later Susan had a cable: "I am coming." Of course she was coming, and her speech, Susan declared, would be the event of the whole affair. When she arrived Elizabeth confessed that she had prepared no speech. Well, Susan simply shut her up in a room at the Riggs House, with a guard at the door, and would allow no one to see her until the speech was written. Elizabeth probably expected nothing less.  So at last, after many years, Susan, Elizabeth Cady Stanton, Julia Ward Howe, Lucy Stone, Henry B. Blackwell, Frederick Douglass, Antoinette Brown Blackwell, Isabella Beecher Hooker, all that were left of the narrowing circle, stood together again in amity.  There was a reception at the White House with charming Mrs. Cleveland receiving, the President apparently impressed, teas and dinners and receptions in many Senatorial abodes; women from a dozen countries of Europe; columns of praise in the newspapers—everything but votes for women.  Forty years of work. Thirty years yet before the end.

# CHAPTER XXIII

## A HOME AT SEVENTY

THE merger of the two suffrage associations really meant the absorption of the American by the National, for the vitality of the old Massachusetts organization had been running low for a number of years, and the younger and more progressive members were glad to enlist under the supreme leadership of Susan B. Anthony. Among the "come-overs" were two women destined to become internationally famous during the closing decade of the Nineteenth Century, Rev. Anna Shaw and Carrie Chapman Catt. In 1890 they were in the very prime of life, rarely endowed mentally, and blest with those indefinable qualities called magnetism and charm. Susan recognized both as future leaders, but it was to Anna Shaw that her affection went out, and it was Miss Shaw who thereafter became her close friend and co-worker. From one point of view it was a peculiar, not to say an incongruous association, Susan the radical, the utterly unconventional, the agnostic in religion; and Anna Shaw the roly-poly little Methodist preacher, rather narrowly educated, rather inexperienced in life, brimming with harmless egotism, loving applause, yet as unselfish as a saint where her ideals were concerned. In very little except their selflessness were the two women alike. Susan loved her for that one quality, and she came to depend on her, as she had depended, so many years ago, on

Mrs. Stanton, for her ready and eloquent gift of speech. Just as she and Elizabeth used to collaborate perfectly on the platform, so now Anna Shaw supplied a certain fluency, a suave and flowing, persuasive style, which Susan lacked. Susan was never suave. She presented a solid fact argument, dazzling and stimulating to the mind, but sometimes over the heads of people who listened only with their emotions.

To such audiences Anna Shaw made an irresistible appeal. She had a perfect pulpit manner, made people laugh and cry in the best Beecher tradition, yet never descended to Talmage buffoonery. Had Anna Shaw been a man the little country parishes she served would never have held her long. Some rich Methodist summer visitor to Cape Cod would have heard her but once before summoning her to a large city church, for her sermons inevitably held the attention even of people to whom most sermons are deadly bores. Susan knew her United States, for in forty years of "plodding on" she had visited the farthest corner of practically every State and she knew, that taken as a whole, we are a church going people. Hence the value of a suffrage worker like Anna Shaw. The moment she rose to speak two thirds of the audience settled in their seats exactly as they did in their cushioned pews of Sundays, knowing by instinct that they were going to hear their own language spoken, knowing also that not one of their familiar fetishes would be assailed. Later there was another reason why Susan liked to have Anna Shaw constantly with her. After seventy-five she suffered at times from a little nervous constriction of the throat, the first sympton of which Miss Shaw instantly recognized, and was ready at once to intervene with a

*From the painting by Mary Foote*

### MRS. CARRIE CHAPMAN CATT
President for Many Years of the International Woman Suffrage Alliance

question, a flash of wit, a story, which gave Susan a chance to recover before the audience suspected that her voice had halted.

Mrs. Catt, a younger woman, was—and is still, as every one knows, a remarkable speaker, but of the same intellectual, unemotional type as Susan herself. Her first value to the movement was her genius for organization, her executive ability and her power of raising money. Precisely the qualities Susan had possessed in the 1850's. Mrs. Catt developed into a fine presiding officer, her handsome face and figure, her great dignity and her knowledge of parliamentary law combining to make her a perfect chairman. As President for many years of the International Woman Suffrage Alliance she was ideal.

With these two gifted women, and others, added to the National forces, the movement should have gained great momentum during the last decade of the Nineteenth Century, and the fact that it did not was due to the fact that the 1890's were so torn with social and political strife that the dominant political parties were completely occupied with keeping themselves intact. It was a time of crisis peculiarly American, one more struggle toward self-direction. The '80's had seen the liquidation of Civil War reconstruction problems, but in 1890 began another struggle, between the wage earners and the farmers on the one hand and the holders of vast wealth on the other. The labor troubles of the '80's, culminating in the murderous anarchist riots in Chicago, had spelled the doom of the badly led Knights of Labor, who were succeeded by the orderly and more powerful American Federation of Labor. But the principle of organization was stubbornly re-

sisted by many large employers, and a bitter antagonism
between labor and capital in the '90's, added to an even
more bitter feeling between farmers and what they
call "Wall Street," created a political situation which
left the women helpless. The farmers of the Middle
West, whose causes of discontent closely resembled
those which exist in 1928, had little in common with
industrial workers except a general sense of wrong, a
feeling that they were not sharing in the nation's un-
precedented prosperity, and the only remedy which
occurred to them was to unite with the workers and
"wipe the two old parties off the face of the earth."
In general, the combine may be called the Populist
movement, though it attracted to it many radicals of
all political faiths, with William Jennings Bryan its
perfect flower, and his extemporaneous "cross of gold"
speech, carefully rehearsed for two years, its perfect
expression. After the apotheosis of Bryan in the 1896
Chicago Convention the Populist movement was more
or less swallowed up in the free coinage of silver mania,
and like all our third party movements quickly disappeared. But for years after the Republicans and the
Democrats were too busy with questions of farm relief,
with the tariff, finance, immigration and one or two
foreign complications to notice women.

Yet in "The Mauve Decade," which looked a less
felicitous color to workers and suffragists, the social
importance of American women gained tremendously.
Not only had the higher education of women become
a common-place, but in every State thousands each
year left high school, college and university not for
domesticity but for skilled labor, business and the
professions. The '90's also saw the rise of women's

clubs, organizations of wives, mothers and grandmothers, thirsting for the wider culture denied them in
youth, and avid for social and civic activities. The
settlement movement grew up, hundreds of smaller
Hull Houses absorbing college women who formerly
went into teaching or church work. In a word the
'90's saw women in great numbers leaving "The
Home." Few of their organizations at first touched
politics, and most clubs barred from their platform
radical thinkers like Susan B. Anthony, Charlotte
Perkins Gilman and even Anna Shaw. But in 1892
came the Columbian Exposition, and there for the first
time all the women's groups came together and discovered that they had a common goal, equality with
men. Even the Women's Christian Temperance Union
and the Federation of Women's Clubs embraced the
idea that sooner or later they would have to become
political.

This too was Susan B. Anthony's work. The organizers of the 1892 exposition, but for her, would have
repeated the mistake of the Centennial management
and left women entirely out of their plans. As early
as 1889 Susan began quietly to agitate among friends
in Washington the question of women's participation
in the event. Knowing that the suffragists themselves
would get no recognition she worked with women
prominent in the social life of the capital. For many
years her home, during winter months, had been the
Riggs House, Mr. and Mrs. Spofford, its owners, keeping a suite for her use, counting it their contribution
to the cause. The drawing-rooms were always at her
disposal, and the result of a series of small meetings
held in the winter and spring of 1889, was a commit-

tee of women of which Susan was the director, although her name never appeared in any of its publicity. In January, 1890, when the World's Fair bill came before the House of Representatives, Susan's committee presented her petition, signed by more than a hundred of the most prominent women in Washington, wives and daughters of Cabinet officers, Justices of the Supreme Court, Senators and Representatives, army and navy men of high rank, asking that women be placed on the National Board of Managers. These women could not be ignored, so the exclusively masculine board, when appointed, was empowered to create a Board of Lady Managers, which, as the word lady suggests, was meant to be purely ornamental. One hundred and fifteen women were selected, with Mrs. Bertha Honoré Palmer of Chicago as chairman, an error of judgment on the part of the men who intended to make the appointment complimentary. Mrs. Palmer not only made the women's board a dynamic force in the management of the exposition but she organized a series of women's congresses, a feature of such importance that the proceedings in the printed report of the exposition filled six large volumes.

Having achieved her great object Susan stepped aside, refusing to accept any office for herself or any of her coadjutors, and even declining to appear at official functions for fear of embarrassing Mrs. Palmer. But when in May, 1893, there convened in Chicago the World's Congress of Representative Women, the first in the world to assemble, it was discovered that the most conspicuous woman there was Susan B. Anthony. Twenty-seven countries, one hundred and twenty-six organizations, represented by five hundred and twenty-eight delegates from the United States, Canada, South America, Europe, Asia, Africa, Australia and New Zealand, took possession of the Art Palace for one week, holding seventeen or eighteen simultaneous sessions every day. Only ten thousand persons could enter the building at a time; hundreds stood outside every hour, patiently waiting to get in on one or another meeting. And of the 150,000 who passed the gates not one but who demanded to see and hear the woman whose name was known—all unsuspected by Americans—the world over, Susan B. Anthony. She could not enter a room as a spectator without creating a sensation. The speaker, however distinguished, simply had to halt her discourse until the audience ceased cheering and Susan was seated on the platform. On days when she was advertised to speak a squad of police had to be sent to keep the corridors from a dangerous jam, and it required two stout policemen to get Susan through the crowds to the platform and afterward out of the building to her carriage. When she rose to speak men and women climbed on their seats, threw hats and handkerchiefs into the air and cheered themselves hoarse before she could utter a word. Every speaker in departments of education, religion, philosophy, art and science, paid her tribute, and every mention of her name provoked long applause. No woman, not even a reigning queen, ever received greater homage. It was as if the world suddenly woke up to the fact that but for her women would not be there at all. After fifty years of poverty, hard and grudgingly requited labor, misrepresentation, abuse, villification, Susan, as poor at seventy-three as she had been at thirty, the black silk gown she wore a gift, was lifted into the ranks of the immortals.

All that she would ever say of that extraordinary demonstration in her honor was: "It advanced the cause by twenty-five years."

But it would not have been Susan B. Anthony if she had not made a few new enemies. Very early she clashed with the evangelical churches on the subject of Sunday opening of the fair. Susan wanted it open all day Sunday, for, as she said to one particularly truculent clergyman: "If I had charge of a young man in Chicago at this time, I would far rather have him securely locked up in the fair grounds all day Sunday than let him roam the streets."

"Would you allow him to go to the Wild West Show on Sunday?" asked the clergyman in horror.

"Of course I would," said Susan placidly. "In my opinion he'd learn more from Buffalo Bill than from listening to an intolerant sermon."

The delighted Col. Cody, on hearing this, sent Susan a box for one of his performances, asking her to bring some of her suffrage friends. Not knowing that a box held only six persons Susan brought twelve, so two boxes had to be given her. Buffalo Bill, opening the show as usual by riding in under a spotlight on his splendid horse, rode directly to Susan's box, and reining his steed to his haunches, swept his hat to the saddle in a magnificent salute. Susan rose and bowed low, and for a moment these two typical Americans faced each other to the wild applause of thousands.

Another memorable meeting in Chicago was between Susan and the great singer Nordica. At every social function given during the summer Susan had to appear, if only for half an hour, and no one would leave without speaking to her or touching her hand. At this affair Nordica asked the privilege of singing especially for Susan, who knew nothing of music and pretended, like Grant, to distinguish the national hymn from the others only because people stood up. But Nordica's singing moved Susan almost to tears. Afterward she put her arms around the beautiful artist and said: "Dear Nordica, I could die listening to your voice." It was the sigh of a soul which had put away everything, even beauty, for the achievement of a single object in life.

To crown her happiness Colorado that year added a woman suffrage amendment to its State Constitution.

In the early autumn Susan went home for a brief rest, for in her seventy-fourth year Susan had actually achieved a home. After the death of Lucy Read Anthony in 1880, Mary, the home-keeping daughter, rented the lower story of the modest brick house in Rochester which Daniel had bought when he sold the farm, and lived herself in the upstairs rooms. Mary Anthony now, after years of teaching in the public schools, was ready to retire, and she begged Susan to go to housekeeping with her and henceforth direct the work of the National Woman Suffrage Association from a home. Elizabeth Cady Stanton urged her to do it. "My advice to you, Susan," she wrote, "is to keep some spot you can call your own, where you can live and die in peace, and be cremated in your own oven if you desire."

The idea appealed to Susan, but she hardly knew how she and Mary were going to afford to furnish and maintain a whole house. Mary had saved money and

invested it wisely, but, Susan argued, that was her
sister's money, and how was she to pay her share of the
enterprise? All the money she earned by lecturing had
gone to pay the debts of the *Revolution,* and after that
to help the movement. She often wrecked her bank
account to pay the expenses of women attending conventions, even buying sometimes the gowns they wore.
Never in her life had she been paid a salary, or more
than part of her expenses during State campaigns. Her
own "best" gowns, her bits of jewelry, the lace collars
she loved so dearly, even her famous red silk shawl,
always worn with everything, were birthday or Christmas gifts from rich friends. But Mary was determined, and so Susan came back to Rochester to the
house which remained their own until both ended life.

To her wonder and astonishment she found that the
Political Equality League of the town had solved all
her difficulties by furnishing the house from garret to
cellar, friends from all over the country contributing.
Susan entered to find beautiful rugs on the floor, easy
chairs in living rooms and bedrooms, a study for herself
and one for Mary, tables piled with books and magazines, china, linen, silver, and gifts of great historic
value. Mrs. Stanton sent the mahogany table on which
in 1848 she and Lucretia Mott, Martha C. Wright and
Mary McClintock, had written the call for the first
woman's rights meeting. Relatives had sent bits of old
family furniture, a chest of drawers, a dressing table
and mirror which had been part of Lucy Read's wedding outfit more than eighty years before. Even the
spinning wheel at which she had sung as a girl, stood
beside the wide open fire in the living room. Mary's
treasures and Susan's, of pictures and photographs, old

daguerreotypes and prints, preserved through a lifetime, hung on the walls. Pictures of Garrison, Phillips, Douglass, Elizabeth Cady Stanton, Margaret
Fuller, Mary Wollstonecraft, Lydia Maria Child,
Ernestine Rose. It was a complete home, though its
simplicity, and the sight of Susan and Mary cooking
their own dinners, of Susan sweeping off the porch and
walks, or running to the corner late at night to post
letters, would have amazed the European notables who
paid her such deference at Chicago.

The only trouble about a home presented to an old
and honored leader by admiring disciples is that the
old leader is rather expected henceforth to stay in it.
Invariably as organizations grow large and prosperous
they tend to bureaucracy and officialism. Politics enter
in, an intrigue here and there. The younger members
think they ought to be advanced. New leaders want to
exercise their leadership. Many of the new generation
of suffragists thought it just as well that Mrs. Stanton
had grown so stout and elderly that traveling was no
longer possible. Her radicalism offended the church
members. Even Susan, although, of course, no convention was a success without her, often said such caus-
tic and unexpected things. At a convention of the New
York State Federation of Women's Clubs in 1899 some
one introduced a resolution against the seating of Sena-
tor-elect Brigham H. Roberts of Utah because he was
a Mormon. The President of the Federation wanted
to keep the resolution from passing, so she asked Susan
to say a word. Susan, according to some of the suffragists, might merely have said that Mr. Roberts had
no chance of being seated, which was a fact. But instead she told the women that she saw no reason for

protesting against the seating in Congress of a Mormon who had violated the law of monogamy, when they had never yet raised a voice against Gentile men in Congress or any other high official body who were known to be violators of that and many other laws for the protection of women and girls. Such things got into print, furnished material for sermons against suffrage. The women never understood that what Susan wanted was not merely votes, but the wiping out of sex caste. She had no patience with what she called palliatives, but what small-town women called vital reforms. She and Mrs. Stanton fully agreed, and Susan often said so, that petty reforms, special legislation restricting individual freedom of habits, smoking, Sunday observance, etc., was a dangerous thing. It would, the two women pointed out, eventually lead to Government interference with personal liberty, and even to a system of espionage amounting to tyranny. How prophetic was their vision is hardly necessary to remark.

Mrs. Stanton made her last appearance at a national convention in January, 1892. She received the ovation she deserved, after forty years of devoted service. In a noble speech she announced her retirement and asked that Susan be named her successor. She and Lucy Stone were made honorary Presidents of the National American Woman Suffrage Association, and Anna Shaw Vice-President-at-large. For a number of years afterward Mrs. Stanton sent letters to be read from the platform, and these finally resulted in open discontent in a considerable faction, because Elizabeth, instead of growing conservative in her old age, as people, especially women, are expected to, tended more and more to become a social rebel. Susan did not always agree with the ideas expressed in those controversial letters, but no matter how distasteful she knew they were to certain groups she insisted that they be read and respectfully listened to. Nothing could swerve her loyalty to the woman who first of all in the world had drawn other women together to battle for their human rights, and nothing could ever swerve Elizabeth's loyalty to her. To a woman who deliberately tried to make trouble between the two by repeating to Mrs. Stanton something Susan, in a flash of temper, had said, Elizabeth wrote: "We have said worse things to each other face to face than we ever said of each other outside. Nothing that Susan could do or say could break my friendship with her; and I know that nothing could uproot her affection for me."

As she grew very old Elizabeth Cady Stanton's mind, so crystal clear on most subjects, became a little obsessed with one idea, the obstinacy of the church in refusing to advance with the times. She could not see that the theological mind had taken any thought since the days when the bloomer costume was denounced as a direct violation of the laws of God. Susan thought the church had advanced about as rapidly as other institutions, but, she said, "it is right that she should express her ideas, not mine." She held to this even when, in 1895, the National Council of Women, with other women's organizations, celebrated Mrs. Stanton's eightieth birthday, and Elizabeth insisted on featuring in her address an attack on the church. At the convention of 1896 the famous Stanton "Bible resolution" came near wrecking the suffrage association. For several years Mrs. Stanton and a committee of women of her choice had been at work on a so-called "Woman's

Bible," no revised version of the Scriptures, but merely a running commentary on chapter and verses of the old and new Testaments relating to women. In 1896 they published their commentaries on the Pentateuch, but Mrs. Stanton in no way sought to impose it on the suffragists. Several members of the executive board of the association, who, as Susan said, were unborn when Elizabeth began the fight for their freedom, were so incensed that they decided to put the association on record as against the publication. Not daring to consult Susan on the subject, they waited a favorable monent and then sprang a resolution that a paragraph of condemnation should be incorporated in the report of the recording secretary. For a moment Susan was too shocked to speak, then with the support of one of her liberal associates, Clara Bewick Colby of Nebraska, she succeeded in tabling the resolution. The next day it cropped up again in the report of the resolutions committee. Stirred to intense anger Susan left the chair and made a speech which almost amounted to her resignation as head of the association. She said:

". . . When our platform becomes too narrow for people of all creeds and of no creeds, I myself cannot stand upon it. Many things have been said and done by our *orthodox* friends which I have felt to be extremely harmful to our cause; but I should no more consent to a resolution denouncing them than I shall consent to this. Who is to draw the line? Who can tell now whether these commentaries may not prove a great help to woman's emancipation from old superstitions which have barred the way? Lucretia Mott at first thought Mrs. Stanton had injured the cause of all woman's other rights by insisting on the demand for suffrage, but she had sense enough not to bring in a resolution against it. In 1860 when Mrs. Stanton made a speech before the New York Legislature in favor of a bill making drunkenness a ground for divorce, there was a general

cry among the friends that she had killed the woman's cause. . . .
You had better not begin resolving against individual action or you
will find no limit. This year it is Mrs. Stanton; next year it may be
I or one of yourselves, who will be the victim."

And she uttered these prophetic words which might
even now with advantage to women's souls be inscribed
on the walls of every one of their club houses:

"If we do not inspire in women a broad and catholic spirit, they
will fail, when enfranchised, to constitute that power for better government which we have always claimed for them. Ten women
educated into the practice of liberal principles would be a stronger
force than 10,000 organized on a platform of intolerance and bigotry.
. . . This resolution adopted will be a vote of censure on a woman
who is without a peer in intellectual and statesmanlike ability; one
who has stood for half a century the acknowledged leader of progressive thought and demand in regard to all matters pertaining to the
absolute freedom of women."

In agony of soul Susan sat for an hour listening to
the women she trusted and leaned on speak against the
woman whom of all others she loved and revered.
Anna Shaw, Carrie Chapman Catt, Rachel Foster
Avery, Laura Clay, were all in favor of the resolution,
as were Henry B. Blackwell and his daughter, Alice
Stone Blackwell. Mary Anthony, Charlotte Perkins
Gilman, Lillie Devereux Blake, Clara B. Colby and a
few others stood by Susan, but the resolution was carried nevertheless.

For a time Susan thought she must leave the association, and Mrs. Stanton urged that they both resign.
Probably a considerable minority in the ranks hoped
they would. After three weeks of miserable days and
sleepless nights Susan decided that she could not resign,
she could not, as she wrote Elizabeth, "leave those half

fledged chickens without any mother." She saw the trend of the association into narrow and bigoted ways, and she determined, in the few years of life left to her, to turn them from it. Years ago she had thought her greatest task was to change the minds of men. Now she saw that Mrs. Stanton was halfway right; the minds of women, enslaved by centuries of churchly domination, were equally loath to relinquish their own taboos.

# CHAPTER XXIV

## PALMS IN THE TWILIGHT

THE last ten years of Susan B. Anthony's life, though crowded with honors at home and abroad, were not her happiest, although she had the immense satisfaction of seeing two more States, Utah and Idaho, add woman suffrage amendments to their constitutions. She saw in the altered tone of the press, the generous space given to woman suffrage news, indications of the changed mind of the community toward the question. Everywhere the leaven was working. Instead of coarse and sneering jests at the mention of women in political life men had begun to say, "Oh, it's bound to come some day," many of them no doubt, devoutly hoping that the thing would happen after they were dead. Even in the anti-suffrage societies which sprang up among the reactionaries, men and women, Susan saw certain proof of the increasing conviction that it was "bound to come some day." But in the political parties suffrage made no apparent advance. Year after year the sixteenth amendment was introduced in Congress, carelessly referred to committees and forgotten. Sometimes a committee granted a formal hearing, but nothing ever came of it. Susan waited for that unknown political situation which she knew would ultimately develop and would foice the party in power to act. Ultimately it did, though not in her lifetime. And the amendment, when passed, was not the sixteenth but the nineteenth.

By 1895 the number and importance of the women in the National American Woman Suffrage Association had increased until every State in the Union sent delegates to the annual conventions. Yet sometimes Susan sighed for the older days when the numbers were fewer and the minds of the women less divided. To her the whole object of the woman suffrage movement was sex equality, the wiping out of every arbitrary distinction in law and custom, that women, as she phrased it, might own and possess their own souls. To many of the newer members of the association, recruited largely from women's clubs and the Women's Christian Temperance Union, the object seemed to be to own and possess the souls of the community. Susan had no objection to their agitating as individuals for "moral" reforms, anti-cigarette laws, anti-racing, anti-gambling, Sunday closing of baseball and amusement parks, but she objected strenuously to any such activities on the part of suffrage clubs or State associations. Even the prohibition movement, although Susan herself was a total abstainer, got no support from her. She waged a constant war with her associates in defense of a rigid adherence to the one question of votes for women, and her indomitable will imposed it upon them as far as the national work was concerned. On the eve of the 1896 campaign in California she almost quarreled with her friend Frances Willard before she forced a promise that the W. C. T. U. should keep out of the fight, and she was obliged to write to Elizabeth Cady Stanton an almost brutal refusal to allow any controversy with the reactionary wing of the churches.

". . . Especially in this California campaign, I shall no more thrust into the discussions the question of the Bible than the manufacturing of wine. What I want is for the men to vote 'yes' on the suffrage amendment, and I don't ask whether they make wine on the ranches or believe that Christ made it at the wedding feast. I have your grand addresses before Congress and enclose one in nearly every letter I write. I have scattered all your 'celebration' speeches that I had, but I shall not circulate your 'Bible' literature a particle more than Frances Willard's prohibition literature. So don't tell Mrs. Colby or anybody else to load me down with Bible, social purity, temperance or any other arguments under the sun but just those for woman's right to have her opinion counted at the ballot box. I have been pleading with Miss Willard for the past three months to withdraw her threatened W. C. T. U. invasion of California this year, and at last she has done it. Now for heaven's sake, don't you propose a Bible invasion."

Yet when Susan reached California she found that religion, social purity and especially prohibition, had arrived before her and had so terrorized the voters that they saw in every petticoat a menace of a world too chilly and house-cleaned for masculine endurance. The very word Reverend, attached to Susan's chief lieutenant, Anna Shaw, was dampening to the spirits of the local political leaders. It was Susan's fixed policy to enter no State campaign unless the dominant party included a suffrage plank in its platform, and this year not only the Republicans but the Populists, the Socialist-Labor Party and the small Prohibition Party had done this, the Democrats alone refusing. Practically every important newspaper in the State was friendly, and the prospect seemed bright for success. Orders were given all suffrage speakers to confine their remarks strictly to the amendment, and for the most part they obeyed. But the Women's Christian Temperance Union, although they kept the letter of Miss Willard's promise to keep out of the campaign, broke it in spirit by advertising widely that as soon as the amendment carried their forces would descend on the State to educate the women to destroy the wine making and distillery industries. It was enough. The wine-growers organized in defense of their business, the newspapers cooled perceptibly, and many of them, just before election, advised their readers to vote against woman suffrage. So the amendment was lost. The women mourned loudly that the saloon had beaten them, but Susan told them plainly that their own political ignorance had beaten them. In deep exasperation she wrote to Frances Willard, who shortly afterward implored her to join the W. C. T. U. crusade against "yellow journalism," and specifically against the Corbett-Fitz-Simmons prize fight which those papers were featuring on the front pages every day:

> "Don't you see, if women ever get the right to vote, it must be through the consent of not only the moral and decent men of the nation, but also through that of the other kind? Is it not perfectly idiotic of us to be telling the latter class that the first thing we shall do with our ballots will be to knock them out of their pet pleasures and vices? If you still think it wise to keep on sticking pins into the men you will have to go on doing it. I certainly shall not be one of your helpers in that particular line of work."

The "reformers" could not understand Susan. Some reminded her that she had once delivered a lecture on social purity, but she could not take their minds back to the days of the Beecher-Tilton trial, or make them see that her lecture at that time was practically a defense of the suffrage organization. Some of the women openly expressed the wish that she would stay at home and write the biography on which she and Ida Husted Harper had agreed to collaborate. "The bog," as

Susan irreverently called it, was undertaken as a promise to the association, but it moved slowly because Mrs. Harper, a trained and expert journalist, had the greatest difficulty in persuading Susan that it was to be the story of her life rather than the life of every woman in the movement, past and present. Susan could not bear to leave out a single name, even those of women who had entertained her in their homes during all the years of her wanderings. Thus the writing could be done only when Susan was at home, and she was never at home very long at a time. She continued to travel, to lecture, to attend State and National conventions and to direct with a firm hand the affairs of the organization. She rarely missed a National Republican or Democratic convention, and she invariably called on every new President about as soon as he was installed in the White House. Always she was received as a distinguished guest—say a prince from some foreign land. President McKinley took her upstairs to see his invalid wife who afterward sent her a pair of the bedroom slippers she knitted interminably on her couch. Susan was past seventy years, but bedroom slippers were not what she wanted from the White House.

Her hair was gleaming silver now, her strong face was lined and seamed, and behind her gold-rimmed spectacles the keen blue-gray eyes looked a little tired. But not until the summer of 1895 did she give the slightest sign of failing physical powers. It was in July, and although the weather was excessively hot, she readily consented to go to a Chautauqua assembly at Lakeside, Ohio, as a substitute for Anna Shaw who had been taken ill at Cape Cod. She spoke with all her usual fire and fluency, but toward the close of her address she stopped abruptly, groped for her chair and fell into it unconscious. Because of her advanced age the physicians pronounced her prolonged fainting spell a grave symptom and all over the country telegraphic reports went out that Susan B. Anthony could not live until morning. Obituary notices were hurriedly prepared, one large Chicago daily wiring its correspondent at Lakeside to send "5,000 words if living, no limit if dead." This message gave Susan a good laugh, even in her impatience at having to remain in bed for several weeks under the care of hospital nurses. "If I had pinched myself right hard I needn't have fainted at all," she said defiantly.

Letters and telegrams by thousands poured in begging her to take at least a year's rest, and many urged her to retire altogether from active life. Even Elizabeth Cady Stanton wrote: "Let me urge you with all the strength I have, and all the love I bear you, to stay at home and rest." At the time Elizabeth wrote in her journal: "I knew at the time that it would be torture for Susan to stay at home." Susan did make the concession of refusing an offer from the Slayton Bureau for a lecture tour that winter, and for the first time in her life she indulged in the extravagance of a stenographer to help her take care of her enormous correspondence.

She was well and strong again, but she felt vaguely that something had slipped away from her, a little of her control over the affairs of the National Association. Her policy of holding the annual convention only in Washington was attacked, a majority of the executive board voting to carry it, on alternative years, to distant States. Susan agreed with them that this would edu-

DR. ANNA HOWARD SHAW
Vice-President-at-large of the National American Woman Suffrage
Association, 1892-1904, and President, 1904-1915

cate a wider public, and possibly bring more States into the suffrage ranks. But much as she desired to see new States added to the four in which women now voted, she adhered to her conviction that the ballot would never be given women by popular vote. In every State campaign since the Civil War more and more alien citizens, immigrant peasants considered bet-ter fitted than American women to govern the country, had piled up adverse votes against woman suffrage. Better, she thought, to bring to the capital once a year women from every State to force on Congress the fact that their women constituents were determined to press the amendment through. She was overruled, and she submitted, just as she submitted to being shielded from draughts, seated in cushioned easy chairs and being "spared" many of the details of business affairs. The women loved her, she knew, but why did they keep re-minding her that she was, after all, seventy-five years old, and why, oh why, did they begin to allude to her, even in the newspapers, as "Aunt Susan?" She loathed the title, not because of its undue familiarity, but for its plain suggestion of superannuation. Still there is noth-ing you can do about such things when friends shower you with gifts at birthdays and Christmas, and finally on one birthday make you a present of an annuity which insures you against poverty for the rest of your days. Yes, at seventy-five, Susan B. Anthony who had lived on the uncertain returns of a wage earner since she was nineteen, now had an income. Eight hundred dollars a year, less than sixty-seven dollars a month, a little less than a primary school-teacher would consider a good beginning wage. To this the next year Rachel Foster Avery, out of her own purse, added enough to bring

Susan's income up to $100 a month. Not a fortune, but with the house, with what the thrifty sister Mary had saved and with the lectures Susan could give each year, it sufficed.

In 1899 the third convocation of the International Council of Women was held in London, and Susan decided that with strict economy in the matter of dress, hotels and cabs, she could afford to go. Like Lindbergh in Paris she innocently thought that she would be called upon to pay all her own expenses. She did pay for her steamer tickets and a modest room in an hotel, but from the hour she set foot on English soil she was so beset with invitations, so swamped with hospitality, that she hardly ever during her entire stay ate a meal in private. Even more than at Chicago she found herself the heroine of the congress. She looked despairingly at her small wardrobe and went shopping with May Wright Sewall, President of the American women's section, for a more modish black satin gown and a purple velvet evening cloak lined with white satin. It would be more sensible, she protested, to buy a plain black cloak, but Mrs. Sewall was firm for the purple velvet, and very regal Susan looked in it when she appeared at the first of a dozen great functions given by society to honor women from every quarter of the globe. At the opening session of the congress Susan spoke for an hour on "The Position of Women in the Political Life of the United States," giving a complete résumé of all that had been accomplished through organization since the passing of the first married women's property act in 1848. That speech, a masterpiece of concise brevity, of compressed facts and eloquent logic, established her, as all the newspapers agreed, as without question the colossal figure of the women's convention. "At nearly eighty years of age," said one paper, "her voice has still the best carrying quality of any of the fine voices heard during the meetings. In these large halls, filled with thousands of people, she has been able to reach the farthest corners without apparent effort." In every meeting, as in all the notable social gatherings, she was indeed the colossal figure. The *London Times* said: "Miss Anthony is being entertained by all the lords and ladies of the United Kingdom. She dines with Lady Somerset, stops overnight with the Countess of Aberdeen, lunches next day with the Duchess of Sutherland, is received by the Queen, and threatens every day to call on the Princess of Wales."

The meeting between Susan B. Anthony, who demanded the fullest measure of freedom for all women, and Queen Victoria, who thought woman suffrage a most detestable heresy, was brought about by the Countess of Aberdeen, President of the International Council, and herself, at that time, not entirely converted to suffrage. The Queen consented to entertain the most distinguished delegates at Windsor, at a breakfast over which Princess Christian presided. Afterward the guests were to be received in the Queen's own drawing-room, but age and infirmity made it impossible to speak to more than two, whom she herself named, Lady Aberdeen and Susan B. Anthony. When Victoria appeared, supported on the arms of two ladies in waiting, nearly sightless, worn with the labors of one of the longest reigns in history, Susan, only a year younger, but strong and upright as a forest pine, was affected almost to tears. The Queen held out her hand to Lady Aberdeen, who sank on her knees to kiss it. Then the old hand

and the wonderful smile went out to Susan. Totally ignorant of royal etiquette, but moved to her very heart, Susan grasped the Queen's hand and murmured: "Oh, how *do* you do." Afterward she said: "I know it was all wrong, but the words just came out."

Probably Queen Victoria was less disturbed by that breach of etiquette than the elderly owner of an ancient title whom Susan casually introduced to two abashed newspaper women, with the apologetic remark, "I am afraid I can't remember your name." The noble lord did not furnish it.

In her high necked black satin and old lace collars and ruffles Susan was honor guest at the garden party given by the Lord Bishop of London at Fulham Palace, built by Henry VIII; at the tea given by Ambassador and Mrs. Choate at Carlton House Terrace; at the magnificent reception given by the Countess of Aberdeen and the Countess of Warwick, and at the great banquet given by the Society of American Women in London at the Hotel Cecil. She made speeches everywhere, always without fatigue. Like a soldier Susan felt at her best in action.

After the congress she spent a month visiting old friends, the Jacob Brights, Mrs. Fenwick Miller, Margaret, Mary and Anna Priestman, sisters-in-law of John Bright, Priscilla Bright McLaren, eighty-four years old, and Rebecca Moore, eighty, who years back had been the English correspondent of the *Revolution*. She held conferences with the English suffragists, beginning to hope that the Government would within a reasonable time bring in a reform bill which would include at least a limited number of women. Among those who attended those conferences was a friend of

Harriot Stanton Blatch, the wife of a barrister in Manchester, Emmeline Pankhurst.

Home again in late August Susan permitted herself the luxury of a week in Geneva, New York, with Elizabeth Cady Stanton and Elizabeth Smith Miller, the inventor of the historic bloomer costume. Then she went west on a lecture tour, for purple velvet evening cloaks must be earned. During that journey Susan fought with a depression of spirits new to her and which she could hardly understand. "Oh, if I were only thirty years younger," she wrote. "The plans crowd upon me, and everywhere I see new opportunities for pushing this work, but I can't rouse the women to take advantage of them. They are willing, but they don't know how." Something, she realized sadly, had gone out of American life, the hard fiber of the pioneers. No women any more would work as she and the early suffragists had worked, although none of them were now pointed out as eccentric or strong minded because they demanded woman's rights. Was it perhaps because of this? Susan suspected that this might be true. The worst of unrestricted immigration was not that it filled New England and the western prairies with alien faces and strange tongues and lowered standards of living, but that it took the ax and the plow out of native hands, created caste, and made Americans rich and soft.

Susan knew of no way of keeping the movement alive and virile except by shifting the responsibility of it on the shoulders of those who were to outlive her, so in 1900, when she was eighty years old, she resigned as President of the National American Woman Suffrage Association. Although many had wanted her to retire, the resignation when it came threw even those who loved her least into a confusion of grief. They suffered a shock almost comparable to that in England when Victoria died. The oldest woman in the association could not remember a time when Susan's dominant personality did not rule the conventions. It did not comfort them to hear her say, "I am not retiring now because I feel unable, mentally or physically, to do the necessary work, but because I want to see the organization in the hands of those who are to have its management in the future. I want to see you all at work while I am alive, so I can scold you if you do not do it well."

For her own reasons she had chosen for her immediate successor, not her closest associate, Anna Shaw, but Carrie Chapman Catt. And when she took the younger woman by the hand and led her forward, saying simply, "I present to you your new leader," every one in the great auditorium, even the hard-boiled men reporters at the press table, shed tears. Susan would come again for a few years, but only as a guest. This was her farewell to public life, her disappearance as one of the unique characters among American history makers.

In 1902 Susan read to the convention Elizabeth Cady Stanton's last annual message. In June she went to New York and spent a week in the quiet apartment on Central Park West where Elizabeth was living out her peaceful, busy old age. Hardly able to walk unassisted from one room to another, practically blind from cataracts over both eyes, she was still, with the aid of a secretary, writing newspaper and magazine articles and reading all the important new books. She and

Susan quarreled jestingly as of old, Elizabeth still insisting that the churches were women's worst enemy and reproaching Susan for growing conservative in her old age. Thank heaven that was one disease of time she had escaped. At the moment of parting, Susan held her hand for a long time, struggling to speak without too evident emotion.

"Shall we meet again, do you think?"

"Oh, yes," answered the game old heretic, "if not here, then in the hereafter, if there is one. And if there isn't we shan't know it."

Four months later she died, and all afternoon Susan sat tearless and mute, the telegram clasped in her hand. "I cannot talk," she told newspaper men who came to the house. "She would have found beautiful phrases to describe our friendship, but I cannot put it into words."

At the austere funeral, without prayers or eulogies, with only children and grandchildren, a few close friends and two women clergymen to say what they liked just so they mentioned no theology, Susan sat with eyes fixed on Elizabeth's face, white as the satin pillow on which she lay. Even in the noble calmness of death, Susan thought, the lips wore a slightly amused expression. Life had always amused Elizabeth Cady Stanton.

Susan went to Woodlawn and the grave, saw the friend she loved best in all the world laid in earth. When it was over she let her head sink on her breast, knowing suddenly that she was an old, old woman.

# CHAPTER XXV

## SOLDIER SLEEP

THREE last things Susan was determined to accomplish before she died. She wanted to see woman suffrage established on an international basis, women in close organization the world over demanding their political freedom; she wanted to collect a permanent fund, $500,000 or more, the income to be used for national work; and she wanted the University of Rochester opened to women. This last, by comparison with the more ambitious projects may seem trivial, but it proved to be the most difficult of the three, for few of the alumni, scattered all over the United States, favored the admission of women students, nor were the trustees especially enthusiastic about it. But Rochester was Susan's own city, and after working since her school-teaching days for coeducation, it wounded her pride to see the doors of the old institution closed to girls seeking collegiate training for positions in high schools, in the higher ranks of business and the professions. She formed a committee of Rochester women to help raise the required endowment, and in the end it was secured. But it was that little piece of local work that really cost Susan her life.

Her first task, after resigning the presidency of the National Association, was to complete and distribute the last two volumes of the "History of Woman Suffrage." Before the end of 1901 it was done, and very successfully. Colleges and universities which a few years ago disdained such a work now accepted it eagerly. Harvard University, which had returned a complimentary set of the first three volumes, as unworthy of a place in its library, now asked for the complete set, sending payment in advance. Literary critics reviewed it as an important contribution to American history, and editorial writers commented interestedly on Susan's preface to the last volume.

Susan's foreword to the last volume of the History may be regarded as her final message to the American suffragists, for it painstakingly explained why, in her opinion, the women's vote must come to them through an amendment to the Constitution, and not by State action. A change in the electorate so sweeping, she declared, could come only by the consent of one of the dominant parties. Never should it be sought from any third parties, which, in our history emerge only to disappear. Third parties usually endorse woman suffrage, partly because they grasp at any straw, and partly because they rely on the idealism of women to help them in any reforms they happen at the moment to advance. Women must not be deceived. "Reformers," once in office, could be depended upon no more than the most conservative of the "regulars." They, in time, would be converted, but only when a peculiar political situation arose to make it expedient for the party in power. It was well to win in all the States possible, for each one added to the strength of opinion in Congress. But Susan reminded women that after fifteen State campaigns only two States, Colorado and Idaho, had voted favorably on the amendment. Utah and Wyoming, for purely local reasons, had adopted woman suffrage in their territorial constitutions, and had kept it, on reaching statehood, by consent of Congress, not of their voters. Great reforms were never adopted by the masses, but always by intelligent minorities.

"If it had been necessary to have the consent of the majority of men in every State for women to enter the universities, to control their own property, to engage in the various professions and occupations, to speak from public platforms, and to form great organizations, in not one would they be enjoying these privileges to-day. It is very probable that this would be equally true if they had depended upon the opinions of a majority of the women themselves. They are more conservative even than men, because of the narrowness and isolation of their lives, the subjection in which they have always been held, the severe punishment inflicted by society on those who dare step outside the prescribed sphere, and stronger than all perhaps, their religious tendencies through which it has been impressed upon them that their subjected position was assigned by the Divine will."

Every advance, she pointed out, had been won by small groups of women.

"Between three and four million women engaged in wage earning in occupations outside domestic service. Would this be possible if they had been obliged to have the duly recorded permission of all the men over twenty-one years of age?"

The ripe political wisdom of this advice was justified, for though women went on begging the general electorate in the separate States for the franchise, they had gained, at the end of the World War, only seven more amendments to State constitutions, New York being the only suffrage State east of the Mississippi. Illinois, by legislative action, had given its women partial suffrage. Yet the National American Suffrage Association, grown very conservative after Susan's passing, concentrated on State action, letting their weak

Congressional Committee lapse into practical oblivion. Another organization, fired with Susan's own militant spirit, had to rise to carry out the instructions of the great leader.

That the work in Washington seemed to Anna Shaw and Mrs. Catt, and all officers of the association, entirely without promise is understandable. The only President who seemed to afford a particle of hope was Theodore Roosevelt, for he, as Governor of New York, had once sent a message to the legislature recommending a woman suffrage measure. But Roosevelt, either because he was in love with the idea of enormous families as the salvation of society, or because he was over-mindful of his political fences, changed his mind after becoming the nation's chief executive. Twenty-four hours before she died Elizabeth Cady Stanton wrote him a statesmanlike letter asking him to dare to become the emancipator of women, but to this and to another letter written immediately afterward by Susan B. Anthony, Roosevelt never made any response. For Susan he professed both admiration and affection, and when she went with delegations of suffragists to the White House he received her as a personal friend. In one of the last years of her life he gave her a private interview on the suffrage question, though on that occasion he was cold and formal.

It seems possible that had she seen him alone Theodore Roosevelt would have been unable to resist the plea of that venerable soldier, that woman worn out with the battles of more than half a century, marble pale, and fragile as a wraith, more beautiful in old age than in youth. But with Susan in the President's office were two women of whom he was decidedly wary.

Ida Husted Harper, journalist and historian of the movement in that day; and Harriet Taylor Upton, a Republican Party worker, closely associated with what was known as the "Ohio gang," of which Roosevelt's pet enemy, Mark Hanna, was the leader. Before these women he seemed afraid to express his personal opinions or plead his party exigencies.

Susan asked President Roosevelt first if he would not, as often as possible, mention women in his speeches and messages, which gave him a chance to say with his broad smile: "But I always mention women."

"Yes," said Susan, "as wives, mothers, and sometimes as wage earners. Never with any reference to their political rights."

She asked him next if he would not appoint experienced women on boards and commissions relating to such matters as they would be competent to act upon, and Roosevelt said that he was not unfavorable to the idea. She asked him to recommend to Congress the appointment of a special commission to investigate the practical workings of woman suffrage in the four States where it existed. The President frowned, but said: "Let me have that in writing and more specifically." After this he grew more coldly official, and when Susan asked him if he could not say a word in encouragement of the Oregon campaign for suffrage, then in prospect, he said bluntly that he never interfered in any State matter. Which was hardly accurate. Susan then called his attention to the surprising action of Congress in forbidding the legislatures of Hawaii and the Philippines to confer voting rights on their women, a privilege never before denied any American Territory.

"What!" cried Roosevelt, "you would have the vote granted to those oriental women?"

He professed astonishment when Susan told him that both Governor Taft and Archbishop Nozaleda in the Philippines had reported that if any natives were given the ballot it was the women who were best fitted to use it. But he gave permission to have this testimony sent him.

"President Roosevelt," said Susan, at last, "this is my principal request—and it is almost the last request I shall ever make of anybody. Before you leave the Presidential chair, recommend to Congress a Constitutional Amendment which will enfranchise women, and thus take your place in history with Lincoln, the Great Emancipator. I beg you not to close your term of office without doing this."

There was a silence. Mrs. Harper reminded the President of his message to the New York Legislature, and ventured to say that if he refused Susan B. Anthony's request, the American people might think that he had receded from a great ideal.

"They will have no right to think that," said Roosevelt testily, and the interview came to an end. Was it one of fate's little ironies that the President who finally did recommend the woman suffrage amendment to Congress was Woodrow Wilson, the man denounced by Theodore Roosevelt as a musty schoolman and a reactionary in politics? He might have derived some small consolation from the fact that Woodrow Wilson did it under compulsion.

Susan's dream of an International Suffrage Alliance came true in 1904, at the Berlin congress of the International Council of Women. This International

Council was made up of every kind of women's societies the world over, clubs, philanthropic, cultural, political, and until 1904 it was in no way, as a council, committed to woman suffrage. Just before it convened a suffrage committee of women of many nationalities was formed, with Susan B. Anthony as its chairman. Still the Council, meeting in Germany, only by sufferance of the Emperor and his Ministry, they thinking it a clever gesture to make in the face of the Powers, was a little afraid of the suffrage committee. Susan, at eighty-four, crossed the Atlantic and journeyed to Berlin, confident that she would see opposition broken down, and because of her presence there, it was. A great mass meeting had been arranged, but the leaders, frightened for the prestige of the congress, asked Susan, as the greatest suffragist in the world, to stay away until the temper of the public was tried out. But when the meeting opened the presiding officer, glancing around the stage where were seated the most distinguished guests, asked: "Where is Susan B. Anthony?"

The response from the audience was an overwhelming ovation. Every person in the vast hall sprang up, men throwing their hats and walking sticks, women their handkerchiefs into the air, cheering without a break for nearly fifteen minutes. They called for Susan again and again. Susan did not come. She wanted the Council to act of its own will, without any emotional impetus. The International Woman Suffrage Alliance was formed that week, with Carrie Chapman Catt as President, and thereafter women's full political freedom became the goal of women in every civilized country in the world. It was the crowning triumph of Susan's life. The obscure school teacher who, in 1853, left her classroom to crusade for what seemed an impossible ideal even in a republic, saw herself the leader of a world movement which needed only time, a short time, as it proved, to win an eternal victory.

Whenever in Berlin Susan entered a room every one rose until she was seated, and when the delegates were received at the Palace in Potsdam the Empress insisted on Susan's being seated even while she herself was standing. "You are the guest of honor at this gathering," said the gentle Augusta, when Susan sat beside her for a short conversation. Whereupon Susan, who never missed an opportunity, said that she hoped the German Emperor, who had raised his country to be a commercial equal of the United States, would go still further and give German women a higher place than was allowed as yet to her own countrywomen.

"Ah," sighed the Empress with a wry little smile, "the gentlemen are all very slow to comprehend this movement."

Susan journeyed home by way of England, the country she loved next to her own. She longed to see once more the few friends left, and the younger women who were carrying on the work of John Stuart Mill, Jacob Bright and Lydia Becker. She was very well and happy, and in the atmosphere of English homes, the most comfortable homes in the world—except in winter—her light humor returned, her youthful, bantering spirit. Anna Shaw, who was with her, tells entertainingly Susan's encounter with Annie Besant, whom she had always liked, but with whose Eastern religion she had little sympathy. It was in the home of Mrs. Bright, and Mrs. Besant, barefooted, clad in a mystic white robe, smoked her endless cigarettes and discoursed on Karma and the Yogi philosophy.

"Annie," demanded Susan, "why don't you make that aura of yours do its gallivanting in this world, looking up the needs of the oppressed, and investigating the causes of present wrongs? Then you could tell us what to do about it all."

Mrs. Besant explained that æons were long, earth life short, and while every one would be perfect some day it was useless to try to deal with individuals here. And she gazed upwards as if contemplating æons.

Susan wickedly turned the conversation to Charles Bradlaugh, refused a seat in the House of Commons because he was an infidel, a little notorious also because in past years he had been Annie Besant's lover.

"When your aura goes visiting in the other world, does it ever meet your old friend, Charles Bradlaugh?" asked Susan. "And wasn't he very much surprised to discover that he was not dead? I should think he would have been. He was so sure that death was going to end him for good and always. What is he doing with himself in the other world?"

Mrs. Besant sighed heavily. Charles Bradlaugh, it appeared, was an uneasy spirit. "He is hovering too near this world," she said. "He cannot seem to get away from his mundane interests. He is as much concerned with Parliamentary affairs now as when he was on this plane."

"Well!" cried Susan, "that's the most sensible thing I've heard yet about the other world. It encourages me. I've always felt sure that if I entered the next life before women were enfranchised, nothing in the glories of heaven would interest me so much as women's freedom on earth. I shall be like Mr. Bradlaugh. I shall hover around and continue the work here."

A great shock awaited Susan and Mary on their return to the peaceful Rochester home. A letter that their last remaining brother, Col. Daniel R. Anthony, was dying in Leavenworth. They took the long journey to Kansas to see him once again. Both brothers, Daniel and Merritt, had forsaken their Quaker traditions to fight through the Civil War, and both had won honors. Merritt died, a comparatively young man, in 1900. Daniel, a man of wealth, left his sisters money to insure their comfort while they lived, and $5,000 to Susan's suffrage fund.

They lived only a short time to enjoy this new wealth, for the great effort Susan had made to complete the co-educational fund in Rochester University had fatally sapped her vital forces. She had never doubted that the money would be raised, but returning to Rochester after a hot and wearisome journey, she was called on the telephone by the secretary of the women's committee, Mrs. F. R. Bigelow, told that after exhausting every resource the fund was $8,000 short, and that the time limit was to expire the next afternoon at four o'clock. Without waiting to take off her hat Susan went into action. Mary had made a provision in her will devising $2,000 to the university if women were admitted, and Susan said: "Mary, you must give that money now." Then she started, driving to department stores, banks, and offices. In vain. Apparently all had been canvassed. Next morning she set out again, this time to the homes of old and wealthy families. From the pastor of her church, Rev. William Gannett, and his wife she secured a pledge of the second $2,000, and late in the morning, from another friend, a third pledge. The fourth seemed impossible, for at three o'clock not another person had given a dollar. They "had so many calls." They were "under unusual expenses" that year. They didn't like to see things change at the university. In desperation Susan made a last minute visit to a man she knew to be in no very affluent circumstances, but he generously agreed to pledge, for her sake, the final $2,000. With Mrs. Bigelow she drove rapidly to the University to a meeting of the trustees. They scanned her list, said kind and congratulatory words, but told her regretfully that the fourth subscription could not be accepted, as the donor was a very old man, and his estate, they feared, would not be good for the amount. For a moment Susan was too stunned to move or speak. Then rising she walked to the table and said: "Gentlemen, I asked Mr. Wilder to loan me his name that this question of coeducation in the University of Rochester might not be hurt by connection with me or with woman suffrage. I now pledge my life insurance for the last $2,000. Will you accept it?"

The next day she was too exhausted to leave her room, but on Sunday she went, as usual, to Mr. Gannett's church. The entry in her journal that night is almost illegible. "Went to church to-day, but had a sleepy time—such a sleepy time. It seemed as if something was the matter with my tongue. I had a feeling of strangeness—could not think what I wanted to say. A queer sensation all the afternoon—Mary asked me several times if anything was the matter. I shall be better or worse to-morrow."

She woke up dazed and almost speechless, but in the

afternoon braced herself to go to the office of the trustees to make certain that all the pledges had stood legal examination. The next entry in the journal is a mere scrawl: "They let the girls in. He said there was no alternative."

The following evening the house was full of girls bringing armloads of flowers, and expressing their gratitude. Susan, after greeting a few of them, turned suddenly very white, moved uncertainly toward the door and slipped upstairs. Mary followed her, and there on the bed she found Susan in profound unconsciousness. This time it was no fainting spell, but a slight lesion of the brain, a light stroke of apoplexy. For a week she lay speechless, and for a month afterwards her speech was much impaired. Too clear minded to ignore the warning she called in an eminent specialist, Dr. Edward Mott. He told the truth, that she could never be restored to perfect health. The second stroke might come at any time, and it might be delayed for years. She must never again waste a particle of her strength, never mingle in crowds or risk taking cold. Susan smiled. She had a few things to attend to yet, and she did not propose to work from an invalid's chair. Never afterward, however, did she attempt to speak without the devoted Anna Shaw near her, to go on with the speech if her throat suffered that odd contraction.

The 1906 annual convention of the National American Woman Suffrage Association was held in Baltimore. Susan knew that it would be her last, and she wanted it to be a great success. Miss M. Carey Thomas, President of Bryn Mawr, and her friend, Miss Mary Garrett, both women of wealth and great influence in

Baltimore, had recently come into the association, and at Susan's request Miss Thomas arranged a college evening at the convention, and Miss Garret opened her Baltimore home, usually closed at that season. In her beautiful house were entertained besides Susan and Julia Ward Howe, the college women, Mary E. Woolley, President of Mount Holyoke; Lucy Salmon, Professor of History at Vassar; Mary A. Jordan, Professor of English at Smith, and Mary W. Calkins, Professor of Philosophy at Wellesley. On that notable evening, at which President Ira Remsen of Johns Hopkins, presided, Susan seemed well and perfectly happy. Julia Ward Howe and Clara Barton sat with her on the platform and all three spoke briefly. But she attended no more meetings. Anna Shaw reported to her between sessions, and at last brought her the joyful news that the permanent fund was at last secured, for Miss Thomas and Miss Garrett had jointly pledged themselves to give $60,000 to complete it. This was a guarantee that the work would go on as planned, and Susan was so elated that she rose from her bed declaring that she was well enough to go to Washington to the celebration of her eighty-sixth birthday. Doctors forbade it, but Susan said: "The hammer may as well fall one time as another now. I am going." Miss Garrett insisted on sending a trained nurse along, and by the time the train reached Washington both the nurse and Miss Shaw feared that she had reached the end. After a day's rest in bed she got up again and dressed for her birthday dinner. Susan was dying on her feet, dying as she had lived, a stoic. At the dinner many men prominent in official Washington spoke, and letters from President Roosevelt and others were read. After

© Denver Times, 1920

ENTER MADAME

*Ding in Denver Times*

listening to the President's tribute to her Susan rose, and with more than a touch of her old fire, said: "One word from President Roosevelt in his message would be worth a thousand eulogies to Susan B. Anthony. When will men learn that what we ask is not praise, but justice?" Then followed her last speech, ending with the dauntless words, "Failure is impossible."

In Baltimore, at the time of the convention, there was an epidemic of bronchitis, and both Susan and the ninety-year-old Julia Ward Howe, took severe colds. Mrs. Howe survived it for a time, but in a month Susan was dead. She hated to have any one see her ill, and for the first three weeks no one but Mary, the doctors and nurses, entered her room. In the last hours she kept Anna Shaw close beside her. Miss Shaw was president of the association now, and Susan made her swear that she would keep the office as long as she was strong enough to do the work.

"It will be harder for you than it has ever been for me," she whispered. "I was so much older, and I had been president so long, that you girls have all been willing to listen to me. With you it will be different. . . . There will be jealousies, . . . misunderstandings, criticisms. . But take your stand and hold it . . . like a good soldier."

Kneeling beside her pillow Anna Shaw solemnly promised, and Susan, with a sigh, closed her eyes. Presently she began to speak, and Mary and Miss Shaw, leaning over, heard her utter a long roll call of remembered names, women's names out of the past, all the old comrades in the fight. They seemed to be passing before her, and she greeted them with joy. Elizabeth, Lucy Stone, Ernestine Rose, Isabella Hooker, Rhoda de Garmo, Amy Post, Lucretia and Lydia Mott, Martha Wright . . . Some of the names Anna Shaw had never heard, and Mary had almost forgotten. But Susan forgot not one.

Then she slept, half conscious, until, an hour after midnight, on March 14, the flame which had been burning lower and lower since dusk, flickered palely and went out forever.

The day of her funeral a furious blizzard swept the city, a shrieking wind and snow that heaped the streets with drifts. Yet ten thousand people stood in the bitter cold outside the church where she lay in a flag-draped coffin. Beside it all day stood a guard of honor of girls from Rochester University. After the last words of the short funeral service were spoken the doors were opened and crowds of shivering people filed in, past the gray casket and the mounds of flowers, seeing her only a little more marble white than she had been in her last years, dressed in the familiar black silk gown and rich lace collar, fastened with a pin which the Wyoming women had given her on her eightieth birthday, a jeweled flag with a diamond for each of the suffrage States. Just before the coffin was closed the pin was taken from the still breast and given to Anna Shaw, her badge of succession.

All the flags of the city were at half mast as Susan rode through the driving storm to her rest beside her father and mother in Mount Hope Cemetery. Roses and lilacs dropped their frozen petals into the open grave. The wind tossed waves of snow over the piled mound.

In every newspaper office in the country obituaries

were rushed into type. A great woman had passed. Hundreds of columns in her praise were written.

A few complacent editors said: "She was the champion of a lost cause." "Her peculiar views on this question will soon be forgotten." "There is reason for the belief that it will gradually subside."

Susan had said: "Failure is impossible." She knew.

# CHAPTER XXVI

## CARRY ON

In January, 1912, the National American Woman Suffrage Association is meeting in annual convention in Philadelphia. At the opening session the Governor of the State and the Mayor of the city extend an official welcome. So many distinguished men and women are taking part in the program that Philadelphia's finest homes open their doors in a succession of receptions, teas, dinners. The flowers alone in the convention hall represent a greater outlay of money than Susan and Mrs. Stanton were able to collect for a three days' meeting. The press table, at which in old times they would have been grateful to see a few local reporters, are crowded with correspondents, representatives of the national press associations, news photographers. To great applause the President, Rev. Anna Shaw, rises to make her annual address. On the high bosom of her black silk dress the plump little Methodist preacher wears a jeweled pin, that pin which, just before the coffin lid was closed, was taken from Susan's breast and given, as a badge of office, to her successor. In 1906 it bore four diamonds, one for each of the suffrage States. In six years Anna Shaw has added two more stones, and she tells the assemblage that next year the symbolic pin will sparkle with nine. In November, 1912, suffrage amendments are to be submitted in three States and the prospects of success are bright.

The dismal prophecies of the obituary writers have not been fulfilled. The cause marches, and there is everything to help it march. No longer does the association have to plod on with little money, few friends and only amateurs to work with. The old crusaders, in their Kansas, South Dakota, Missouri and Ohio campaigns, paid all their own expenses and endured incredible hardships that they might have money enough for halls and a little advertising. Now there is plenty of money not only to pay the expenses but the salaries of expert organizers and speakers. Money to hire the largest halls, to command fleets of motor cars, to employ secretaries and stenographers, to make the freest use of telegraphs and telephones. Far from being buried in Susan's grave, the woman suffrage agitation is flourishing both in the United States and Europe. In England an aggressive campaign of militancy is going on—though militancy is not spoken of in the American association except to be denounced. Since 1909 Miss Shaw has refused to meet Mrs. Pankhurst, and to newspaper interviewers she has said that the Suffragettes have destroyed the chances of the English women for at least a generation. Nothing of that sort will ever be allowed to spring up in the United States. The American association will win its fight, but only by peaceful and dignified methods.

Neither Miss Shaw nor any one else has placed even a tentative date for final victory. There is, in fact, one item on their ledgers which continues to be written in red ink. The Federal Suffrage Amendment, Susan's great obsession, has made no progress at all. Year after year the bill is introduced in Congress and is regularly referred to the Senate Judiciary and the

House Rules Committees, those bournes from which no traveler not officially summoned e'er returns. Once in a while a bored and indifferent committee grants a hearing to the women. Nothing is expected to result, and nothing does. But some work in Washington must go on, if only out of respect to Susan's memory. The women think that Susan wasted her time beating at the doors of Congress. They agree that it is much better to concentrate on State referendums, for is it not plain that when a sufficient number of States are won, the Federal Amendment will be forced through by the women voters?

The theory has this underlying weakness. A sufficient number of States can never be won. In at least twenty American States the constitutions were deliberately framed to make amendment difficult if not altogether impossible. In some, for example, after a proposed amendment has been rejected by the electorate it cannot again be submitted for a long term of years, ten or even twenty. In one or two others only one amendment can be submitted at an election, and it is plain that that one would never be spared to women. Then there are the States of the solid South. Whatever their constitution, no Southern legislature would pass a woman suffrage amendment, and in no Southern State would the voters ratify such a measure. The national association leaders know all this, for Susan had taught them. Out of her long experience she had learned that great reforms are never achieved through the consent of majorities. Woman suffrage, submitted to the mass of the voters, even women voters, would inevitably be rejected. The largest endorsement the question can ever expect is a two-thirds vote in both houses of Congress, and ratification by three-fourths of the State legislatures. But since Congress will not consider the amendment, and some State legislatures will, the successors of the pioneers stick to their method. They do not know what else to do.

Disraeli—among others—declared that "a party is lost if it has not the constant reinforcement of young and energetic men." It is a long time since the National American Woman Suffrage Association has had any such reinforcement, but at the Philadelphia Convention, modestly sitting in the back of the hall, two young and extremely energetic women represent that saving element. At a point where committees for the ensuing year are being considered these two women call on Miss Shaw with what seems a very generous proposition. If they can be placed on the Congressional Committee they will agree, entirely at their own expense, their own responsibility, to get the moribund Federal Amendment to the floors of Congress. Miss Shaw is pleased with the young women, university graduates both, one a high school teacher in Brooklyn, the other a social worker with experience in New York, Chicago and London. The single drawback is that both girls had been associated in England with Mrs. Pankhurst and her wild women. Miss Shaw asks if this is true and they admit it candidly. Alice Paul and Lucy Burns had been in the mobs thrown back from the House of Commons, they had suffered arrest and imprisonment, known hunger strikes and forcible feeding. These things, they say, are not necessary in a country where even a few women are voters. All that is necessary here is to persuade Congress to consider the amendment, and to show the women voters how to influence Congress to pass it. Miss Shaw hesitates, but on the strong recommendation of Jane Addams, then a member of the executive committee, she authorizes the appointment of the two women. They suggest four others to be placed on the committee, four very able women, Mary Beard, wife of Charles A. Beard of Columbia, since co-author with him of "The Rise of American Civilization"; Mrs. William Kent, wife of a Congressman from California; Mrs. Lawrence Lewis of Philadelphia; and Crystal Eastman of New York. There is not much immediate work for the committee, says Miss Paul. In November a new President and a new Congress will be elected, and it is with them that they will have to deal. Meanwhile Miss Paul thinks she can collect a little money for expenses.

In November, 1912, the Democrats reaped an amazing victory, the first they had known since Grover Cleveland's second election in 1892. Woodrow Wilson came in with a substantial majority in both Houses of Congress. That election was a gift of the gods to the new Congressional Committee, for it rendered much simpler the policy they meant to pursue. In effect it was the Pankhurst policy, although Mrs. Pankhurst did not invent it. She borrowed it from the greatest of Irish Home Rule leaders, Charles Stewart Parnell, who may have borrowed it from the ancients. Parnell did not carry it to complete success, but the England of his day knew that had not a scandal in his private life caused his political overthrow and premature death, he probably would have made it succeed. Parnell was determined to win home rule for Ireland, not by violence but by constitutional methods. Mr.

© by G. V. Buck, Washington, D. C.

**ALICE PAUL**
Who Led the Final Fight for the XIXth Amendment

Gladstone, when he formed his Government in the early Eighties, was theoretically in favor of home rule, but he would not advance the bill, so Parnell and his group in the House of Commons went over to the opposition. In all succeeding bye elections they campaigned against every Liberal candidate, and at length they forced out the strong Liberal Party, or helped importantly in forcing it out. Not because the Conservatives were friendly to home rule, for they were not. Parnell fought the Liberals because they were the party in power and hence responsible for the fact that the Irish bills were blocked. When the Conservatives assumed power he asked for a Government bill for Ireland, and when this was refused he opposed the Conservatives. Sooner or later, he knew, one of the parties would need the Irish vote so badly that they would make home rule part of their Government policy. Mrs. Pankhurst and the Suffragettes adopted this method. They fought the Liberals simply because they had power to pass the suffrage bill and refused to do so. The older suffragists, both in England and the United States, thought that the Pankhurst policy put back the final victory of woman suffrage by many years, but Mr. Asquith and Mr. Lloyd George were under no such delusion. They knew that if Mrs. Pankhurst lived long enough, woman suffrage was inevitable.

Alice Paul and Lucy Burns believed that the same policy would win in the United States, that as a matter of fact it had a better chance to win in the United States, because even as far back as 1912 women voted in nine States, and that vote, if properly organized, could play havoc in elections. In the United States, it is true, it is not always possible to hold a national party responsible, for the President does not always have a majority in both Senate and House, nor does one party invariably control in both houses. But in 1912 the situation was, for the suffragists, ideal. Woodrow Wilson in his first term had a clear majority in both Houses of Congress, and he controlled his party more completely than any President since Andrew Jackson. Even those Democrats who disliked him personally yielded him implicit obedience. Their party was in power after many years of famine, and as a minority group in the country they knew that they could retain power only by uniting under a strong leader. Every measure introduced in Mr. Wilson's first Congress had to have the seal of his approval beforehand. Any measure he wanted introduced and passed was instantly accepted by the Democratic caucus. Hence the first appeal in behalf of the Susan B. Anthony Amendment must be to the President himself, although a President has nothing whatever to do with Federal amendments. He does not even have the power to veto them. President Wilson was known to be an anti-suffragist, so it was taken for granted that he would refuse to advance the suffrage measure. It was taken for granted also that Congress would refuse to act independently of the President. This would place the Democratic Party on record as blocking the bill. The National American Woman Suffrage Association could then go into the nine suffrage States, and in the next election ask the women voters to withold their support of the Democratic Party until it ceased to block the woman suffrage amendment.

When this plan was unfolded to Anna Shaw she was horrified. She denied that there was or ever could be

in the United States a party in power. The women
had friends in both parties and all they had to do was
to make more friends. She did not see how it was
possible to ask the women voters to oppose the Democratic candidates in their States, because all the men
were suffragists. They could not be held responsible
for the narrow-minded obstinacy of their party leaders.
Besides, if women voters showed themselves so un-
grateful to men who had helped them get their citizenship, how could the association ask other States to pass
suffrage amendments? Miss Shaw would not countenance any militant movement. As soon as possible
she caused Alice Paul and Lucy Burns to be removed
from the Congressional Committee, and she gave the
Congressional Union, the suffrage society they had
organized in Washington, the instant choice of abandoning the Paul policy or getting out of the national
association. They chose to stay by Alice Paul and
Lucy Burns. Miss Paul had collected a fairly large
amount of money—in the first year she raised and spent
$27,000—and the militant campaign was launched.

The Congressional Committee made no secret of its
plans. On the contrary they did everything they could
think of to advertise them. They wanted the President,
the Congress and the country to know that woman
suffrage had progressed from its propaganda to its
political stage, that the women knew perfectly well
why the suffrage amendment was held up, and that
they intended to hold the proper persons responsible.
When Woodrow Wilson arrived in Washington on
March 3, 1913, for his inauguration, the militants met
him with a suffrage parade, and very soon after he was
installed in the White House they sent a deputation

to call on him.   The speakers did not try to convert
President Wilson to woman suffrage.   They merely
requested him *as responsible head of his party* to direct
his Congress to pass the bill for the Susan B. Anthony
Amendment.   Very much puzzled, the President explained that he was not the head of his party, but its
chief servant.   He could not possibly advise Congress
to pass a woman suffrage bill, because the Baltimore
platform, on which he had gone to the country, had
made no mention of woman suffrage.   He was firmly
resolved never to initiate or put through any important
piece of legislation which was not provided for in the
Baltimore platform.   He admitted that he was opposed
to woman suffrage, especially by Federal action.   The
Democratic Party were committed to the doctrine of
State rights, and any change in the electorate, in his
opinion, must come as a result of State legislation.

Every word a President of the United States utters
publicly is news, and President Wilson's pronouncement on the suffrage amendment was instantly telegraphed to every corner of the United States.   The
women turned their attention to the Democrats in
Congress and as they, of course, heartily endorsed
everything their leader had said on the subject, this too
went out to the country.   Thus it was definitely
established that the Democratic Party was blocking the
amendment.   A party, not individuals in Congress, was
keeping women out of citizenship.   The Washington
correspondents, who had never paid the least attention
to woman suffrage, now began to treat it as news of
importance.   They probably did not believe that the
woman vote of the country could ever be organized to
defeat Democratic candidates, but the mere threat of

it made a good story, and thereafter the militant movement got all the publicity it needed.

Congress convened on April 7, 1913, the suffrage amendment was reintroduced, and on that day women from every Congressional District in the United States marched to the Capitol with petitions to their representatives to pass the bill. The militants next organized in a score of cities from coast to coast simultaneous demonstrations, parades, mass meetings, pageants, in favor of the bill. In all meetings the speakers announced that the Democrats were expected to act favorably, and unless they did they would have a very difficult time when the next elections occurred. The result was that the party in Congress caucused on the subject of the bill and decided on a course of action which they thought would effectually silence the militants. They would have the bill reported favorably by the Senate Judiciary Committee, they would give a day for debate, vote the bill down and decently inter the whole question, at least for that session. In June the Judiciary Committee did report favorably, and in July the Senate devoted a day to a woman suffrage debate, the first time in twenty-one years such a thing had happened. Senators from the suffrage States spoke warmly for the bill. This was to convince the women voters that it was not their fault that the Susan B. Anthony Amendment failed of the necessary two-thirds majority. The next day the bill was reintroduced by a Republican Senator, referred as a matter of routine back to the Judiciary Committee and left to its slumbers.

Militant activities did not cease with this defeat. The Congressional Union, which had begun as a local society in Washington, extended its membership throughout the country, especially in the nine suffrage States. In Washington the Congressional Committee became a strong and skillful lobby, interviewing Congressmen, attending every open meeting of the committees having charge of the bill, bringing every argument to bear to induce the committees to bring it to the floor of the House and Senate. They sent deputation after deputation to the President, especially after he departed from his policy of rigid adherence to the Baltimore platform. Every visit was most carefully planned to place him on record as a foe to the amendment, which by his party's deliberate intention was allowed to languish in committee pigeon holes. With the mind of the country thus prepared and enlightened, the militants went out in the Congressional elections of November, 1914, and in all the suffrage States campaigned against the Democratic candidates. It is not possible to say exactly how successful their efforts were, but it is certain that in that election many Democrats failed to be returned to Congress. Of forty-three candidates only twenty went back to Washington.

To Anna Shaw and the executive board of the national association this performance savored of insanity. Every man defeated was a suffragist and in favor of the amendment. It was true that the men who replaced them were also suffragists, at least officially, but that did not absolve the women who voted against the old candidates from black ingratitude. In letters and telegrams to the President and Congressmen, in newspaper interviews and in public speeches the National American Woman Suffrage Association repudiated the policy of the militants. They assured the

Administration and the public that those women were a small and irresponsible group, in no way representative of the suffragists of the United States. The Congressional Union, which in 1916 became the National Woman's Party, was comparatively speaking a small group, never claiming more than 50,000 members, but every member was an active and aggressive force. The party was very well financed also, Mrs. O. H. P. Belmont, who became a member of the executive board, giving lavishly to the campaign fund, and other women of wealth contributing generously.

A singular situation was thus developed in the suffrage ranks. The National American Woman Suffrage Association, heirs of Susan B. Anthony, the radical, now became the right wing of the movement, just as Lucy Stone and Julia Ward Howe had been in 1869. They went even farther in their antagonisms to the left wing, for they actually abandoned Susan's child, the Federal Amendment. Their new Congressional Committee, of which Ruth Hanna McCormick was chairman, caused to be introduced in Congress a rival amendment providing for suffrage referendums in the separate States whenever one-eighth of the legal voters petitioned for them. Mrs. McCormick, who is credited with inheriting much of the political sagacity of her father, the late Mark Hanna, must have known the utter futility of such a measure, for while a legislature might be forced to submit a suffrage amendment to the electorate, no law could force a majority of the voters to endorse it. The Shafroth-Palmer resolution, as the new amendment was called, failed so completely to capture the public imagination that it was soon dropped by the national association.

The World War, whose flames now approached even the distant shores of the United States, gave another turn to the activities of the militants. In the national election of 1916 the Woman's Party chartered a special train and campaigned across the country against the Democrats, planting beside the Wilson banners, "He Kept Us Out Of War," their own slogan, "He Kept Us Out Of Suffrage." It was not expected that President Wilson could be defeated, but it was expected that he would soon cease to keep us out of war, and within five weeks from the date of his second inauguration he did go to Congress with his stirring war message. Immediately began that picketing of the White House which was so severely condemned by those who did not perceive its logic and its effectiveness. The United States was going into a European war. American women were being called upon to give their husbands, sons and lovers to wounds and death for democracy and freedom, while they themselves were denied democracy and freedom. It was time for them to demand that the suffrage amendment be passed immediately. Therefore with banners bearing striking quotations from the war message, from public speeches, from notes to the Allies and to the Central Powers, the women walked back and forth before the White House every day. At four o'clock, when the President and Mrs. Wilson went for their daily drive, they saw a group collected at the gate, saw huge banners inscribed: *"We shall fight for the things we have always held nearest our hearts—for Democracy, for the right of those who submit to authority to have a voice in*

ADELAIDE JOHNSON'S PORTRAIT MONUMENT
Elizabeth Cady Stanton, Susan B. Anthony and Lucretia Mott in the
Capitol at Washington, D. C.

*their own government."* Nothing ever fired the hearts
of women more. They came from distant States to do
a single day's picketing. On Capitol Hill the Democratic majority, now somewhat diminished, knew that
sooner or later they would get a message from the
White House that the suffrage amendment must be
passed.

"If a creditor," said Alice Paul, "stands before a
man's house all day long demanding payment of his
bill, the man must either remove the creditor or pay
the bill." President Wilson made one attempt to remove the creditor when he permitted the arrest, on the
absurd charge of blocking traffic, of two hundred and
eighteen women pickets. They went to prison, but
public opinion made it impossible to hold them there
long. As soon as they were released they began to
burn the speeches of President Wilson in Lafayette
Square, facing the White House. By this time our
soldiers overseas were beginning to die in battle. The
splendid efforts of the American Army in behalf of
world democracy, while their mothers and sisters were
being kept in political bondage at home, while all
American women were being entreated to help win the
war by every personal sacrifice, made further resistance on the part of the President and Congress impossible. In December, 1917, a committee from the
House of Representatives called at the White House—
or were summoned—to confer with the President on
the suffrage amendment. He told them that "now they
had sought his advice" he very frankly and earnestly
advised them to vote for the amendment "as an act of
right and justice to the women of this country and of
the world." The House therefore passed the bill.

The Senate, acting on their own responsibility—or on orders—delayed action for a time. The President advised them to follow the example of the House, assuring them that he had not been influenced by the voice of "foolish and intemperate agitators." Still they waited. But in 1918 a Republican Congress was elected, convening in May, 1919, in special session. On May 21 the amendment was again voted on, passing both House and Senate by more than the requisite two-thirds majority. Thirty-seven State legislatures quickly ratified, and in November, 1920, the women of the United States went to the polls full voters. Seventy-two years from the date of the Seneca Falls Convention, that obscure gathering of women, bond slaves under the law, and so poor that the very wages of their toil belonged to others. Between those women who possessed nothing, not even their own children or their own persons, and these women citizens who possessed everything, since opportunity is everything, seventy-two years. In terms of ordinary human progress a thousand years. For liberty came to this subjected class only incidentally by act of Congress; it came, in reality, through a completely altered mind of a nation.

There is drama in the circumstance that the year of victory was the centennial year of Susan B. Anthony, who more than any other succeeded in changing the minds of men toward women, of women toward themselves. That tremendous task to which she gave her life and her genius was nearly finished when she died. It was nobly continued by those to whom she bequeathed it. It was brilliantly brought to triumph by a younger generation which, reborn in her spirit, knew how to carry out her almost forgotten plan of campaign. In that last difficult advance it was the soul of Susan B. Anthony that went marching on.

# INDEX

HOUSTON PUBLIC LIBRARY

RO1029 49726

SSCCA $^5$ B
AN8D

DORR, RHETA LOUISE CHILDE
SUSAN B. ANTHONY, THE
WOMAN WHO CHANGED THE
MIND OF A NATION

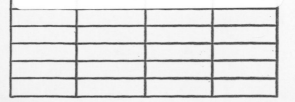

SSCCA $^5$ B
AN8D

HOUSTON PUBLIC LIBRARY
CENTRAL LIBRARY